The Enterprising Musician's Legal Toolkit

The Enterprising Musician's Legal Toolkit

DAVID R. WILLIAMS

ROWMAN & LITTLEFIELD
Lanham • Boulder • New York • London

Published by Rowman & Littlefield
An imprint of The Rowman & Littlefield Publishing Group, Inc.
4501 Forbes Boulevard, Suite 200, Lanham, Maryland 20706
www.rowman.com

6 Tinworth Street, London, SE11 5AL, United Kingdom

British Library Cataloguing in Publication Information Available

Library of Congress Cataloging-in-Publication Data

Names: Williams, David R., 1964– author.
Title: The enterprising musician's legal toolkit / David R. Williams.
Description: Lanham : Rowman & Littlefield Publishing Group, 2020. |
   Includes bibliographical references and index. | Summary: "The
   Enterprising Musician's Legal Toolkit takes musicians from business
   ideation through actual development and ultimately protection of content
   and the brand with annotated contracts and other legal content. It
   expands upon the author's previous book, 'The Enterprising Musician's
   Guide to Performer Contracts'"—Provided by publisher.
Identifiers: LCCN 2020003563 (print) | LCCN 2020003564 (ebook) |
   ISBN 9781538135075 (cloth) | ISBN 9781538135082 (paperback) |
   ISBN 9781538135099 (epub)
Subjects: LCSH: Music trade—Law and legislation—United States. |
   Music—Vocational guidance—United States.
Classification: LCC ML3795 .W49362 2020 (print) | LCC ML3795 (ebook) |
   DDC 780.68/1—dc23
LC record available at https://lccn.loc.gov/2020003563
LC ebook record available at https://lccn.loc.gov/2020003564

For Esther, my guiding star.

Table of Contents

PART V: PROTECTING YOUR BUSINESS & PROTECTING YOURSELF

Preface

This book, written for musicians, is about entrepreneurial risk-taking. Its central purpose is to better position you to make a living doing what you love by helping you to clarify and plot out your ideas no matter what they are. I've learned through my teaching, consulting work, and nonprofit service that musicians often feel paralyzed with entrepreneurial decision-making. The creativity and ideas are there, but they often don't know how to get started. Fear of the unknown looms large.

It's no small wonder why a musician would feel uncertain about taking the risk of launching a business. Traditionally, the music industry has long been one of exclusion. Artists were considered a commodity to be exploited by a seemingly endless line of gatekeepers including artist managers, booking agents, music publishers, producers, and recording executives comprising a human fortress between talent and their potential audience.

Today, however, the fast-paced march of technology has been the single greatest influence on the music industry and its practices since the invention of the phonograph. Paul Pacifico, the CEO of Association of Independent Music (AIM) sums it up saying:

> Artists today are pretty much by definition music entrepreneurs and owner-operated companies, building their businesses and their brands. For them, technology has been the principal driver, reducing the barriers to entry in terms of lower costs and the democratization of industry supply chain resources, such as production equipment and support services.[1]

The combined forces of digitalization and rapid expansion of the Internet may have been the music industry's biggest disruptor. It's never been easier to create your own content, record and distribute your own album, market yourself inexpensively on a global scale, and speak directly to your audience. And there's no better time—the creative economy is thriving. A 2018 PricewaterhouseCoopers outlook report tells us that there is an upward growth trend in global revenue generated from the entertainment industry with future growth predictions of up to 5% topping $2.2 trillion in 2021.[2]

I teach entrepreneurial musicianship to graduate students in two different programs at The New School in New York City. The students I work with are extraordinary in their creativity, energy, and passion. I've not met one student who lacked an opinion about the career they wanted for themselves or what each expected from their studies. They're fortunate that the programs they've chosen are so forward-thinking.

University training programs and conservatories have been slow to come to the understanding that a practice-based curriculum alone will not adequately prepare students to thrive in the modern creative economy. Today, emerging artists need to embrace the reality that they are small business owners. Each is the CEO of his own brand—a brand each can and should define for themselves before someone else defines it for them. The issues students grapple with most often are those involving organizational focus and follow-through.

Specifically, I see two distinct entrepreneurial mind-sets: The first is *"I'm just going to do it and I'll work out the details later; what's the worst that can happen?"* These people jump in and sometimes make a real mess of things. I know this firsthand because I'm often called upon to untangle the knots (such as the regulatory sailor's knot resulting from the well-intentioned folks who, without statutory authority, moved their nonprofit corporation to another state).

The second mind-set is more common. These people never set fire to their ideas because they are frozen in place. They're afraid of what they don't know and are not in a position to waste precious start-up money by going down the wrong path. Every avenue they see available to them seems to end with *"I have no idea how to do this. Is there a right order for these things?"* I admit to being in this latter category myself. In corporate America, we call this "paralysis by analysis." Its hallmark is spending an inordinate amount of time gathering information and endlessly weighing the pros and cons of some strategic decision that, by the time a decision is finally reached, the opportunity is gone; it was swallowed up by a more nimble organization who saw the same opportunity and decided that the risk in waiting eclipsed the risk in acting.

This book is written for musicians holding both these mind-sets: those who need a pathway laid down for them and those firebrands who find themselves with a business currently underway, but who are bumping up against compliance or other legal obstacles they wish they considered earlier. I'm here to help all of you.

NOTES

1. Alison Coleman, "In the 21st Century, to Be a Musician Is to Be an Entrepreneur," *Forbes*, January 19, 2018, www.forbes.com/sites/alisoncoleman/2018/01/19/in-the-21st-century-to-be-a-musician-is-to-be-an-entrepreneur/#4c61fef64470.

2. "Global Entertainment & Media Outlook, 2018–2022," PricewaterhouseCoopers, 2018.

Acknowledgments

I am grateful to the folks at Rowman & Littlefield for their support of this undertaking, especially Natalie Mandziuk, Michael Tan, and John Cerullo. Maureen Coleman, Susan Mojave, Aferdian Stephens, and Justin Rosin provided critical feedback and advice, making the book more user-friendly. Finally, I want to thank Christine and John Lancaster, Stephanie Blythe, and Tammy Mesic for their deep kindness and unwavering support.

Introduction

This is a reference book about entrepreneurship for musicians. It assumes you are a musician or other creative type looking for some direction for planning, launching, and formalizing some enterprise in the cultural and creative industries. My first book, *The Enterprising Musician's Guide to Performer Contracts*, walks readers through contract basics, then focuses on clauses commonly found in contracts that performers are regularly handed to sign: engagement (gig) contracts and artist-management contracts. That book provides self-help tools for those who find they don't have a written contract and need to determine whether the promises made to them are actionable, or those who have performed but can't get paid. The genesis for that book was the accumulation of sample contracts and problems my friends and clients brought to me during and immediately after I finished law school.

I wrote this book for musicians interested in taking action and launching a creative enterprise without regard to any specific artistic practice. It doesn't matter whether your plans include you being an artist/sole proprietor, being an artistic collaborator co-authoring songs, being a band member, forming a theatrical production company, or starting an arts festival or community music school. All new businesses begin with the idea, passion, and hard work. This book will help steer you through the uncertainty and decision-making that can easily mire you in frustration and self-doubt.

Divided into five parts, this book contemplates a chronology from business ideation through actual development and ultimately protection of your content and the brand you are putting out into the world. Like my first book, it's not necessary to read this book straight through, although you may save yourself some time if you read Chapter 1 before reading all the specifics provided in Parts II and III. Chapter 1 will help you organize your thoughts and help steer you to the chapter(s) most relevant to you. You'll also find the index to be a great navigational tool.

Part I focuses on getting started. It walks you through basic concepts for organizing your thoughts and planning the overall architecture of your business. It will get you thinking early about how you expect your business to develop and change over time. It asks you to consider your tolerance for personal financial risk as you look ahead. Anticipating these issues now will save you headaches later.

Part II introduces the four most common for-profit legal structures for businesses in the U.S.: sole proprietorships (Chapter 2), partnerships (Chapter 3), limited liability companies (Chapter 4), and corporations (Chapter 5). Each structure is discussed in detail including their benefits and drawbacks. In each chapter, you'll find a basic formation checklist and, where applicable, sample documents to use as a basis for creating your own.

Part III introduces alternatives to traditional for-profit business models: nonprofit entities (Chapter 6) and hybrid structures, which are for-profit entities that share the public benefit characteristics common to nonprofit businesses (Chapter 7). If the mission of your for-profit business is intended to benefit society in any way, consider reviewing these newer, hybrid legal structures. If your enterprise is one that fits squarely within a typical public donation/grant-funded model, then a nonprofit organization is likely best.

Part IV focuses on state and federal compliance matters. Chapter 8 introduces regulatory topics relating to naming and launching a business once the legal structure has been decided. Chapter 9 discusses some of the legal issues relating to hiring employees and engaging independent contractors to help expand your business. Protecting your business through the purchase of insurance is also discussed.

Part V is about protecting your interests while making money from your creative output. Chapter 10 provides guidance for those who work in active collaboration with others distinct from forming a partnership legal structure. Chapter 11 walks you through the basic principles of copyright law. It also contains a ten-question quiz at the end of the chapter to test your understanding of concepts presented. Chapter 12 introduces various types of licenses common to the music industry. Finally, Chapter 13 discusses several other types of contracts musicians should understand and have some facility with to protect their interests.

There are three appendixes: Appendix A is a comparison chart of the upsides and downsides of the business structures introduced in Parts II and III. Appendix B is an analysis of the copyright quiz questions from Chapter 11, and Appendix C contains a chart to help bring some clarity to the main types of music industry licenses and the typical rightsholders for each.

Finally, because there is a fair amount of regulatory information throughout the book, there are many references to "states." In addition to states, the United States is also comprised of districts, territories, and possessions. In every instance, *states* should be interpreted to mean *jurisdiction* without regard to any specific legal distinction.

THIS BOOK DOES NOT PROVIDE LEGAL ADVICE

It's important to understand what legal advice is and what it is not. Legal advice is something specific: it's when a lawyer gathers and considers all relevant facts, determines which laws apply, and predicts how a court is likely to apply the laws to that specific situation. This book cannot provide legal advice because specific facts are not known, therefore applicable law can't be identified, and the likely outcome can't be predicted. The best any author can do is introduce concepts in a general way, along with explanatory examples, and make readers aware of potential risks. It's up to you to weigh your tolerance for risk against any course of action.

My hope is that this book will help you reach your goals by introducing options, facilitating decision-making, and providing some tools to advance your progress.

Ready? Let's get going.

PART I

GETTING STARTED

1

Choosing the Business Structure That's Right for You

The steps to forming a new business aren't particularly difficult, but the process does require planning and decision-making. There's a lot to think about, and the process can be daunting, but you can do it—one step at a time. If you've done any reading about business formation, you've likely seen articles referencing considerations for choosing a legal structure for your business including contract requirements, regulatory paperwork, ongoing recordkeeping and reporting, exposure to personal liability, and challenges relating to financing growth, among others. Any one of these considerations will point you in one clear direction, while another will challenge you to reconsider that choice. The truth is there is no *one* business model that is best overall. Each entrepreneur must decide, based on all of the criteria including individual personality, which structure is best.

What follows in this chapter are what I consider to be the baseline factors for getting started, but which are often overlooked or underappreciated by entrepreneurs. They are (1) whether your enterprise will be for-profit or not-for-profit; (2) the nature of ownership and degree of control you expect; and (3) your tolerance for financial risk. Giving some early thought to these topics will help steer you toward the legal structure that will best suit your plans and provide for a more organic unfolding of your business as it expands.

FOR-PROFIT OR NONPROFIT

What is the mission of your business? Is the central purpose of your business to make money from your music, or is it to provide a public good such as creating access to used musical instruments for school districts in need? Honest answers to fundamental questions like these are necessary to determine whether your business will be for-profit or nonprofit.

Despite the name, you can still make money via a reasonable salary as a principal in a nonprofit organization. The two central issues between for-profit and nonprofit organizations are ownership and profits. No one "owns" a nonprofit; those organizations exist to benefit the public (or a segment of the public) in some way that is recognized by state and federal governments.

In for-profit enterprises, once business expenses have been paid, any profit becomes available to the owner(s). In a nonprofit enterprise, any profits that remain after paying expenses must, by law, be reinvested back into the organization to further its stated mission.

Traditional for-profit business structures are a sole proprietorship, one of the partnership models, a limited liability company (LLC), or a corporation. If your plans include starting a mission-centered business, the traditional option was forming a nonprofit organization, but now there are newer, hybrid business models available in many states that allow business owners of mission-centered enterprises to make a modest profit.

Formation costs are low for sole proprietorships and for general partnerships because of the lack of formalities and state approvals inherent in those two business structures. Setting up an LLC, corporation, or a hybrid entity involves filing paperwork with the Secretary of State (or the functional equivalent). Formation costs for these structures will include state filing fees, possible franchise tax payments (on a state-by-state basis), and attorney fees if you decide to engage one. Each of these legal structures will be discussed in detail in Parts II and III.

Here are some things to consider when deciding between launching a nonprofit business or a mission-centered, for-profit hybrid enterprise:

1. Will you want to sell your mission-centered business one day and cash out? If so, then forming a nonprofit isn't for you because that model doesn't allow for personal inurement. A hybrid model might better meet your needs; see Chapter 7.
2. Does the central purpose of your enterprise fall within one of the enumerated Internal Revenue Service (IRS) categories for qualifying as a charitable organization? If so and if you are more interested in community-based

governance than an entity-focused board of directors and you can see the possibilities for your enterprise to raise money through fundraising and grant writing, then forming a nonprofit corporation is likely a better option; see Chapter 6.

OWNERSHIP AND CONTROL

Ownership is about control—control of decision-making and, ultimately, profits. But ownership is also about liability for business losses and responsibility for strategic thinking. Not having a co-owner will challenge the single owner to avoid seeing strategy through one lens. It will require the single owner to proactively seek advice outside the organization to help weigh options and strategize the company's path to growth.

How many owners do you expect to have in the future? Consideration of the degree of control you prefer will require you to take an honest inventory of your personality, strengths, and weaknesses. Are you a strong collaborator, or do you prefer to be solo? Sole proprietorships have only one owner. If you invite a business partner into your enterprise—even if you never formalize it with a written agreement—your business just became a general partnership unless you have elected some other structure formalized by a state filing. Unless you have a formal partnership agreement that outlines each partner's rights and duties to the partnership, state partnership law will fill in the details. Be warned, those rules rarely reflect what partners intended or even anticipated because the law will make assumptions that may not be true for you and your business partner(s). See Chapter 3 for a discussion of general partnerships.

If you are someone who relishes independent decision-making, a single-owner business structure might be best for you. A sole proprietorship is the most obvious choice, but some states also allow single-member LLCs and single-owner corporations. But while the day-to-day operations of a corporation are executed by corporate officers, you would still need to periodically report to a board of directors who provide corporate governance. If answering to a board isn't for you, forming a single-member LLC might be preferable because that business model does not require a board.

How do you want to spend your workday? What is your tolerance for completing paperwork? Are you good with deadlines? Will you want to be keeping track of filing deadlines and filling out paperwork, or will you want to be focused on the primary responsibilities of making product or providing services? Running a corporation involves a fair amount of ongoing compliance reporting—usually more than that of an LLC. Will you have the money to hire someone to handle payroll, bookkeeping, and other administrative tasks?

Another consideration is growth. How quickly do you plan to expand your business and how will you bring in capital to do that? Many small businesses start as a sole proprietorship or partnership and, over time, evolve such that the simpler business structure no longer makes sense. These enterprises morph into LLCs or corporations. If you plan to grow quickly and want to be able to attract outside investors, you likely will want to form a corporation. See Chapter 4 for a discussion of LLCs and Chapter 5 for a discussion of corporations.

PERSONAL LIABILITY: EVALUATING YOUR TOLERANCE FOR RISK

Entrepreneurs tend to focus on the excitement of launching and operating a business, but often underappreciate the degree to which their choice of legal structure will expose their personal assets to risk. Once you understand liability, generally, you'll be in a better position to evaluate your tolerance for risk, which will inform your choice of legal structure. The term *liability* refers, in this instance, to the extent to which your personal assets (your bank accounts, home, and the other assets you own) are subject to seizure and liquidation to satisfy a business debt of one kind or another.

Let's take a look at the five main types of liability that arise as a business owner. They are (1) liability resulting from unsatisfied business debts; (2) other business-related liabilities; (3) *vicarious liability*; (4) *agency law* and *joint and several liability*; and (5) *tort liability*. The choice of legal structure for your enterprise will either minimize your personal liability or expand your exposure to it.

Unsatisfied Business Debts

Liabilities relating to business debts are fairly obvious: debts assumed by the business. Examples of these are business credit cards, commercial loans, balances due on inventory purchases, equipment leases, property leases, and other types of contract-based obligations owners commit to in the name of the business, including instances in which owners personally guarantee a business commitment. Don't be put off if a potential creditor asks you for a personal guarantee—owners of newer enterprises are often asked to personally guarantee business debts because the business has not yet had the opportunity to establish its own credit history.

Other Business-Related Liabilities

Other liabilities that arise out of business obligations include duties imposed on business owners who rent commercial spaces or otherwise provide goods or services to clients. For example, if you rent office space, your landlord will typically require you to provide proof of commercial general liability insurance intended to provide financial protection against both you and the landlord for specified risks inherent in operating a business—specifically, premises coverage (nicknamed "slip and fall" coverage). If a client is injured on the rental premises, they can sue you alleging that you were negligent (breached your legal duty) by failing to maintain safe premises for your business guests. Similarly, if you rent a performance venue, you will often be required to provide proof of insurance before signing that lease and will be required to indemnify the venue for your negligence. If you don't purchase this insurance coverage, don't have adequate limits of insurance, or your policy language isn't broad enough to contemplate the risks presented in your business, you will have personal liability for the remaining exposures.

Your clients could also sue you for professional negligence in the provision of services or goods that they allege caused them a financial loss. For example, if you are commissioned to score music for a television commercial and your client is later sued for copyright infringement, they will bring you and your business into that lawsuit seeking indemnification from you. If you are not careful in choosing your business trade name, you could also be sued for trademark infringement for using a name already in use even if that name doesn't appear on the federal registry. Some of these exposures can be covered by insurance, so ask your insurance professional about this possibility, but be sure to provide that person with a complete picture of your business so you get a policy that fits your needs.

Finally, other liabilities include tax liability for failure to pay income tax or, if you sell merchandise, failure to remit sales or use tax to your state and, in some cases, municipality. Business owners with employees are also financially liable for uninsured workers' compensation losses when an employee is injured on the job and your insurance is inadequate to cover the loss as well as the amount of taxes you, as the employer, failed to withhold from employee paychecks.

Vicarious Liability

Vicarious liability is liability imposed on us as the result of the actions or inactions of others. As the name suggests, vicarious liability does not necessarily flow to the business owner from their own actions or decisions, but rather it is imposed on the business owner by virtue of their status as owner. Owners of businesses that are not structured to limit or completely shield the owners from liability are vicariously liable for the actions of their employees within the course of their workday. In this context, vicarious liability most often arises in the following two scenarios: (1) business owner liability arising out of the employer-employee relationship;[1] and (2) business owner liability arising under agency law in which the actions or inactions of your business partners are imputed to you.

The best way to limit your exposure to vicarious liability claims brought by third parties relating to actions of your employees (and to protect your employees from personal injury) is to have a detailed employee handbook that every employee is required to affirmatively sign on an annual basis indicating that they have read, understand, and will comply with the protocols that the business owner has developed including those regarding on-the-job safety and complying with general business protocols.

EXAMPLE 1.1

For example, if an employee of your sole proprietorship music business is preparing a musical arrangement for an event and fails to secure the music rights, you can be sued for copyright infringement arising out of your employee's lack of diligence for failing to procure the rights from the rightsholder(s). Your personal assets are at risk to satisfy any resulting legal judgment rendered against you.

Agency Law and Joint and Several Liability

The general partnership legal structure presents the greatest exposure to personal liability because, in addition to the risk inherent in operating any business including being vicariously liable for employees, two additional concepts expand partner liability: the application of *agency law* and *joint and several liability*.

Agency law is an area of law that governs our lives whenever we engage someone else to do something for us—we give them the power to make decisions on our behalf and bind us to those decisions as though we ourselves made them. In this situation, we are the *principal*, and the person to whom we've given authority to act on our behalf is our *agent*. It's always a risk to give another person decision-making authority because we are bound by their acts providing they didn't abuse their authority. In a partnership, each partner is considered to be both a principal and an agent of the partnership; each partner can bind the partnership, themselves, and the other partners. A solid partnership agreement can restrict partners' authority, thereby reducing risk to the enterprise and to other partners.

Joint and several liability is a legal theory applicable to partnerships that means if the partnership is sued and lacks the funds to pay the full judgment awarded, the plaintiff can pursue the balance of the judgment against any one of the partners individually. So, the partner with the greatest personal assets can be legally called upon to pony up the money to satisfy the judgment. In this scenario, the partner who paid the judgment would then have to pursue indemnification/reimbursement from the other partners. For this reason, it is critically important to trust your partners as though each is granted check-writing authority on your personal bank account.

Tort Liability

Tort is the French word for a "wrong." A "tortfeasor" is a wrong-doer. Tort liability is an area of law that includes both intentional and unintentional acts that cause injury to another. One example of an unintentional tort is negligence, which means you failed to do something you had a legal duty to do. For example, if you backed your car into a pedestrian in the grocery store parking lot, you breached the duty to exercise reasonable care owed to that person by failing to safely operate your automobile.

Examples of the business tort of negligence include *wrongful hiring* and *wrongful supervision* of an employee. Business owners can be held liable for negligently hiring someone if the employee caused harm to another and the employer didn't conduct a background check on the employee that would have revealed criminal conduct such as theft or violence or even drug abuse. Similarly, business owners who fail to provide adequate training and supervision of their employees can be held liable for injuries or property damage caused by their employees in executing their work duties.

An intentional act is doing something deliberate and with intent such as running another car off the road in a fit of road rage. No insurance policy may cover intentional or reckless acts like that. Similarly, it is generally against public policy for a business to indemnify a business owner, board member, officer, or employee for such acts. Regardless of whether we injure someone negligently or intentionally, we are all liable to one another for the injuries we cause.

CONCLUSION

Business models with public benefit missions are no longer limited to the non-profit sector. Today, for-profit, hybrid models are available to entrepreneurs, making it possible to provide a public benefit without requiring owners to forgo the traditional benefits of ownership and profit. Not all entrepreneurs are alike—understanding how you want to spend your time, make decisions, and manage your business should factor into the legal structure best for you. Evaluating your tolerance for risk in conjunction with the exposures your business plan presents will help you choose a legal structure that will best shield you against those risks.

I hope this chapter helped you anticipate some of your business needs and introduced options available to you in preparing to meet those needs. Getting a handle on these foundational issues will be critical to understanding the legal structures discussed in Parts II and III and, ultimately, choosing the legal structure that is right for your business. Appendix A provides a comparison chart of business structures.

NOTE

1. Under the legal doctrine *respondeat superior*, which loosely translates to "let the master answer."

PART II

TRADITIONAL FOR-PROFIT LEGAL STRUCTURES

2

Sole Proprietorships

Most musicians in the United States are sole proprietors without even knowing it. They often refer to themselves as *freelancers*. A freelancer is someone who (1) works multiple jobs; (2) earns income reported via Form 1099 as an independent contractor; and (3) does not have employees. Few working musicians in the United States are actually employees of an organization that pays them a salary reported via Form W-2, but some examples are members of a large orchestra.

Generally defined as a single-owner, self-employed person operating a business for profit, the sole proprietorship is the most common legal structure for a business in the United States. In 2014, 75.9% of all businesses were non-employer businesses representing nearly 25 million entities.[1] In 2016, there were 25.5 million non-farm owner sole proprietorship tax returns filed in the United States.[2] According to census documents from that same year, the Arts, Entertainment, and Recreation sector of sole proprietorships reported business receipts of $12.4 billion.[3]

A sole proprietor can have employees, but there can be only one owner of the business enterprise. Common examples include your neighborhood barbershop or the grandmas across town who babysit kids after school. You've likely heard the term *Mom and Pop Shop*. If one of those two people working at the business is its owner and one is an employee, it's a true sole proprietorship. If both people own it, it's likely a general partnership unless state paperwork was filed to specify another structure.

Sole proprietorships are very easy and inexpensive to start because there's little paperwork, no contracts among co-owners to negotiate, and few approvals required from local authorities. The business owner must comply with local zoning laws, inquire about any required business permits, and obtain permission to use a trade name for the business if other than the owner's name.

OWNERSHIP AND CONTROL

The upside of a sole proprietorship is that, as the sole owner, you get to make all the decisions without having to negotiate with a business partner. You have full authority to execute your business strategy and are entitled to 100% of the profits earned from the business. The downside is that without a business partner, you'll need to look outside your business for advice or strategy ideas.

PERSONAL LIABILITY

Another downside of the sole proprietorship business model is liability. Business owners are 100% personally liable for their business debts including business credit cards, loans, letters of credit, and other contractual obligations. Sole proprietors are also vicariously liable for the actions of their employees. See Chapter 9 for a discussion of both employees and personal liability.

PROFIT AND GROWTH

Because of the high level of transparency that exists between the sole proprietor business owner and their business, it can be difficult to get your hands on capital (money) to expand your business. Typically, business owners apply for bank loans, but for sole proprietors these can be difficult to obtain because they look so much like personal loans. Similarly, because sole proprietors don't have stock to sell to raise money to expand their business, it can be difficult to attract investors.

TAX TREATMENT

The sole proprietorship, as a business entity, is not considered to be separate from its owner for tax purposes. Because of this, business profits or losses are recognized on the owner's individual income tax returns. Sole proprietorships file federal Form 1040, Schedule C (where they recognize profits and losses), and Schedule SE (the form used by self-employed people to calculate the amount of tax due, if any).

FORMING A SOLE PROPRIETORSHIP

The sole proprietorship business model is attractive to many entrepreneurs because it's so easy and inexpensive to launch—you just start conducting business.

Formation Steps

1. Choose a business name.
2. If using a trade name, conduct a search to determine whether it's available.
3. Reserve your trade name with the state (optional).
4. Research and obtain any required local permits or licenses.
5. Determine whether you need business insurance (and any insurance required of employers if you plan to hire employees).
6. Obtain federal and, if relevant, state employer identification numbers (EINs).
7. Open a bank account using your EIN.

CONCLUSION

With the simplicity and ease of launching a sole proprietorship comes a trade-off: it can be difficult to raise money or obtain loans to expand your business. Similarly, the benefits of being in control of all strategic decision-making and resulting profits must be balanced against the financial liability inherent in the sole proprietorship business structure. Appendix A provides a chart that compares sole proprietorships against other business models.

SOLE PROPRIETORSHIP RESOURCES

U.S. Small Business Administration, "Choose a Business Structure," www.sba .gov/content/sole-proprietorship-0

NOTES

1. United States Census Bureau, "Having a Boss vs. Working for Yourself," May 24, 2016, www.census.gov/library/visualizations/2016/comm/cb16-94_nonemployer .html.

2. Adrian Dungan, "Sole Proprietorship Returns, Tax Year 2016," *Statistics of Income Bulletin* (Spring 2019), www.irs.gov/pub/irs-soi/soi-a-inpr-id1905.pdf.

3. Dungan, "Sole Proprietorship Returns."

3

General Partnerships

A partnership is generally defined as an association of two or more persons (or even entities such as other partnerships or corporations) conducting business as co-owners for profit. Anyone old enough to execute a binding contract (usually eighteen years old) can legally form a partnership. The partnership model is a common legal structure for creative people who frequently collaborate, whether co-writing a musical, co-producing a film, forming a band or string quartet, or working on an interdisciplinary project. The right to form a business and work with others as co-owners is a well-established right under the common law. Typically, each partner contributes money, property, and/or services to start the enterprise.

TYPES OF PARTNERSHIPS

There are three basic types of partnerships: (1) general partnerships; (2) limited partnerships; and (3) limited liability partnerships. This chapter will focus on the general partnership model because, of the three, that structure is the best fit for musicians and other creative collaborators.

GENERAL PARTNERSHIPS

General partnerships are the most common type of business structure in which there are two or more owners. There are two statutes that govern general partnerships in the United States: the Uniform Partnership Act (UPA) and the Revised Uniform Partnership Act (RUPA). The UPA was promulgated in 1914, but only adopted by about thirty-seven states. The RUPA was amended several times over the years, most recently in 1997. Every state, except Louisiana, has adopted a version of one of these statutes. Despite the existence of these laws, they only exist as a backstop. In other words, if you and your creative team start doing business as a partnership, but never sat down and hammered out a partnership agreement, one of the versions of these laws will apply to your situation by default depending on your state and which law (or version of it) was adopted, if either. You may not want, for example, profits and losses shared equally by default. A better approach is to have a written general partnership agreement that spells out every aspect of how your enterprise should operate.

The hallmarks of a general partnership are that each partner intends to (1) conduct business on an ongoing basis for profit; (2) participate in the day-to-day operations of the business; and (3) share in partnership profits and losses. A key benefit of a general partnership is that, like sole proprietorships, a general partnership is easy to form. Generally, few to no state forms or approvals are required. However, sometimes this simplicity leads to partners rushing into a business relationship without understanding or appreciating the full range of decisions that will need to be made—something that a formal, written partnership agreement would have addressed up front for everyone's benefit and peace of mind.

OWNERSHIP AND CONTROL

Like Limited Liability Companies (LLCs), partnerships are self-governing, so the partners enjoy full oversight and control of the enterprise—there is no board of directors to answer to. The partners make all the decisions and equally participate in carrying out the enterprise's purpose. The partners control day-to-day business operations including those relating to real property (real estate), personal property (tangible things like computers, guitars, and speakers), and creative decisions related to intangibles such as the partnership's trade name (*assumed name*) and the intellectual property that flows from the creative work of the partnership (such as musical compositions, recordings, ringtones, etc.). Partners usually share profits and business liabilities in proportional share to their ownership interest.

PERSONAL LIABILITY

Notable in partnerships is the extent to which partners are financially liable for both the partnership itself and, to varying degrees, the actions of the other partners. A partner's liability exposure is generally high due to the applicability of agency law including the legal doctrine of joint and several liability. Partnership law varies by state; the degree of variance depends largely on the version of partnership law a state has adopted and the application of judicial precedent for applying those rules to past disputes in that jurisdiction.

Agency law applies to general partnerships. Agency law governs situations where one person is the *principal* and another is the principal's *agent* with authority to act on the principal's behalf. In a general partnership, each partner is both a principal and an agent for the partnership. Each partner can act on behalf of the partnership with full partnership authority unless a partnership agreement restricts that partner's authority in some way. So, any partner can bind the partnership to a deal that another partner may not feel is in the partnership's best interest. Because of the rules that apply under agency law and of the high potential for partner liability, partners owe each other and the partnership a fiduciary duty—the highest level of loyalty. Thus, partners are expected to exercise the highest level of responsibility to the other partners including not misappropriating partnership opportunities for personal gain. Every partner must act in the best interests of the partnership and of the other partners.

Partners generally have joint and several liability for partnership debts and for the actions of the other partners. Joint and several liability means that each partner could be held financially liable, up to 100%, for partnership debts or other liabilities. For example, if a band is organized as a general partnership and suffers financial difficulties and can't repay business debts, any one of the band members can be held 100% personally liable for remaining partnership debt after the partnership's assets have been depleted.

Similarly, if one of the band members is in a car accident while on partnership business and is held legally liable for bodily injury and property damage suffered by a third party as a result of the accident, then each of the other band members' personal assets can be seized to satisfy a legal judgment made against the partnership. Despite the increased exposure to personal liability in the general partnership business structure, liability can be managed contractually through a well-drafted partnership agreement and the purchase of insurance. On a more personal level, individual partners may work with a financial advisor to organize their assets in a way that reduces their exposure to the liability inherent in a general partnership legal structure. See Chapter 1 for a discussion of personal liability.

PROFIT AND GROWTH

Similar to sole proprietorships, raising money is difficult because a general partnership doesn't have investors and doesn't have stock to sell to potential owners. Additionally, the partnership can find it difficult to obtain bank loans because of the relative transparency of most general partnership tax structures in which the partnership is not considered a separate entity for tax purposes.

TAX TREATMENT

General partnerships have options for how they will be taxed. These options reflect the decision to either have the partnership, as an entity, recognized for tax purposes (and be taxed like a C corporation) or to allow the profits and losses to pass through the entity for recognition on the individual partners' tax returns (under a principle known as "pass-through taxation"). Choosing to be taxed as an entity means that the partnership will be taxed twice: first it will be taxed at the entity level, then the individual partners will be taxed on their respective profits. Where no election is affirmatively made, pass-through taxation is the default.

Under a pass-through taxation scheme, partnerships file an informational tax form (IRS Form 1065) and the individual partners are given a document by the partnership called a Schedule K-1 under which they report their individual profits, losses, and deductions relating to their participation in the partnership. Because partners are considered business owners and not employees, each partner will also file IRS Form SE (for calculating self-employment tax owed for social security and Medicare).

TYPICAL STATE DEFAULT RULES

As stated above, state default rules apply to general partnerships whose partners have not reduced their intentions to a formal partnership agreement that serves as the enterprise's governing document. If you don't want the default rules to apply to your arrangement, then you and your partners should hammer out a formal, written partnership agreement that spells out your intentions. The chart below shows basic partnership default rules you can expect to apply in the absence of a partnership agreement. When you begin to draft your partnership agreement, it may be a good idea to check with an attorney to determine whether there are any default rules in your jurisdiction that cannot be changed by contract.

Issue	Default Rule
Ownership	Shared equally.
Profits	Shared equally on the assumption that each partner contributed the same amount of start-up capital; no partner receives a salary unless provided for in the partnership agreement.
Losses	Shared equally on the assumption that each partner contributed the same amount of start-up capital.
Ending the partnership	Partnership dissolves automatically when any partner dies, becomes disabled to the extent that they can no longer participate in the business, or decides to leave the business.
Partnership physical property (musical instruments, recording equipment, tour gear, office equipment, etc.)	Ownership of partnership tangible property (or funds resulting from liquidation of that property) is shared equally among partners upon termination of the partnership.
Partnership's intellectual property (music)	Ownership of partnership intellectual property is shared equally.
Ownership of the trade name	The partnership owns the trade name. Once the partnership ceases to exist, no partner may use it for another enterprise.
Management	Equal right to management regardless of capital contribution.
Voting rights	All partners have equal voting rights for important decisions (majority voting).

GENERAL PARTNERSHIP DECISION POINTS

There are several up-front decisions you'll need to make before you sit down to formalize your general partnership agreement. These include basic matters like the stated purpose and primary location of your business to details requiring negotiation among your partners including how profits and losses will be allocated and whether those should tie directly to each partner's ownership interest. The categories that follow will help you get your arms around the things you should be thinking about in preparation for finalizing the details of your partnership and committing those details to a formal agreement.

Personal Property

One thing that musicians often forget to handle up front, but which is central to who we are as creative people, is ownership rights in intellectual property (IP). IP is a form of personal property, the same as a car or laptop, except IP is intangible. IP rights can be owned, licensed, or sold just as tangible personal property can be owned, licensed, or sold. Protecting your IP rights is especially important for those who work in collaborative settings. If you are a member of a band, you need to know who owns the band's trade name so issues don't arise after the band splits up and one or more people want to continue to use the existing name in a new group. Names can be protected under federal trademark law. A trademark is a name or symbol that indicates the source or owner of goods or services. See Chapter 8 for a discussion of trademarks and trade names.

If you co-write songs, you need to decide up front what your ownership interest will be in the songs you write with others unless a future situation arises that calls for an exception. If the standard percentages agreed upon don't seem right after a particular songwriting session, ask to negotiate a different arrangement for that one song, but you'll need to get that deviation from the primary ownership plan in writing as soon as is practicable. Song ownership is important because that ownership percentage will determine the percentage of money due you from all future licensing income. For a discussion of copyright and music licensing, see Chapters 11 and 12.

If you are collaborating on a project with others, such as writing a musical, you'll need to decide who owns what. In the annotated collaboration agreement provided in Chapter 10, the composer, book writer, and lyricist decided that they want to retain copyright ownership in the individual elements each contributed to the musical so each can exploit their element independently of the musical as a whole. For example, if the book writer chose to lead an acting workshop using dialogue from the musical for technical work with acting students, they could do that without compensating the composer and lyricist or even having to ask their permission to do so.

If you want this type of flexibility in your partnership, you'll need to have a formal, written agreement that spells this out because in the absence of such agreement, federal copyright law will assume that the works resulting from your collaborative efforts are "joint works." This means that all contributors to a given project will own an undivided interest in the whole. For joint works, independent revenue streams are not possible; all income from other sources would need to be split equally among the contributors. Not wanting your state's partnership default rules to apply to your arrangement is another important reason to have a formalized partnership agreement. See Chapter 10 for an example of a collaboration agreement in which the collaborators make clear that they have not formed a partnership and that they do not intend that their project (a musical) be considered a joint work under copyright law.

Management

All contracts must outline each party's rights and responsibilities under the contract because these will form the basis for the binding promises each makes to the others. My first book goes into detail about the four required elements all contracts need to be valid: an offer, acceptance of that offer, terms that are definite, and consideration (which is defined as a bargained-for exchange of values). If you are concerned whether a contract provides terms that are definite enough, look for the agreement to spell out what you have promised to do and what was promised to you by the other partners. All agreements should make clear what promises were made among the partners.

Partnership agreements are a type of contract, so the rules of contract law apply to agreements between two or more individuals who form a partnership regardless of whether the partnership is a pop duo, wedding band, string quartet, or any other collaborative enterprise in which the group is intending to form an ongoing partnership and share profits in some way.

Partnership agreements between musicians should clearly outline the following:

- The role each partner will play in the partnership
- Who is responsible for what and when those duties must be executed
- Who has decision-making authority on specific issues
- What limitations exist on those authorities, if any
- Voting, tiebreakers, and dispute resolution

Partners' Roles

Partners can, but don't need to, have equal roles in the partnership. Some partners might contribute more money than time. You and your partners might choose for this to remain fluid, but you'll need some mechanism, like voting, to allow for every partner to have a voice in partnership decision-making. For example, if you're in a band, who decides what venues you'll play, what music will be played at those gigs, and whether the band will accept a gig that pays less than what the band normally agrees to?

Authority

As noted above, general partners can be held financially and legally liable for the actions of their partners. If you give a specific partner authority to do something, you should also consider how that authority should be limited in a way that allows for that partner to move the partnership forward without unnecessarily tying up every single decision. For example, if you are a band and a partner needs to purchase equipment, your agreement could allow for each partner/band member to incur up to $500 in equipment expenses before they need to bring the purchase decision up for vote. Similarly, if you don't yet have a booking agent, you might decide to provide a salary to a partner to contact venues and book gigs, but the group might decide that all potential gigs that fall within a certain geographic radius and fee fall within that partner's authority, but anything outside those parameters needs to be brought to the group for vote.

Voting

Voting rights are one of the most important things to consider in any collaboration, regardless of whether you're a member of a band, a board of directors, or part of a group project. There are two basic issues to consider: (1) what things do you want to put up for vote; and (2) what kind of voting do you want for each of those things?

Issues for Vote

There are countless things collaborators might want approval rights for: publicity expenditures; choosing business partners (such as publicists and agents); monetary deals that exploit your work; touring; merchandising; or adding or removing a partner. For project collaborators, you'll likely want to vote on how best to exploit the project to allow for an income stream from your contribution. You may also want to put the following items up for vote: whether to hire professionals to help market your work (an agent, personal manager, publicist, social media expert, etc.) and who, specifically, should assume those roles and how to compensate them for their work (flat fee, percentage, etc.).

Type of Vote

Voting can be by simple majority or unanimous, one vote per partner or you might allow for unit voting to be used where two people representing a voting bloc receive one vote. Unit voting might be used where there is more than one person contributing to a single element of the collaboration (e.g., two lyricists).

Unit Voting Example

Voting shall be by unit; it being irrelevant the number of persons comprising a unit.

a. Each unit shall be entitled to one vote.

b. In the event two or more persons constituting a unit cannot agree upon a voting decision, then the vote of that unit shall be the will of the majority.

c. In the event there is a tie vote within a unit containing an equal number of persons, the parties within the unit appoint _____ to determine the result of the vote.

If your partnership involves an even number of people, you may want to decide early, prior to a dispute, who the group might want to cast a vote as a tiebreaker. You can delineate a tiebreaker for artistic decisions and another person for business decisions or have the same trusted person serve in both capacities. The person chosen as tiebreaker can be shown on your agreement by name or by title (whomever is in that role at the time the tiebreaking vote is needed, for example, "the individual currently serving as our tour manager").

You may also want to vote on how to remove and replace a partner. Once someone leaves your enterprise, you may want to allow the voting rights to pass to their replacement, allow the voting right to die, or provide for some other alternative. You may also decide that some issues are so important that a unanimous vote is required, but keep in mind that unanimous voting can result in stalemates. You don't want to miss out on a critically important, time-bound opportunity because the partners can't reach a unanimous decision.

FINANCIAL MATTERS

The partnership agreement must contain provisions for the following:

- How profits are distributed
- How much capital, if any, each partner will contribute
- Whether any contribution will be considered a loan and how the loan will be repaid
- Whether any partner's contribution will be non-monetary ("sweat equity")
- Whether any partner will receive a salary
- How losses and expenses are shared among partners

Distribution of Profits

In the absence of a partnership agreement, general partnership law assumes that all the partners have an equal ownership interest in the enterprise. That assumption leads to the conclusion, right or wrong, that each partner is entitled to an equal share of profits. If this is not true for your enterprise, you'll need a written agreement that makes the details of your situation clear. For example, if you formed a three-person partnership in which you all agreed that you, as Partner A, would contribute $2,500 as start-up capital, Partner B would contribute $1,500, and Partner C would contribute only sweat equity initially, your agreement should make this clear.

Allocation of Losses/Repayment of Loans

Continuing with the example immediately above, your agreement should also address whether Partners B and C will perform their partnership duties without sharing in any profits until all partners have contributed the equivalent of $2,500 in one form or another. An alternate approach would be to set the contribution amount lower at $1,000 and treat Partners A and B's contributions as loans, $1,500 and $500, respectively, that must be repaid by Partner C before any partner participates in profit sharing. Whichever approach is taken, these decisions must be formally captured in a written partnership agreement.

Like income, partnership expenses are likely to be prorated equally among the partners (such as hiring an agent or attorney), but other expenses may not be. You'll need to hash those details out early. If a songwriter needs to update their music-writing software program, should that be considered a personal expense or an expense to be shared among all partners? What if a band member wants to buy an expensive piece of equipment? Should expenses be allowed to accrue, or should they be submitted on some agreed-upon timeframe for approval and reimbursement?

Non-Monetary Contributions

If personal equipment will be contributed (loaned, donated, or sold) to the collaboration, it would be wise to spell those details out in the agreement to avoid a dispute in the future when memories have faded and tensions are high. For example: "The partners agree that Johnny X intends to donate his Fancy Speakers, Serial Number 123pdq, to the Band without compensation." If you anticipate a lot of equipment or other non-monetary items brought to the partnership, it might make sense to list them under each person's name and the specific disposition of those items (loaned, donated, or sold to the partnership).

PARTNERSHIP CONTINGENCIES

The topic no one ever wants to discuss at the beginning of an exciting business collaboration is one of the most important that should be hashed out thoroughly and early in the discussions: what happens when something goes wrong? Specifically, when it comes to general partnerships, this topic can be broken down into four contingencies: (1) death of a partner; (2) disability of a partner; (3) partner disassociation; and (4) partnership dissolution. Related to death, disability, or disassociation is the question as to whether the partnership should continue and, if so, under what terms can a new partner be brought into the partnership, if at all?

Death of a Partner

You already know that in the absence of a formal partnership agreement, state partnership law will apply to disputes among partners. The general rule that is applied in that instance is when any partner dies, the partnership automatically dissolves. Having a partnership agreement will allow you to control what should happen if a partner dies including whether the partnership should continue, how the estate can be compensated for the deceased partner's interest in the partnership, and whether the partner should be replaced by a new partner and how that process will work.

Disability of a Partner

What should happen if a partner becomes mentally or physically disabled to the extent that they cannot effectively contribute to the partnership? What constitutes a "disability," and who decides whether that partner is disabled? Should the disabled partner be replaced and, if so, how?

Some partnership agreements provide a broad definition of "disabled" that effectively says that if a partner cannot contribute to the partnership in X number of consecutive days or X number of days in a given 365-day period, they will be considered disabled for the purposes of the partnership. Language like this could be triggered by anything including depression, addiction, disinterest in working, or more traditional understandings of "disabled" including being physically unable to actively participate in the business any longer.

Disassociation from the Partnership

Disassociation refers to being separated from the partnership. Separation can be a voluntary resignation from the partnership or can mean being voted out for some reason. People should be able to leave business arrangements if they choose to; after all, who wants to force someone to continue participating in a venture for which they no longer have any passion? Similarly, if someone's poor attitude or work ethic begins to take a toll on the business and the other partners, there should be a mechanism to remove that person without the partnership dissolving because of it. A voting rule for involuntary disassociation is an important issue to work out early: should something this important be left up to a majority vote or should it be unanimous for the partners who will undertake that vote?

Adding a Partner

The time may come when a partner disassociates from the partnership and the remaining partners must decide whether to carry on without anyone in that role or bring a new person into the enterprise. If the partnership decides to replace the former partner, you'll have several decisions to make, including the following:

- What type of vote will be required to approve the new partner?
- What role and authority (including voting rights) will the new partner have?
- Will the new partner be required to make a financial contribution?

Partnership Dissolution

People change; our lives and our priorities change. The time may come when no one is interested in continuing with the partnership. So, then what happens? The partnership's business affairs need to be wound down. How would you like this to work? It might be a good idea to set out some rules for who gets what and when. Should partnership assets be liquidated and distributed to the partners in accordance with each partner's ownership interest? Or would that plan not properly take into account longer-serving partners who have deeper investments in the partnership?

The typical order of winding things down involves allowing for time to be sure that all outstanding income has been realized (except for any future sales including royalties from recordings and publishing). Next is liquidating partnership assets such as equipment and real estate. Following that, the process begins of paying partnership debts: first are contractual debts owed to third parties (like lines of credit, agents, vendors, and others), then outstanding loans, if any, to partners. After all debts and loans are paid, the original investment capital should be paid back to each partner and finally, splitting the remaining funds, if any, to the partners in accordance with their ownership interest in the partnership.

In the sample partnership agreement below, all four partners are equal. Each partner will share equally in ownership, profits, and liability for losses, and has equal ownership of all partnership assets—both tangible and intangible. Contrast this agreement with the sample collaboration agreement provided in Chapter 10, which demonstrates a completely different intention. In the latter example, there are three people collaborating on writing a musical—a composer, a lyricist, and a book writer. There, the collaborators make clear that they do not want state partnership law to apply to their collaboration, and they expressly state their intention that the resulting musical they produce will allow for each of them, as individuals, to make licensing income from the individual elements contributed and that the piece will not be considered a joint work for copyright purposes. Contrast those intentions with what is provided in the sample partnership agreement at the end of this chapter.

FORMING A GENERAL PARTNERSHIP

General partnerships are easy to form—just start working with one or more people with the intention of forming an ongoing business for profit. The troublesome aspect of general partnerships include (1) how easily these enterprises spring into life; (2) the consequences of not working out basic contingencies for how the enterprise should operate; and (3) the application of state partnership default rules in situations where no formal partnership agreement exists.

Formation Steps

1. If not using partners' last names for your partnership name, make sure the name you want to use complies with state naming rules.
2. Check on the availability of your proposed trade name, if any.
3. Be sure you and your partners have made all the decisions crucial to your enterprise to be captured in your partnership agreement.
4. Research and obtain any required local permits or licenses.
5. Determine whether you need business insurance (and any insurance required of employers if you plan to hire employees).
6. Obtain federal and, if relevant, state employer identification numbers (EINs).
7. Open a partnership bank account under your assigned EIN.
8. Formalize your partnership agreement, take a member vote on its acceptance, and distribute copies to all members.
9. Take other action required by the state in which the general partnership will be domiciled.

See Chapter 8 for a discussion of trade names and EINs.

CONCLUSION

General partnerships are the most common business structures for collaborators in the creative industries because of how easily they're formed. However, the ease of formation can cause issues later for those who didn't take the time to consider all the contingencies that could arise and provide solutions for addressing them. Additionally, the application of agency law and the legal doctrines of vicarious liability and joint and several liability considerably increase partners' exposure to personal liability for partnership debts. Appendix A provides a chart that compares general partnerships against other business models.

GENERAL PARTNERSHIP RESOURCES

B Plans, "Creating a Partnership Agreement," articles.bplans.com/creating-a
-business-partnership-agreement/

B Plans, "How Partnerships Are Taxed," articles.bplans.com/how-Partnerships
-are-taxed/

B Plans, "Partnership Basics," articles.bplans.com/Partnership-basics/

IRS, "Small Businesses and Self-Employed Partnerships," www.irs.gov/busi
nesses/small-business-&-self-employed/partnerships

IRS, "Tax Formation for Partnerships," www.irs.gov/businesses/partnerships

U.S. Small Business Administration, "Choose a Business Structure," www.sba
.gov/content/partnership

The sample agreement that follows is intended to be equal in all respects.

SAMPLE PARTNERSHIP AGREEMENT
FOR FOUR EQUAL PARTNERS

This Agreement is made and entered into this *<date>* day of *<month>*, by and between the following individuals, referred to in this Agreement as Partners:

<name of Partner>
<name of Partner>
<name of Partner>
<name of Partner>

The foregoing individuals, hereinafter individually referred to as Partner and in the plural as Partners, set forth in this written agreement the terms and conditions by which they will associate themselves in the Partnership.

1. Name of Business
   The Partnership, whose registered name is *<insert registered name>*, will conduct business under the Trade Name *<insert trade name>*.

   This is the place to insert the partnership's registered and assumed name (aka DBA name), if any.

2. Place of Business
   The principal place of business shall be *<insert location>* until amended by agreement of the Partners.

   The principal place can be wherever the partners want it to be. It can also be changed later.

3. Duration
   The Partnership shall commence as of the effective date of this Agreement and shall continue until terminated as provided herein.

   Partnerships last until they are dissolved according to state law or in accordance with the rules set forth in the agreement. If there is no agreement, state partnership law determines when partnerships end—usually when any partner dies, becomes incapacitated, leaves the partnership, or the partnership can no longer operate as a business.

4. Purpose
   The purpose of the Partnership is *<insert purpose>*.

   This is where a partnership such as a band would list all business activities including co-writing songs; making recordings; performing live; making videos, films, and television appearances; commercially exploiting musical compositions for publication; contracting with business partners to develop and sell merchandise; touring; and otherwise promoting the partnership under its trade name.

5. Exclusivity
   The Partners agree that each will contribute his services on an exclusive basis to the Partnership in all purposes identified in Paragraph 4., above.

Partners further agree that each will contribute such services diligently, professionally, and to the best of his ability for the duration of this Agreement.

Having an Exclusivity Clause clarifies the commitments made by each Partner to the others and to the enterprise that each is investing 100% of their time and talent into this enterprise. This agreement doesn't allow the partners to split their time and perform the same services elsewhere.

6. Management
The Partners agree that each Partner will be responsible for and account to the other Partners for the following in support of Partnership operations:

This is the place to insert specific partners' duties and authorities. For example: check-writing authority, booking gigs, and signing contracts. No partner can draw a salary unless the agreement provides that authority, so if someone is drawing a salary, the agreement must outline that person's duties to the partnership that are outside the general duties shared by all partners.

7. Contributions
The following schedule is acknowledged whereby each Partner has contributed an initial investment of capital or loan, as indicated, for the purpose of launching the Partnership:

This is where you would insert after each partner's name, the amount of money each has contributed to the partnership's start-up fund and indicate whether that amount is a loan or an investment. Where investment amounts differ, you'll need to decide whether the individual partner's ownership interest will parallel the amount of investment, by percentage. If any partner makes a loan to the partnership, you'll need to decide and capture here (or by a separate contract) how and when that loan will be repaid and under what interest terms, if any.

8. Exploitation of Partnership Assets
Partners agree that any and all leases of Partnership assets are void unless reduced to a writing and signed by all Partners following a vote.

This is an important clause. It requires that all "leases" must be contained in a writing signed by all the partners. "Leases" is a broad legal term and, in this context, includes licenses of the partnership's intellectual property. In other words, it means that an individual partner cannot unilaterally license a musical composition to a third party without the other partners' approval. The reason this is so important is partnership law would generally allow a unilateral license because every partner is considered to be an agent for the partnership and, as such, could dispense with partnership assets, like copyrighted material, on behalf of the partnership. This clause illustrates another reason to have a formal, written agreement that makes the rules and authorities clear.

9. Partnership Loans
   Partners agree that no loan shall be taken out and no encumbrance made as collateral against any Partnership property, whether real or personal property, including any intellectual property interests, unless reduced to a writing and signed by all Partners following a vote.

   Similar to Clause 8., above, this clause also restricts individual partners from unilaterally using partnership assets as collateral for a loan or otherwise obtaining a loan on behalf of the partnership without the other partners' unanimous written consent following a vote.

10. Partnership Property: Ownership, Profits, and Losses
    Unless otherwise provided for, or by mutual consent of all Partners, ownership in the Partnership and in all Partnership assets whether real property or personal property, including the Partnership's Trade Name and any and all intellectual property arising out of the work of the Partnership, shall be in equal parts as follows:

    <name of Partner> 25%
    <name of Partner> 25%
    <name of Partner> 25%
    <name of Partner> 25%

Similarly, any and all Partnership losses, expenses, or deductions shall be equally shared according to the schedule provided by this Paragraph unless otherwise agreed.

This Profits and Losses Clause spells out each partner's percentage interest in the partnership (and in the partnership's income) and their liability for partnership losses. This sample agreement is one in which each partner has an equal share in the enterprise, but it doesn't have to be this way. Sometimes one or more partners' contribution might be greater than the others, so that partner might be entitled to a higher ownership interest and a greater percentage of the profits. Further, these percentages can change; a newly admitted partner might start out with a smaller ownership interest or even no ownership at all—they might merely be an employee or independent contractor initially, then later invited into the enterprise as a true partner-owner. Nothing needs to be set in stone; consider your needs and how they might change, and have the agreement reflect this flexibility. Even if you end up hiring a lawyer to assist with drafting a number of complex contingencies, having thought through all these details will serve you well and save the partnership money in attorneys' fees.

11. Other Partnership Compensation

No Partner shall be entitled to collect a salary or other compensation from the Partnership unless and until the Partners agree, in writing, to provide such compensation for services rendered to the Partnership.

This is a general rule of partnership law. All general partners are expected to contribute to partnership operations and decision-making. That participation is where the output of creative work comes from and from where the profits flow. If a partner is understood to receive a salary or other compensation on top of the basic partner income from jointly produced profit, then that should be laid out clearly in the agreement that governs the management of the partnership.

12. Assignment

This Agreement may not be assigned or transferred, except an interest in the net receipts as provided herein, without the express written consent of all the other Partners; however, nothing contained herein shall prevent a Partner from transferring or assigning his rights by will, trust, or other testamentary instrument to any person(s) and/or entities, for estate planning purposes.

As the heading states, this is an Assignment Clause. Assignment Clauses usually do exactly what this one does: they restrict someone from subcontracting out their duties to another person. Here, the partners don't want anyone to decide to leave the partnership, even for a time, and hire someone else to take their place. In contracts involving creative people, particularly musicians, these are common clauses. You were hired for your talent and creative energy; you are not allowed to sub out your gigs to another person without the hiring entity releasing you and allowing a substitute musician. Also common is the second part of this clause, which does not restrict partners from assigning their interests in income to someone else. Assigning your duties and assigning your rights (to income) are very different things.

13. Books and Records
     All Partnership books, records, and bank accounts shall be kept at the principal place of business unless and until the Partners agree to change such location. All such books, records, and accounts shall be made available to each Partner, or his designated representative, for review at all reasonable times. Should the Partners agree to hire an accountant or other professional to maintain Partnership books, the Partners agree to share those expenses on a prorated basis.

Partners should always have reasonable access to partnership accounts including contracts, bank records, and licenses. If the place for storing these important documents needs to move, the new location should be discussed and put to a vote so any partner can have access to the records without undue burden. The costs of hiring professionals to maintain the records should be shared equally. It's also a good idea to have an independent professional be responsible for keeping partnership records even if one of the partners volunteers and is experienced with accounting or other recordkeeping. Doing so may guard against allegations of self-dealing or obfuscation of partnership records.

14. Representations and Warranties

Each Partner hereby represents and warrants that:

a. he is under no legal disability and has the right to enter into this Agreement and perform its terms;

b. no act or omission by any Partner will violate the rights of any person, firm, or corporation or will subject the Partnership to any liability or claims;

c. all material each has or will contribute to the Partnership is and will be original to each party (except for public domain sources) and has not been adapted or derived from any other copyrighted and/or trademarked material owned by a third person or entity not a party to this Agreement. Furthermore, to the best of the contributing party's knowledge, his material does not infringe upon or violate the rights of others, including any rights of publicity or privacy belonging to any third persons or entities; and

d. each Partner further warrants and represents that he will not sell, assign, transfer, or pledge as a security any right, title, or interest in or to any asset of the Partnership without the prior written consent of all the other Partners, and any attempt to do so will be null and void.

The Reps and Warranties Clause provides the foundation for the promises that each of the partners make to the others and to the partnership itself. This one has four parts:

14a. relates to each partner's legal capacity to enter into the agreement, generally. When each partner says that they are not "under a disability," they're saying that they're old enough legally to contract and have the requisite mental capacity to contract because they know the extent of what they're doing and their obligations under the contract.

In 14b., the partners are agreeing that entering into this contractual arrangement will not interfere with a similar contract they have with anyone else. If a similar contract did exist, then the person or entity who had earlier contracted with one of these partners could bring a lawsuit alleging tortious interference with contract.

14c. is especially important in enterprises where people collaborate to write songs or otherwise co-author something. This clause says that the creative contributions each partner will bring to partnership projects will be original to that partner and no content will infringe on any person's rights.

Finally, 14d. is a double down on the concepts outlined in Clauses 8. and 9. that any unilateral attempts by any partner(s) to sell, license, or pledge as loan collateral any material that belongs to the partnership will be ineffective unless unanimously agreed to as evidenced in a document signed by all partners.

15. Indemnification

    Each Partner shall defend, indemnify, and hold harmless the other Partners from and against any and all liability, loss, expense including reasonable attorneys' fees, or claims for injury or damages arising out of the performance of this Agreement, but only to the extent such liability, loss, expense, attorneys' fees, or claims for injury or damages are caused by or result from the negligent acts or omissions of each Partner and relates to the services provided to the Partnership.

Indemnification clauses like this one require partners to protect one another and the partnership against legal claims made by outsiders against the partners and the partnership entity based on the actions of the individual partners. Specifically, these clauses (also known as Hold Harmless Clauses) say two things: (1) each partner will hire an attorney to defend the others against any legal claims that arise out of the actions or non-actions of an individual partner; and (2) each partner will pay any monetary judgment awarded to a plaintiff in those matters on behalf of the others.

These clauses have real punch as they relate to the promises outlined in clause 14. For example, if a partner participating in songwriting provides music later determined to be the original work of another artist, the owner of that content can bring a copyright infringement lawsuit against the partnership and the individual partners. In this example, the partner who contributed the infringing material would be responsible for providing a legal defense (hiring an attorney) and paying any resulting monetary award because their conduct precipitated the lawsuit.

16. Voting

Whenever any consent is required, the Partners agree that voting shall be by majority vote. Each Partner shall have one vote; however, it is understood that the Partners have the discretion to amend the voting apportionment to unanimous voting on matters the majority of Partners agree is one requiring unanimous consent.

In the event the Partners cannot agree upon a decision or because votes are tied, the Partners hereby appoint the following person(s) to break the deadlock:

Artistic Decisions: _____

Business Decisions: _____

Voting rights should be spelled out. Specifically, the items subject to voting should be provided throughout the agreement as well as the type of vote. For example, some items up for vote may be by simple majority while others may be so important that unanimous vote is required. These issues need to be worked out by the partners in advance and captured in the partnership agreement. Partners should also anticipate the need for a tiebreaker which, as indicated in the example immediately above, can be split between artistic decisions and business decisions or in any other way the partners agree. The tiebreaker doesn't need to be named specifically; you could insert a title such as "the band's current manager" or "the individual currently serving in the role of partnership accountant."

17. Partnership Dissolution

This Agreement shall terminate, and the Partnership shall be dissolved by operation of law, except as otherwise provided herein, or upon written agreement of all Partners following a unanimous vote of dissolution.

Upon a unanimous vote of dissolution, the Partners shall liquidate all Partnership assets whether real property or personal property, including the Partnership's Trade Name, with reasonable promptness. After the collection of Partnership receivables, the balance of the remaining proceeds, if any, shall be distributed first to any outstanding Partnership debts to third parties, then to any debts owed to any Partner(s).

After payments of all Partnership debts have been made in full, any remaining Partnership assets shall then be distributed among the Partners in a manner consistent with the terms set forth in Paragraph 10., above.

Dissolution of the Partnership shall in no way restrict the Partners from receiving continuing income, individually, as provided for in Paragraph 10., from the exploitation of intellectual property resulting from the Partnership.

If you've read the introductory material to this chapter, you know that under general rules of partnership law, if no partnership agreement exists to state otherwise, a partnership will automatically dissolve when any partner dies, becomes disabled, or leaves the partnership for any reason. Having a clause that addresses dissolution is usually the last thing anyone wants to discuss when preparing to launch an enterprise, but it's important to work these details out in advance of these contingencies.

In this dissolution clause, the partners have agreed that dissolution can result from a unanimous vote reduced to a writing. Further, this clause outlines the liquidation of partnership assets and how the profits, if any, will be distributed once partnership debts are satisfied. This clause also recognizes that partners expect to receive continuing income from the exploitation of partnership assets (income from completed recordings, music publishing, etc.) even after the partnership has dissolved. "Music publishing" refers to music licensing income (see Chapter 12 for a discussion of music licensing).

18. Disassociation
    a. Disassociation from the Partnership can occur upon death or disability of a Partner, through voluntary resignation from the Partnership, or removal by vote of the other Partners. Partners wishing to disassociate voluntarily shall provide thirty (30) days' written notice to each of the other Partners indicating his intention to disassociate from the Partnership. Partners removed by majority vote of disassociation shall be entitled to thirty (30) days' written notice by the voting Partners.
    b. Disassociated Partners shall be entitled to that Partner's share of the Partnership valued as of the effective date of disassociation and net

earnings from the exploitation of Partnership intellectual property including net royalties from recordings and publishing; however, such net royalties shall only be due upon actual receipt of same by the Partnership. Disassociated Partners shall have no liability for expenses or other liabilities following the date of disassociation except for those previously agreed to prior to the date of disassociation.

c. Disassociated Partners shall not be entitled to any value or interest in the Partnership's Trade Name or to any Partnership profits following the date of disassociation except for continuing earnings from exploitation of Partnership intellectual property including recording and publishing earnings as indicated in Paragraph 18b., above.

d. Partnership valuation shall be conducted by an accountant unanimously agreed to by all Partners. If a disassociated Partner disagrees with the accountant's valuation of the Partnership, he may, upon thirty (30) days' written notice to each of the other Partners, submit the matter to mediation or arbitration pursuant to Paragraph 20d. herein.

Disassociation is the term for when one or more partners leaves the partnership.

18a. lays out how partner disassociation can happen: death, disability, voluntary resignation, or voted out by the other partners.

18b. provides for what a disassociated partner is financially entitled to and when that entitlement is due (in this example, net royalties don't need to be paid to the disassociated partner until the partnership has actually received those funds from third parties). The partnership doesn't need to front any money to a disassociated partner.

18c. speaks to what the disassociated partner is not entitled to. Specifically, that partner is not entitled to any interest in the partnership's trade name nor any income beyond the date of his disassociation except for his share of royalties that flow from his work prior to disassociation.

18d. states that when disassociation takes place, the partnership must be valued by an independent professional (unanimously agreed to) in order to determine the disassociated partner's financial interest and what happens if they disagree with that valuation (the issue must be submitted for mediation/arbitration). Some partnerships will provide more detail in this area by including a specific schedule for when and how the disassociated partner should be paid.

19. Addition of a Partner

    Neither the disassociation of an existing Partner nor the addition of a new Partner will dissolve the Partnership. In the event of disassociation of a Partner for any reason, the remaining Partners may elect to admit one or more new Partners upon the mutual, unanimous consent of remaining Partners. New Partners are required to sign an agreement which will bind such Partners to the terms set forth in this Agreement. However, no Partner(s) admitted to this Partnership after the date this Agreement was executed by the original Partners shall be entitled to any Partnership assets, net profits, receipts, or any other property (whether real property or personal property, including the Partnership's Trade Name and any and all intellectual property arising out of the work of the Partnership) that predate his/her admittance to the Partnership.

    Providing rules for admitting new partners is important. This clause makes a few things clear: (1) exiting or entering partners will not dissolve the partnership (which would likely be the case in the absence of an agreement); (2) new partners must be voted in; (3) the vote for new partners must be unanimous; (4) new partners must sign a document referencing this agreement and their consent to be bound by its terms; (5) new partners are not entitled to any profits or other assets created or contributed by the others that predate the new partner's admission to the enterprise; and (6) new partners shall have no financial interest in the partnership's trade name (presumably because the new partner did not participate in building any goodwill in it).

20. Miscellaneous

    a. Integration

    This Agreement constitutes the entire agreement among the parties and shall supersede all prior agreements, arrangements, negotiations, proposals, and understandings, if any, relating to the obligations and matters set out herein, whether oral or written.

Also known as a Merger Clause, the purpose of an Integration Clause is to trigger a rule of evidence that disallows any party from offering into evidence any proof, written or oral, that in any way contradicts the terms in the agreement. For this reason, all partners should carefully read the agreement and be sure each understands it. Further, there should be no side deals outside this agreement because evidence of those will be disallowed in a legal setting. If a side arrangement does come up, this agreement should be revised or a completely separate agreement should be drawn up that addresses that specific situation.

b. Amendment

No additions, amendments, deletions, or substitutions will be valid unless made in writing and duly signed by all Partners.

This is a basic Amendment Clause which makes it clear that no party can unilaterally change the terms of the arrangement without the others' formal written consent.

c. Applicable Law

The laws of the State of _____ shall govern the interpretation of this Agreement.

This is a Choice of Law Clause. Technically, these clauses are not necessary since there are legal tests in every jurisdiction for determining which law or laws apply to a situation or dispute, but they can be helpful in business arrangements involving musicians because some states (and even specific courts) have more experience handling music industry issues than others.

d. Remedies

Any dispute arising out of this Agreement which cannot first be resolved through mediation shall be conclusively resolved by an arbitrator or panel of arbitrators with recognized expertise in the subject matter of this Agreement. The Commercial Arbitration Rules of the American Arbitration Association will apply unless otherwise agreed upon by the parties. The resolution will be binding upon the parties and any court of competent jurisdiction may enter judgment upon the award rendered. The losing party agrees to pay the costs of arbitration as well as the prevailing Partner's (or Partners') reasonable costs and attorney fees.

This is a Remedies Clause. These spell out, in advance of a dispute, what the agreed-upon rules will be for handling any issues that arise. This one requires mediation as the first step. Mediation is one form of alternative dispute resolution (ADR). It is a confidential, structured process for parties to a dispute to discuss their grievances with the others in front of one or two impartial mediators. Mediation is low cost, private, and the parties (in conjunction with the mediators) can set the terms and rules of the mediation. Mediation can only work if all parties participating in it are willing to be reasonable and compromise. Volunteer Lawyers for the Arts has a strong mediation program, but there are others as well.

In this agreement, if mediation doesn't result in a resolution, arbitration, another form of ADR, is the final step. Arbitration is slightly more formal and is also private, unlike litigation. Both mediation and arbitration are designed to be faster and cheaper than litigation. To my thinking, mediation aims to get people talking, hearing one another, and possibly preserving the relationship. Arbitration, like litigation, is adversarial and once parties to a dispute have adopted an adversarial posture, the professional relationship is likely lost.

e. Notices

In the event of any default hereunder, the aggrieved Partner(s) will send written notice to the other Partners outlining the nature of the alleged default and provide two (2) calendar weeks for the other Partner(s) to cure the alleged default before taking steps to declare a material breach of this Agreement.

All notices required hereunder shall be in writing and shall be given by personal delivery or certified or registered mail (return receipt requested). Said notices shall be effective upon the receipt thereof. All notices shall be addressed to the parties at the street addresses following their signatures below or to such other addresses as any party may otherwise specify in writing.

This clause combines a Default and Notice of Cure provision as well as a general Notices provision. The default and notice of cure portion of the clause provides a protocol for instances where one or more partners are unhappy with one or more of the other partners' behavior in the partnership and, in this case, requires the aggrieved partner to formally let the partner with whom they have a grievance know the nature of their displeasure and give the aggrieving partner two weeks to modify their behavior. The idea here is that the person who is believed to be causing disharmony in the partnership is given an opportunity to turn things around before the others begin the process of taking a vote to remove them from the partnership. The Notice portion of the clause lays out how that notice should be given (in writing, by certified or registered mail).

I like these clauses because they require people to communicate with one another even if the communication is an uncomfortable one. In addition to communication, these formalities remind the individuals that this is a business; there are baseline expectations that need to be followed, and consequences for not complying with their contractual duties.

f. Successors and Assigns

This Agreement binds the Partners and permitted executors, administrators, personal representatives, successors, and assigns. Nothing in this Agreement, express or implied, confers on any other person any legal or equitable right, benefit, or remedy of any nature whatsoever under or by reason of this Agreement.

This clause provides that if a partner dies, becomes disabled, or otherwise has another individual standing in their place as their representative, the terms of the contract will operate the same in those situations. The partner's death or disability doesn't change the operation of the contractual arrangement.

g. Severability

In the event any term or provision of this Agreement is or becomes illegal, invalid, or unenforceable, in any jurisdiction, such illegality, invalidity, or enforceability shall not affect any other term of this Agreement or invalidate or render unenforceable such term or provision in any other jurisdiction.

The purpose of a Severability Clause is to save the contract from failing completely if a specific clause or element of it is determined by a court to be against the law. These clauses aim to prop up the entire contract if a portion of it gets knocked away because the law changed or the contract ends up being interpreted in a state other than the one whose laws are intended to govern the arrangement.

h. Construction

Captions of individual clauses contained in this Agreement have been provided as a matter of convenience and in no way define, limit, extend, describe, or otherwise affect the scope or meaning of this Agreement or the intent of any provisions hereof.

In my experience, it is not very common to see headings above clauses in a contract. When headings are provided, they can present a problem for the party who drafted the contract. The issue is one of potential ambiguity: if the title given to the clause is deemed to differ substantially from the actual content or functionality of the clause, considered together they can be determined to be ambiguous, which can be fatal to a contract under long-standing, commonly understood rules of contract interpretation. For this reason, drafters commonly include a Construction Clause (sometimes labeled Headings or something similar) that states that the captions or headings should not be read as part of the contract but are merely provided as a way to help readers maneuver through it.

In witness whereof, the parties thereto have executed and sealed this Agreement on the date indicated above.

_____	_____
Partner's Printed Name	Partner's Signature
_____	_____
Street Address	Preferred Email Address
_____	_____
Preferred Phone	Date

Assume there are three more such signature blocks here.

4

Limited Liability Companies

A Limited Liability Company (LLC) is a legal structure created under state law that combines aspects of both a partnership and a corporation. Specifically, LLCs combine some of the operational flexibilities and tax benefits of a general partnership with the limited liability of a corporation. Being a relatively new[1] hybrid as compared to other legal structures, state laws vary more distinctly with LLCs than for other business structures like corporations and partnerships.

Like corporations, LLCs must follow state formalities with respect to both formation and ongoing compliance reporting. One such formality is the Operating Agreement, which, for musicians, should contain details about rights to income (including royalties), who holds company property (such as equipment), how the company can be dissolved, and other contingencies such as what happens in the event of a member's death, disability, or member disassociation (much like a partnership agreement).

TYPES OF LIMITED LIABILITY COMPANIES

There are two basic types of LLCs: (1) member-managed; and (2) manager-managed. In a member-managed LLC, the members have decision-making authority, and each member is an agent for the company. In this model, each member-owner can bind the company contractually much like a partnership. In a manager-managed LLC, the members cannot participate in the day-to-day operations of the company, but they can have a say in the larger, strategic decisions. Only the managers in manager-managed LLCs can bind the company as its agent.

OWNERSHIP AND CONTROL

LLC owners are called members. There are no limits on the number of members an LLC can have, but some states limit the minimum number to one or two. An LLC with only one owner is called a single-member LLC. Members can be individuals, including foreign persons, or even an entity. Unlike a corporation, LLCs don't have boards of directors, so control is more directly in the hands of the members. Centralized control is attractive to business owners who aren't interested in obtaining approvals for larger, strategic decisions (or for declaring a profit distribution) as is typical with corporate officers and their boards of directors.

PERSONAL LIABILITY

LLC members' personal liability is typically capped at the amount of a member's financial investment in the company as is the case for owners of a corporation. No one member is liable for the entirety of business liabilities. Unlike a general partnership, there is no duty to indemnify the other members even though in member-managed LLCs, each member is an agent for the company. Exceptions to LLC liability protection include instances where an owner personally guarantees company debt obligations. See the discussion of liability in Chapter 1 for more details on this important topic.

PROFIT AND GROWTH

Business owners (in this case, members) are compensated once the company starts to make money. A member's interest in the company is maintained in the member's capital account, which records their initial contribution, percentage of profits over time (which generally correlates to the member's ownership interest by percentage), and any *distributions* made. A *distribution* is how profits are recognized by LLC members. Unlike corporations, LLCs don't issue stock, though they can allow for *profit interests* to designated members. Profit interests provide preferential treatment through increased profit percentages and/or place some members first in line for profit recognition before other members receive their distribution.

Because LLCs don't issue stock, they can't "go public" via an initial public offering (IPO). Some companies decide, after long periods of growth, that it would be beneficial for the company to reorganize from an LLC to a corporation in order to raise capital through an IPO.

TAX TREATMENT

Unique to LLCs are the options available under the IRS code for how the organization wishes to be treated for tax purposes. For tax purposes, the IRS considers single-member LLCs as sole proprietorships and multi-member LLCs as partnerships by default, but it is possible for a multi-member LLC to elect to be taxed like a corporation by filing IRS Form 8832 (or 2553, which is specific to subchapter S recognition). See Chapter 5 for a discussion of C and S corporations.

THE OPERATING AGREEMENT

An Operating Agreement is a contract among LLC members and between the members and the enterprise itself. It sets out the organization's rules for governance. Not every state requires an Operating Agreement, but it is nonetheless a good idea to have one to avoid conflicts between members of a multi-member LLC. Much in the same way that developing a Partnership Agreement requires co-owners to think through possible contingencies to best prepare themselves for smoothly working through issues that inevitably arise, Operating Agreements serve the same purpose.

It's a good idea to develop an Operating Agreement even if you elect to form a single-member LLC model because the agreement helps establish a distinction between its owner and the entity, which can lend legitimacy to the enterprise for obtaining business loans and other purposes. Operating Agreements can also keep a single-member LLC's operations on track with its original purpose.

The life of an LLC begins with filing Articles of Organization with the state. Unlike the Articles of Organization, the Operating Agreement is not usually required to be filed with the state, but most states require that one exists. Because an LLC can be single-member or multi-member, the type of LLC you launch will determine the content of your Operating Agreement (as well as content required by the state).

Basic Single-Member Operating Agreement Decision Points
- Name of your LLC
- Name of member-owner
- Principal place of business
- Date of formation
- Business purpose
- Duration of the LLC
- How the company will be managed
- Capital contributions by member

The Sample Single-Member Operating Agreement that follows was drafted for a New York LLC. New York requires LLCs to have an Operating Agreement, but does not dictate its content. Your state may have specific requirements for Operating Agreements, so before you start working on the content, check with your Secretary of State to determine whether there are any specific requirements you need to be aware of. Also, check to see whether there are any model agreements you can use as a starting point for developing your Operating Agreement.

SAMPLE NEW YORK SINGLE-MEMBER LLC OPERATING AGREEMENT

This Single-Member Limited Liability Company Operating Agreement, entered into on _____, 20____, is entered into by and between _____, LLC, (the "Company") and _____ of _____, hereinafter known as the "Member."

WHEREAS the Member wishes to form a limited liability company under the laws of the State of New York for the purpose of engaging in business activities as described in Item 4 hereof and such other business activities as the Member in his/her discretion shall determine.

NOW, THEREFORE, in consideration of the mutual covenants set forth herein and other valuable consideration, the receipt and sufficiency of which are hereby acknowledged, the Member and the Company mutually agree as follows:

1. Registered Name and Office
   The registered name of the Company shall be _____,
   LLC, whose registered office shall be at _____
   _____, City of _____, in the State of New York
   or at such other place of business as the Member shall determine.

2. Trade Name
   The Trade Name under which the Company will conduct business shall
   be _____ until such time
   as the Member in his/her discretion shall otherwise determine. The Trade
   Name shall not be owned by the Company, but shall be licensed to the
   Company by the Member pursuant to a separate agreement.

   *The LLC doesn't need to operate under a trade name, but performers often
   choose to. Similarly, the trade name need not be owned by the LLC—it
   could be owned by one or more members and licensed to the LLC as is the
   intention here. By licensing the trade name to the LLC, the owner is able to
   retain it for possible use with another group once the existing license expires.
   This license makes most sense in a scenario in which a band operates under
   a trade name that is the name of the person who launched the group (e.g.,
   The Dave Matthews Band).*

   *Additionally, musicians will often create another entity to serve as their
   publishing company, which would be owned by the LLC. The publishing company would serve as the administrator of the song catalogue and
   manage all the music licensing. See Chapter 12 for a discussion of music
   licensing.*

3. Formation
   The Company was formed on _____, 20_____,
   when the Member or his representative filed Articles of Organization
   with the office of the Secretary of State pursuant to the statutes governing
   limited liability companies in the State of New York.

4. Purpose
   The purpose of the Company is to engage in and conduct any and all
   lawful businesses, activities, or functions that advance the interests of
   the Company in the music and entertainment industry including writing songs; making recordings; performing live; making video, film, and

television appearances; commercially exploiting musical compositions for publication; contracting with others to develop and sell merchandise; tour; and otherwise promote the Company under its Trade Name and to carry on any other lawful activities in connection with or incidental to the foregoing, as the Member in his/her discretion shall determine.

The stated purpose of this single-member LLC is detailed, but it often doesn't need to be. Follow your state's rules concerning the company's stated purpose; you can always amend the Operating Agreement if you need to.

5. Term

The term of the Company shall be perpetual, commencing on the filing of the Articles of Organization of the Company, and continuing until terminated under the provisions set forth herein.

6. Organization and Management of the Company

The Company is organized as a member-managed limited liability company. The business and affairs of the Company shall be conducted and managed by the Member in accordance with this Agreement and the laws of the State of New York.

The Member shall have sole authority and power to:

a. act for and/or on behalf of the Company;

b. perform any act that would be binding on the Company;

c. incur any expenses on behalf of the Company; and

d. designate and appoint by separate written documentation, an individual to wind down the Company's business and transfer or distribute the Member's interests and Capital Account as designated by the Member or as may otherwise be required by law.

7. Non-Exclusivity

Except as limited by applicable New York law, the Member may engage in other business ventures of any nature including, without limitation by specification, the ownership of another business similar to that operated by the Company. The Company shall not have any right or interest in any such independent ventures or to the income and profits derived therefrom.

Whether or not a member's services will be exclusive to the LLC is some-thing to be worked out in advance. Usually in multi-member LLCs, there is an exclusivity clause that prohibits members from dividing their interests by providing similar services outside the LLC unless authority is given follow-ing a vote.

This sample agreement allows the member to engage in other business ventures even if those services are similar to the services provided under this agreement. For example, this member can play gigs with other groups because the Operating Agreement does not contain an exclusivity provision relating to professional services.

8. Ownership of Company Assets
   The Company's assets, including both real and personal property (ex-cepting the Trade Name), shall be deemed owned by the Company as an entity, and the Member shall have no ownership interest in such assets or any portion thereof.

   The LLC (not the member) owns all property, both real estate (real prop-erty) and personal property (music equipment, laptops, speakers, etc.) ex-cept the trade name, which is licensed to the LLC by the member.

9. Member Capital Account, Contributions, and Distributions
   The Company shall maintain a Capital Account for the Member that shall reflect:
   a. the Member's capital contributions;
   b. any net income, gains, losses, or decreases of the Company; and
   c. any distributions made to the Member.
   Though the Member is not obligated to make any capital contributions, the Member may make such capital contributions in such amounts and at such times as the Member shall, in his/her sole discretion, determine. The Member may take distributions of the capital from time to time in accordance with the limitations imposed by applicable law.

10. Books, Records, and Accounting
    The Member shall maintain complete books and records accurately reflecting the Company's accounts and transactions on a calendar-year

basis using such cash, accrual, or hybrid method of accounting as in the sole judgment of the Member is most appropriate. The Company shall keep at its registered office or at such other office as shall be designated by the Member the following items:

a. a copy of the filed Articles of Organization and all amendments thereto, together with executed copies of any powers of attorney pursuant to which any document has been executed;

b. copies of this Agreement, and all amendments thereto;

c. copies of the Company's federal income tax returns and reports, if any, for the five (5) most recent years; and

d. copies of any financial statements of the Company for the five (5) most recent years.

The Member intends that the Company, as a single-member LLC, be taxed as a sole proprietorship in accordance with the provisions of the Internal Revenue Code. Any provisions herein that may cause the Company not to be taxed as a sole proprietorship shall be inoperative.

As indicated above, the IRS default rule is that single-member LLCs are taxed like sole proprietorships and multi-member LLCs are taxed like partnerships unless specified otherwise through an election that is completed by filling out a form. Recall from Chapter 1 that income from both sole proprietorships and partnerships, if so elected, "passes through" to the individuals, so the LLC, as an entity, is not taxed.

11. Bank Accounts

All Company funds shall be deposited in the Company's name in a bank account or accounts as the Member in his/her discretion determines. Withdrawals from bank accounts shall be made only in the regular course of Company business.

12. Company Dissolution

The Company shall dissolve and its affairs shall be wound up on the earlier of:

a. a determination by the Member that the Company shall be dissolved;

b. an event specified in the Articles of Organization or this Agreement;

c. upon the death of the Member; or

d. upon the disability of the Member.

With respect to disability of the Member, he/she may continue to act as Manager hereunder or appoint a person to so serve until the Member's interests and Capital Account(s) have been transferred or distributed.

13. Indemnification

The Member shall not be liable for the debts, obligations, or liabilities of the Company, including under a judgment, decree, or order of a court.

The Member (including, for purposes of this clause, any assignee and/or transferee of the Member, estate, heir, personal representative, receiver, successor, or trustee) shall not be liable, responsible, or accountable, in damages or otherwise, to the Company or any other person for:

a. any act performed, or the omission to perform any act, within the scope of the power and authority conferred on the Member by this Agreement and/or under New York law except by reason of acts or omissions found by a court of competent jurisdiction upon entry of a final judgment rendered and un-appealable or not timely appealed ("Judicially Determined") to constitute fraud, gross negligence, recklessness, or intentional misconduct;

This indemnification clause requires the company to legally protect the member for actions taken in good faith. Paragraph a. provides exceptions to such protection including intentional conduct, fraud (stealing), or reckless behavior. For example, if the member injures someone while driving drunk to or from a performance, the company is under no obligation to indemnify them once a final judgment has been made against them.

b. the termination of the Company and this Agreement pursuant to the terms hereof;

c. the performance by the Member of, or the omission by the Member to perform, any act which the Member reasonably believed to be consistent with the advice of attorneys, accountants, or other professional advisers to the Company with respect to matters relating to the Company, including actions or omissions determined to constitute violations of law but which were not undertaken in bad faith; or

Paragraph c. provides that if a member makes a decision to act or refrain from acting based on advice received from a professional such as an

attorney (or if they thought they were following professional advice, but turns out they misunderstood the advice), they are nonetheless entitled to a legal defense and indemnity by the company.

d. the conduct of any person selected or engaged by the Member.

Paragraph d. addresses vicarious liability. It requires the company to indemnify and provide a legal defense to the member, if necessary, in a situation in which liability is imputed to the member based on the acts or omissions of another person for whom the member may be responsible such as an employee under the doctrine of respondeat superior; see Chapters 1 and 9 for details about employer liability.

Provided the Member is indemnifiable under the standards set forth herein, the Company shall indemnify, defend, and hold the Member harmless from and against any and all liabilities, damages, losses, costs, and expenses incurred by the Member (including amounts paid in satisfaction of judgments, in settlement of any action, suit, demand, investigation, claim, or proceeding as fines or penalties) and from and against all legal or other such costs as well as the expenses of investigating or defending against any actual, threatened, or anticipated claim arising out of this Agreement or the Member's association with the Company. All rights of the Member to indemnification under this Agreement shall be cumulative of, and in addition to, any right to which the Member may be entitled to by contract or as a matter of law or equity. Such rights survive the dissolution, liquidation, or termination of the Company as well as the death, removal, incompetency, or insolvency of the Member.

This paragraph is the one that actually lays out the nature of the benefit provided to the member. Specifically, it says the LLC will pay for the legal defense of the member, attorney fees, and any monetary judgment award (damages) rendered against the member.

However, if the Member is judicially determined to not be entitled to indemnification hereunder, the Member shall be entitled to receive interest-free advances to cover the costs of defending or settling any anticipated, actual, or threatened claims against the Member that may be subject to indemnification hereunder. The termination of any actual or threatened claim against the Member by judgment, order, or settlement or upon a plea of *nolo contendere* or its equivalent shall not, of itself, cause the Member not to be entitled to indemnification as provided herein unless and until judicially determined to not be so entitled.

This final paragraph says that the member is entitled to interest-free advances to pay the legal fees or settlements even if there's a question of fact regarding whether this agreement provides indemnification and even if the member is required to sign a settlement decree of nolo contendere. Nolo contendere is a plea made by a defendant in a criminal proceeding that acts as a guilty plea except, in this case, they aren't admitting any wrongdoing.

Further, this paragraph says that if a court determines, following a final judgment, that the member is not entitled to indemnification under this agreement, then any monies advanced to the member will be considered an interest-free loan to be repaid to the company.

14. Applicable Law
    The laws of the State of New York shall govern the interpretation of this Agreement.

    This is a Choice of Law Clause. See the sample partnership agreement in Chapter 3 for a discussion of this clause.

15. Severability
    In the event any term or provision of this Agreement is or becomes illegal, invalid, or unenforceable, in any jurisdiction, such illegality, invalidity, or enforceability shall not affect any other term of this Agreement or invalidate or render unenforceable such term or provision in any other jurisdiction.

    The functional purpose of a Severability Clause is to try to keep the entire contract from failing if one or more portions of it are determined to not be in harmony with the law. See Chapter 3 for a discussion of this clause.

16. Integration of Agreement
    This Agreement constitutes the entire agreement between the Member and the Company and supersedes all prior agreements, whether oral or written, as respects the matters set forth herein.

This is a Merger Clause (sometimes also referred to as an Integration Clause). See Chapter 3 for a discussion of this clause.

17. Construction

Captions of individual clauses contained in this Agreement have been provided as a matter of convenience and in no way define, limit, extend, describe, or otherwise affect the scope or meaning of this Agreement or the intent of any provisions hereof.

These clauses, sometimes titled as this one is or as "Headings" (or something similar), are common to contracts that use titles above individual clauses. The purpose of the clause is to put some distance between the title and the clause it precedes to avoid ambiguity that could arise if the title, caption, or heading does not accurately or sufficiently describe the clause it precedes.

18. Heirs and Assigns

Nothing in this Agreement, express or implied, confers on any other person any legal or equitable right, benefit, or remedy of any nature whatsoever under, or by reason of, this Agreement.

This clause aims to make clear that no rights or other authorities provided to the member under this contract can flow to any other person via a contractual assignment of rights or through operation of law upon the member's death. Also, this clause is an example of an instance in which the caption "Heirs and Assigns" does not accurately reflect the content of the clause because the clause is much broader than the LLC member's heirs and assigns.

IN WITNESS WHEREOF, the parties have executed this Agreement this _____ day of _____, 20_____.

_____, LLC

_____, Managing Member
Printed Name
_____, Managing Member
Signature

Acknowledgment of Notary Public

State of _____

_____ County.

On this _____ day of _____, 20 _____, before me appeared

_____, as Managing Member of this LLC as outlined in this Operating Agreement. The Member provided government-issued photo identification to be the above-named person and in my presence executed the foregoing and acknowledged that he/she executed same as his/her free act and deed.

_____

Notary Public

My commission expires: _____

Having a notary sign your single-member Operating Agreement may or may not be required in your state but, nonetheless, it does lend a single-member LLC some legitimacy because it adds formality and indicates the member's will to be bound to its terms.

MULTI-MEMBER OPERATING AGREEMENTS

Multi-member Operating Agreements are more complicated because they need to contain all of the decision points provided in the sample single-member version above, but also all of the safeguards specific to enterprises with multiple owners. I don't recommend you draft a multi-member Operating Agreement yourself and, for this reason, don't provide a sample.

However, below find the additional decision points for a multi-member Operating Agreement so you are as prepared as you can be when you're ready for that first conversation with a business attorney you engage to help you with drafting an agreement that meets the needs of your multi-member LLC.

In addition to the basic single-member decision points indicated above, what follows are decision points to consider before speaking with an attorney for assistance in drafting your Multi-Member LLC Operating Agreement:

- Each member's name and address
- Member's percentage of interest held
- Member's initial capital contribution
- If manager-managed, who will be the manager(s)?
- Will the manager receive a salary above a profit distribution?
- Roles of manager(s) and member(s)
- Any additional capital contribution requirements
- Distribution rights including any special profit interests
- Voting rules
- Details regarding annual and other meetings
- Whether members can assign their interests to others and, if so, how
- Contingencies for both voluntary and involuntary dissociation of a member (including death and disability)
- Rules for removing a member and admitting new members
- Notice requirements for member communications
- Remedies for handling disputes
- Any other provisions relating to member's interests

FORMING AN LLC

In some states the filing fees can be much higher than the fees for launching a corporation; however, in most states, the fees are comparable to filing corporation paperwork. Additionally, the cost of preparing the LLC paperwork can be more expensive due to the up-front documentation required, which often involves hiring an attorney or other professional to help with the heavy lifting. The upside is that the ongoing compliance-related paperwork for LLCs is generally less than that required of corporations.

LLC formation begins with the filing of Articles of Organization with the Secretary of State, or the functional equivalent, along with the state-required filing fee. Often, states will also require you to have an Operating Agreement prepared and signed by all members even though you typically don't have to file it. The Operating Agreement serves as a contract among all the members and the company itself. Similar to corporate bylaws or a partnership agreement, the Operating Agreement provides a formal document whereby the company states how it will be governed.

Finally, some states have a publication requirement as part of the formation process. New York, for example, requires LLC founders to publish a statement of intent in two newspapers (for six consecutive weeks) in the county in which the company will have its principal place of business. Following publication, the founders need to file affidavits of publication with the Department of State evidencing compliance with the publication requirement.

Formation Steps

1. Be sure you and the LLC's other members, if any, have made all the decisions critical to your enterprise and to be captured in your Operating Agreement.
2. Contact your Secretary of State's office (or the functional equivalent in your state) to determine the filing requirements specific to you.
3. Make sure the name you want for your LLC is available and complies with the state's naming rules.
4. Complete the state's Articles of Organization form and submit with the state filing fee.
5. If the state has a publication requirement, publish the required content in the newspapers required (often in the county in which your LLC is domiciled) for the statutory period of time and pay the publication fees.
6. Once the publication requirements are met, complete an affidavit/certificate of publication, if required, and submit it to the Secretary of State along with any required fee.
7. Research and obtain any required local permits or licenses.
8. Determine whether you need business insurance (and any insurance required of employers if you plan to hire employees).
9. Obtain federal and, if relevant, state employer identification numbers (EINs).
10. Open a business bank account for your LLC under your assigned EIN.
11. If a multi-member LLC, hold a meeting to work through the decision points for your Operating Agreement.
12. Formalize your Operating Agreement, take a member vote on its acceptance, and distribute copies to all members.
13. Send a duly signed copy (or copies, as required) of your Operating Agreement to your Secretary of State's office, if required.
14. Calendar any dates you'll need to track for supplying the state with periodic updates to your LLC.

CONCLUSION

The LLC is a popular choice of legal structure because of the partnership-related operational flexibility it offers business owners, but without the high degree of exposure to personal liability. And while the LLC structure doesn't provide the same level of personal liability protection the corporation structure can, many business owners feel that not having board of director oversight allows them the freedom to make strategic decisions more nimbly than a corporate model would allow. Appendix A provides a chart that compares LLCs against other business models.

LLC RESOURCES

IRS Publication 3402—Taxation of Limited Liability Companies, rev. June 2016, www.irs.gov/pub/irs-pdf/p3402.pdf

NOTE

1. Wyoming, in 1977, was the first state to pass legislation recognizing the LLC statutory entity. See Delaware, Inc., "History of the Limited Liability Company (LLC)," www.delawareinc.com/llc/history-of-delaware-llc/.

5

Corporations

Like a limited liability company, a corporation is a statutory entity recognized under state law in every state. Corporations can do all the things individuals can do: they can borrow money, take tax deductions, declare a financial loss, partner with other organizations, and share profits among their owners. The corporate legal structure is popular for entrepreneurs because it allows for rapid growth through investment opportunities and offers the greatest protection from personal liability for its owners. Unlike sole proprietorships or general partnerships where the enterprise ceases to exist once the proprietor or partner dies, corporations can potentially live on forever, allowing for management and ownership changes over time.

There are considerable formalities associated with forming and operating a corporation—both in the initial state filings, but also in complying with state laws relating to internal operations, recordkeeping, ongoing annual or biennial compliance reporting, and the payment of franchise taxes[1] in some states.

TYPES OF CORPORATIONS

There are two basic types of corporations: (1) the C corporation; and (2) the S corporation. The *C* and *S* designations refer to subchapters of Title 26, Chapter 1, of the Internal Revenue Code. C corporations are recognized as completely separate entities from their owners (known as shareholders). They are the most common type of for-profit corporation and the type people are usually referring to when discussing corporations. C corporations are taxed twice—once at the entity level and once at the shareholder level upon receiving dividends (profits on their investment).

An S corporation is a corporation that has elected to pass corporate income and losses to its shareholders for federal tax purposes, thus avoiding paying tax at the entity level. To obtain subchapter S status, incorporators file state corporation paperwork, then apply for S recognition with the IRS via the Election by a Small Business Corporation (Form 2553) within seventy-five days of formation. Some states will recognize the federal form, but others will require you to refile the subchapter S paperwork with the state each year. Failure to maintain S status will result in an automatic converting of your S corporation to a C corporation, creating tax liability for the entity. Further, some states don't fully recognize subchapter S pass-through tax treatment and will require the entity to pay a state income tax.

Because S corporations have some special (restrictive) rules, they are not the preferred choice for many entrepreneurs. Some of these restrictions include the following:

- Ownership is limited to up to one hundred owners.
- All shareholders must approve and sign the subchapter S election form.
- Shareholders cannot be nonresident aliens (foreign nationals).
- Shareholders cannot be other companies.
- S corporations can only issue one class of stock (no preferred stock options).

OWNERSHIP AND CONTROL

Corporate owners are called shareholders. Shareholders' ownership in a corporation is evidenced by ownership of stock representing their ownership interest, by percentage, in the corporation. There is no limit to the number of owners a C corporation can have. Corporations are governed by a board of directors elected by its shareholders. The board appoints the senior-level officers who run the day-to-day operations of the company. In some states, it is possible for one person to be the corporation's sole owner, director, and officer simultaneously.

PERSONAL LIABILITY

Shareholders are typically not personally liable for corporate debts, although there are exceptions including instances where an owner personally guarantees a business loan as is often required by lenders of start-up businesses. Shareholders (and some officers and directors) can also be held liable for failing to pay federal and state taxes. Another important exception to liability protection is the legal doctrine "piercing the corporate veil" in which a claimant seeks to put aside the limitation on liability and reach the personal assets of the shareholders to satisfy a debt or other financial obligation owed by the corporation. Piercing the corporate veil is rare, but it can be done if a claimant can convince a court that the corporation is a sham to the extent that liability protection wouldn't be appropriate. One of the primary reasons for piercing the corporate veil is if the corporation doesn't follow state compliance formalities and/or hasn't established any internal governance procedures.

PROFIT AND GROWTH

Corporations raise money primarily by selling stock to other investors (who become part owners). When corporations are first formed, they are private until they "go public" via an initial public offering (IPO). Because newly formed corporations are privately held, there is no public marketplace for investors to purchase shares of stock to become owners of the corporation, so it's common for the initial owners of young corporations to be family members and friends.

TAX TREATMENT

C corporations are considered separate tax entities from their shareholder-owners. For this reason, C corporations are said to be taxed twice: the corporate entity is taxed on its earnings at the prevailing corporate tax rates as reported annually via federal Form 1120. Shareholder-owners are also taxed at their individual tax rate when they receive their percentage of corporate profits through the payment of dividends (once the board has declared that dividends be paid). In a privately held corporation, dividends are paid out to shareholders periodically once profits are realized unless the owner(s) chooses to forego dividend payment and instead invest the earnings in the business. Double taxation isn't an issue for corporations capitalized with debt (loans) with the added benefit that the debt load is generally tax deductible by the corporation. Dividend payments to shareholders are not tax deductible by the corporation.

S corporations file federal Form 1120S annually. Similar to a general partnership, S corporations don't pay tax at the entity level; instead, shareholders are given a Schedule K-1 and recognize corporate income or losses on their individual taxes. But some states don't recognize subchapter S status, so in those states, S corporations will owe state tax, which could be just a fixed minimum or be based on a percentage of income. Also, as noted above, some states assess a minimum franchise tax on corporations.

ARTICLES OF INCORPORATION

Individuals undertaking corporate formation are called *incorporators*. The incorporators don't need to be the organization's founders—often the founders will hire a professional to handle the incorporation paperwork. The application is called the *Articles of Incorporation*.

Also referred to as the *Certificate of Incorporation* or the *Corporate Charter*, the required contents of the Articles are few. This document is a contract with the state that makes the case for the corporation's legal purpose for being. Most, if not all, states will have a basic, optional online form to complete for submitting the Articles of Incorporation, but you can often draft your own. Realistically, it will likely be a smoother, faster process if you use the state's form because the person reviewing your materials will have more experience with it than whatever you draft and submit on your own.

Articles of Incorporation Decision Points

- The name of the corporation and any trade name (aka a fictitious name) to be used
- The corporation's business purpose and registered address
- Whether the corporation is organized on a stock or nonstock basis (typically for-profit corporations are stock-based so dividends can be paid based on the number of shares and class type of the stock owned; nonprofit organizations, by contrast, are usually required to be organized on a nonstock basis because they don't have owners and personal inurement is not allowed for charitable organizations)
- Number and classes of shares and their value (the state filing fee might be based off these figures)
- A description and value of any corporate assets (for both real property and personal property)
- How the corporation is expecting to be financed (through stock equity or debt)

- The name and address of the registered agent in the state (sometimes required to be the Secretary of State)
- Name and addresses of the incorporator(s)
- Other information as required by the state of incorporation

FORMING A CORPORATION

Corporations can be formed for any lawful purpose. Formation begins when the company's incorporator(s) file Articles of Incorporation (also known as a Certificate of Incorporation or the Corporate Charter) with the state for what is usually a nominal fee. Corporations can be organized under the laws of the state in which their principal office is located or in another state as a "foreign corporation." Corporate founders often choose to incorporate in a state other than where they live or have their principal place of business for several reasons that usually relate to differences in state corporation law including minimum number or types of directors, state income tax treatment, and franchise tax liability. See Chapter 8 for a discussion of these factors.

Formation Steps

1. Choose a corporate name and search on its availability (see Chapter 8).
2. Reserve the corporate name (optional).
3. Determine the number and makeup of your board of directors and their terms.
4. Pull together the content required for your Articles of Incorporation (also known as the *Certificate of Incorporation* or the *Corporate Charter*).
5. File the Articles of Incorporation and remit the filing fee to the Secretary of State in the state of incorporation.
6. Draft corporate bylaws once the content is determined, including quorum and voting rules, appointing and removing directors, dissolution, and so on.
7. File a franchise tax report and pay state franchise tax owed, if applicable.
8. Research and obtain any required local permits or licenses.
9. Determine whether you need business insurance (and any insurance required of employers if you plan to hire employees).
10. Hold an organizational meeting to vote on any outstanding matters including the issuance of stock to the owners via a stock ledger, adoption of bylaws and rules regarding authorized signers of checks, acceptance of

resignation of incorporator, and appointment of officers. Take meeting minutes documenting all these decisions.

11. Obtain federal and, if relevant, state employer identification numbers (EINs).
12. Open a bank account.
13. Any other actions required by the state of incorporation.

CONCLUSION

The corporate legal structure is common for two important reasons. The first is the opportunity C corporations have for rapid growth made possible once it "goes public" via an IPO. The IPO provides a public marketplace for outsiders (unlimited in number and type) to purchase shares and become owners of the enterprise. The additional owners bring an influx of capital that can be used to expand the business quickly. A second reason for its popularity is the financial protection afforded to corporate shareholders who are not generally personally liable for corporate debts. Appendix A provides a chart that compares for-profit corporations against other business models.

CORPORATION RESOURCES

IRS, "Tax Information for Corporations," www.irs.gov/Businesses/Corporations
U.S. Small Business Administration, "Choose a Business Structure," www.sba
.gov/content/corporation

The following sample Corporate Bylaws is for a corporation organized under the laws of New York State. It is provided courtesy of Scott M. Thomas, Esq. of Thomas Law Firm, PLLC,[2] in New York City, with my annotations.

Sample Corporate Bylaws

of

<Name of Corporation>

A New York Corporation

Article I

Shareholders

1.1 PLACE OF MEETINGS. Meetings of the shareholders of *<Name of Corporation>* (the "Corporation") shall be held at such place, either within or without the state of New York, as designated from time to time by the Board of Directors (sometimes referred to as the "Board" or the "Directors").

1.2 ANNUAL MEETINGS. Annual meetings of the Shareholders shall be held at such times as designated from time to time by the Board. At each annual meeting, the Shareholders shall elect a Board of Directors and transact other business as needed.

1.3 SPECIAL MEETINGS. Special meetings of the Shareholders will be held at such times as determined by the Board of Directors.

I like how these bylaws in items 1.1, 1.2, and 1.3 leave details open for future determination. If you do need to amend your bylaws, it usually just entails raising the change for an affirmative vote of the shareholders in accordance with any notice requirements, then making that change and distributing the revised bylaws to all shareholders while retaining the previous version as part of corporate bookkeeping and records management.

1.4 NOTICE OF MEETINGS. Pursuant to the requirements of Section 605 of the New York Business Corporation Law, written or electronic notice of each meeting of the Shareholders shall be given. This notice will state the place, date, and hour of the meeting and shall be given at least 10, but not more than 60, days prior to the meeting. The notice shall state in general terms the purpose for which the meeting is called.

1.5 QUORUM and ADJOURNMENTS OF MEETINGS. The holders of a majority of the issued and outstanding shares of stock of the Corporation entitled to vote at a meeting, present in person or represented by proxy, shall constitute a quorum for the transaction of business at a meeting of the corporation. If there is less than a quorum of holders of a majority of the shares so present or represented, then the meeting may be adjourned to another time, or place, until a quorum is present, whereupon the meeting may be held, without further notice, except as required by law.

A quorum is the minimum number of persons required to be present (including electronically) in order for official corporate business to be conducted. Establishing quorum rules helps to ensure that the requisite number of people affected by the decision being discussed and/or voted on are present and participating in the process that affects them.

A proxy is a ballot cast by one person for another who is absent from the voting. Proxy voting rules establish that allowing another shareholder to vote in your absence must be in writing and submitted according to corporate formalities established for this purpose.

1.6 VOTING and PROXIES. Pursuant to Section 609 of the New York Business Corporation Law, at any shareholder meeting every registered owner of shares entitled to vote may vote in person or by proxy except as otherwise provided by the New York Business Corporation Law, or in the Certificate of Incorporation or Bylaws of the Corporation. Each Shareholder shall have one vote for each such share standing in his or her name on the books of the Corporation. The Board shall be elected by the procedures outlined in these Bylaws, the New York Business Corporation Law, and the Certificate of Incorporation. In all other matters, unless otherwise provided by the New York Business Corporation Law or by the Certificate of Incorporation or the Bylaws, the affirmative vote of the holders of a majority of the shares entitled to vote on the subject matter at a meeting in which a quorum is present shall be the act of the shareholders.

Item 1.6 in these bylaws provides that the corporation may elect proxy rules via its articles of incorporation, bylaws, or merely follow state corporation law default rules.

1.7 CHAIRMAN OF MEETINGS. The Chairman of the Board shall preside at all meetings of the Shareholders. In his or her absence, an interim Chairman may be appointed by a majority of Shareholders present at the meeting.

1.8 SECRETARY OF MEETINGS. The Secretary of the Corporation shall act as secretary of all meetings of the Shareholders. In the absence of the Secretary, the Chairman of the meeting shall appoint another person to act as Secretary of the meeting.

The corporate secretary records the minutes of each meeting. The usual practice is for meeting minutes to be distributed soon after the meeting so those present have the opportunity to challenge the characterization of what was discussed, or votes taken on an action. Similarly, the secretary sends a meeting agenda to participants in advance of the meeting, so everyone can anticipate the subject matter of the meeting to more effectively participate.

1.9 SHAREHOLDER ACTION WITHOUT MEETING. Whenever shareholders are required or permitted to take an action by vote, such action may be taken without a meeting by written consent, setting forth the action so taken, signed by the holders of all shares outstanding and entitled to vote or, if the Certificate of Incorporation so permits, signed by the holders of outstanding shares having not less than the minimum number of votes that would be necessary to authorize or take such action at a meeting at which all shares entitled to vote were present and voted.

1.10 FIXING RECORD DATE. For the purpose of determining the Shareholders entitled to notice of or to vote at any meeting of the Shareholders or any adjournment thereof, or to express consent to or dissent from any proposal without a meeting, or for the purpose of determining the Shareholders entitled to receive payment of any dividend or other distribution or the allotment of any rights, or for the purpose of any other action, the Board of Directors may fix a record date for any such determination, which shall be not more than 60 nor less than 10 days before the date of any such meeting, and not more than 60 days prior to any other action. In any such case, only the Shareholders of record at the fixed time shall be entitled to notice of and to vote at the meeting or to express such consent or dissent, or to receive such dividend, distribution, or rights, or to be considered shareholders for the purposes of any other action, as the case may be.

Dividends, distribution, or rights refer to one kind of benefit or another. Dividends and distributions refer to a portion of corporate earnings given to shareholders (owners) in proportional share to their ownership interest in the corporate entity. The term dividends is most commonly used in the context of publicly traded corporations while distributions is the term more often used in privately held corporations. In either case, these are funds the board has decided against reinvesting in the enterprise and instead has decided to distribute to shareholders. A "right," in this context, refers to some other shareholder benefit granted by the board such as stock purchase rights.

Article II
Board of Directors

2.1 NUMBER OF DIRECTORS. The number of directors constituting the entire Board of Directors shall be two (2), until changed from time to time by action of the Shareholders or as designated by resolution of the entire Board of Directors. The entire Board of Directors means the total number of Directors that the Corporation would have if there were no vacancies.

2.2 ELECTION AND POWERS. Except as limited by the Certificate of Incorporation or Bylaws, the Board of Directors shall have management and control of the affairs and business of the Corporation. The Board will be elected by the shareholders at each annual meeting or by unanimous written consent in lieu of a meeting. Each Director shall serve until his or her successor is elected or appointed and qualified, unless his position as Director is vacated by resignation, death, removal, or otherwise.

2.3 VACANCIES. Subject to the requirements of Section 705 of the New York Business Corporation Law, whenever any vacancy occurs in the Board of Directors by reason of death, resignation, increase in the number of directors, or otherwise, it may be filled by a majority of the directors then in office, although less than a quorum, or by the sole remaining Director, for the balance of the term, or, if the Board of Directors has not filled such vacancy or if there are no remaining directors, it may be filled by the Shareholders.

2.4 REGULAR MEETINGS. Regular meetings of the Board of Directors may be held without notice at such times and places as the Board of Directors may determine from time to time.

2.5 SPECIAL MEETINGS. Special meetings of the Board of Directors may be called by order of the Chairman of the Board or the President. Written notice (including via email) of the time and place of each special meeting shall be given to each Director by or at the direction of the person or persons calling the meeting at least two days before the meeting. Except as otherwise specified in the notice, or as required by statute, the Certificate of Incorporation, or the Bylaws, any and all business may be transacted at a special meeting.

2.6 ORGANIZATION. Every meeting of the Board of Directors shall be presided over by the Chairman of the Board, or, in his or her absence, the President. In the absence of the Chairman of the Board and the President, a presiding officer shall be chosen by a majority of the directors present. The Secretary of the Corporation shall act as secretary of the meeting, but, in his or her absence, the presiding officer may appoint any person to act as secretary of the meeting.

2.7 QUORUM and VOTE. A majority of the Board of Directors in office shall constitute a quorum for the transaction of business, so long as at least one-third of the total number of Directors participates in the vote. If necessary, less than a quorum may adjourn any meeting to another time or place until a quorum is present, without further notice. Except as otherwise required by the New York Business Corporation Law, the Certificate of Incorporation or the Bylaws, all matters coming before any meeting of the Board shall be decided by majority vote of the Directors present at the meeting, so long as a quorum is present.

2.8 ACTION WITHOUT MEETING. Any action required or permitted to be taken by the Board of Directors may be taken without a meeting if all members of the Board of Directors consent in writing to the adoption of a resolution or resolutions authorizing the action, which resolution or resolutions, and the written consents thereto by the members of the Board of Directors, shall be filed with the minutes of the proceedings of the Board of Directors. Any one or more members of the Board of Directors may participate in a meeting of such Board by means of a conference call, allowing all persons participating in the meeting to hear one another at the same time. Participation by such means shall constitute presence in person at a meeting.

2.9 COMMITTEES. The Board of Directors, by resolution adopted by a majority of the entire Board of Directors, may appoint an executive committee and other committees, each consisting of one or more directors, which, to the extent provided in the resolution appointing them, shall have all of the authority of the Board of Directors, with the exception of any authority the delegation of which is prohibited by Section 712 of the New York Business Corporation Law. Each such committee shall serve at the pleasure of the Board of Directors, which may fill vacancies in, change the membership of, or discharge any such committee at any time.

Depending on the needs of the enterprise and the expertise of individuals serving on the board, the board may decide to assign specific members to a small committee to conduct research, evaluate a specific issue, or otherwise take on some project and report its findings back to the entire board at a future meeting. These can be committees that arise under special circumstances such as conducting an executive director search or merely for ongoing committee work such as a finance or facilities management committee.

New York, in Section 712 of New York Business Corporation Law, places some restrictions on the types of duties a corporate board may delegate to a subcommittee. For example, the board may not delegate filling board vacancies or repealing or amending the bylaws to a subcommittee of the board. The purpose behind the restriction is surely to safeguard against rogue board members trying to circumvent voting rules or otherwise trying to bring change they know the full board would never approve.

2.10 REMOVAL. Subject to Section 706 of the New York Business Corporation Law, the Shareholders may remove any one or more of the Directors with or without cause.

The phrase "with or without cause" refers to reasons for removing a director because of some wrongdoing (for cause) or for no reason at all (without cause). The language is borrowed from employment law, which recognizes "at-will" employment, meaning that unless unlawful (e.g., for a discriminatory purpose), no employment contract is extended to a worker and that worker can be fired for any reason or no reason at all and the worker has no legal recourse to enforce their status as an employee.

Article III

Officers

3.1 GENERAL. The Board of Directors shall elect the officers of the Corporation, which may include a President, a Secretary, and a Treasurer and other officers as the Board of Directors may designate from time to time.

3.2 TERM OF OFFICE, REMOVAL, AND VACANCY. Each Officer shall hold office until the meeting of the Board of Directors following the next annual meeting of shareholders and until his or her successor has been elected and qualified, or until his or her earlier resignation or removal. Any Officer shall be subject to removal with or without cause at any time by the Board of Directors. Vacancies in any office, whether occurring by death, resignation, removal, or otherwise, may be filled by the Board of Directors.

3.3 POWERS AND DUTIES. Each of the Officers of the Corporation shall, unless otherwise ordered by the Board of Directors, have such powers and duties as generally pertain to their respective offices, as well as such powers and duties as from time to time may be conferred upon him or her by the Board of Directors. Unless otherwise ordered by the Board of Directors after the adoption of the Bylaws, the Chairman of the Board, or, when the office of the Chairman of the Board is vacant, the President shall be the Chief Executive Officer of the Corporation.

Article IV
Stock

4.1 STOCK CERTIFICATES. The interest of each Shareholder of the Corporation shall be evidenced by stock certificates in such form not inconsistent with the New York Business Corporation Law or the Certificate of Incorporation and shall be signed by the Chairman of the Board, the President, and Chief Executive Officer.

Stock certificates represent a shareholder's ownership interest in the corporation.

4.2 TRANSFER OF STOCK. Shares of stock of the Corporation shall be nontransferable. The Board of Directors shall have the power and authority to make all such other rules and regulations as it may deem prudent concerning the issue, transfer, and registration of certificates for shares of the Corporation. The existence of restrictions on the sale or transfer of shares or any other matters required by law to be disclosed on stock certificates of the Corporation shall be noted conspicuously on the face or back of every certificate for shares issued by the Corporation.

Sometimes corporations want to put restrictions on stock for one reason or another. Public companies often want to reward highly valued employees with stock rights, but also want to restrict the selling (transfer) of that stock to encourage those employees to remain at the company during some transition period or for other reasons. Privately held corporations will often restrict transferability because they don't want shareholders to sell their stock rights to just anyone. Essentially, private corporations want control over who buys the stock because those individuals (or entities, such as a competitor) become part owners of the corporation and often have proportional share voting rights.

4.3 OWNERSHIP OF STOCK. The Corporation shall be entitled to treat the holder of record of any share or shares of stock as the owner thereof and shall not be bound to recognize any equitable claim or other claim to shares on the part of any other person, whether or not expressly provided by law. The Corporation may issue a new certificate for shares in place of a certificate issued by it, alleged to have been lost or destroyed, and the Board of Directors may require the owner of any lost or destroyed certificate, or his or her legal representative, to give the Corporation a bond sufficient to indemnify the Corporation against any claim that may be made against it on account of the alleged loss or destruction of any such certificate or the issuance of a new certificate.

An equitable claim is one in which the claimant asks a court to flex its muscle and force someone (or some entity) to do something or refrain from doing something (an injunction). A restraining order is a type of injunction and a term many are familiar with. An indemnity bond is a contract purchased by one party because it is required by another party to whom a promise has been made. The contract is intended to step in and provide money to back up the promise made. In this case, the corporation is reserving for itself the right to require a shareholder who claims to have lost their stock certificate (evidencing an ownership interest in the corporation) to purchase a surety bond of an amount high enough to cover the corporation's liability for improperly reissuing a stock certificate.

Article V
Miscellaneous

5.1 FISCAL YEAR. The Board of Directors shall have power to fix, and from time to time to change, the fiscal year of the Corporation.

5.2 DIVIDENDS. Subject to applicable law, dividends may be declared and paid out of earned surplus only, in such amounts, and at such time or times as the Board of Directors may determine, so long as the Corporation is not insolvent when such dividend is paid or rendered insolvent by the payment of such dividend.

Earned surplus means any profits made by the corporation since its inception. So, dividends don't need to be paid with any regularity—whether or not to issue a dividend and how much is always at the board's discretion, but the dividend can be funded by earnings going back in time—not merely from the current quarter or year.

Article VI
Indemnification

6.1 INDEMNIFICATION. The Corporation may indemnify any Director, officer, employee, or agent of the Corporation to the fullest extent permitted by the New York Business Corporation Law and other applicable law.

This is an Indemnification Clause. Indemnification refers to hiring legal counsel and paying any monetary judgment awarded to the plaintiff (the person or entity bringing the legal action). This clause allows for, but does not require, the corporation to purchase Directors and Officers (D&O) Liability Insurance to protect board members and corporate officers from lawsuits brought against them in their capacity as representatives of the corporation. For more on indemnification clauses, see examples provided in different contexts in Chapters 3, 6, and 10.

Article VII
Books and Records

7.1 RECORDS. The Corporation shall keep correct and complete books and records of account and shall keep minutes of the proceedings of the shareholders, of the Board of Directors, and/or any committee which the directors may appoint, and shall keep at the office of the Corporation in the state of New York or at the office of the transfer agent or registrar, if any, a record containing the names and addresses of all shareholders, the number and class of shares held by each, and the dates when they respectively became the owners of record thereof. Any of the foregoing books, minutes, or records may be in written form or in any other form capable of being converted into written form within a reasonable time.

A transfer agent is an entity that handles the paperwork for transferring stock—through sale or otherwise from one stockholder to another. A registrar is the entity that records the transfers and maintains these records on the corporate ledger. Corporations often hire these functions out and usually to the same entity. While there are different classes of shares, share classes most often connotate distinctions in voting rights and dividend treatment. For example, owners of preferred stock shares receive profit (dividends) before holders of common shares receive profit.

Article VIII
Amendment

8.1 AMENDMENT. The Board of Directors shall have the power to adopt, amend, or repeal the Bylaws of the Corporation by vote of a majority of the entire Board of Directors, subject to the provisions of Section 602 of the New York Business Corporation Law and also subject to the power of the shareholders to amend or repeal the Bylaws made or altered by the Board of Directors.

Secretary Certification

The undersigned, as Secretary of the Corporation, hereby certifies the foregoing Bylaws are a true and correct copy of the Bylaws of <Name of Corporation> and that such Bylaws were duly adopted by the Board of Directors on the date set forth below.

Date: _____

Signature: _____

NOTES

1. A franchise tax is a tax levied on a business for the privilege of conducting business in the state; it's not based on earnings or any other merit-based marker.

2. Thomas Law Firm, PLLC, thomaslawfirm.co (212) 203-9975.

PART III

NONPROFIT AND HYBRID LEGAL STRUCTURES

6

Nonprofit Organizations

This chapter will focus on nonprofit organizations. The Internal Revenue Service's (IRS) Statistics of Income (SOI) Division aggregates data from tax filings and publishes its findings by tax year. For 2015, the most recent year available, the SOI states that there were 1,184,547 nonprofit charitable organizations reporting over $3.8 trillion in assets and $2.9 trillion in revenue.[1] The most common structure is the nonprofit corporation, but some start-up companies will choose to try out their nonprofit business model in a less independent and more conservative approach: the fiscal sponsorship model. Some organizations will operate under a fiscal sponsorship model for a few years, then once they are confident in their ability to execute on their mission, have sufficient experience, and have reliable sources of funding, they will incorporate and file for charitable organization status under federal and state law. Most of this chapter will focus on the nonprofit corporation, but the chapter concludes with a discussion of the fiscal sponsorship approach.

More than any of the other standard legal structures, the nonprofit organization is likely the type that is most misunderstood and whose level of complexity is most underappreciated. When most people think of a nonprofit organization, two things come to mind: (1) entities exempt from paying federal and state income taxes; and (2) entities that can accept donations and offer their donors a tax benefit in exchange. While these are both true, only nonprofit organizations qualifying as *charitable organizations* under the Internal Revenue Code (IRC) can be exempt from paying certain taxes and offer their donors a tax benefit. Charitable organization recognition is the central reason many arts organizations choose the nonprofit corporation legal structure.

TYPES OF NONPROFIT ORGANIZATIONS

Nonprofit organizations can choose among a few different legal structures (a trust, an unincorporated association, corporation, etc.), and the IRS recognizes nearly thirty types of organizations whose missions could qualify them as a charitable organization for the purpose of federal tax exemption. The most common setup is a nonprofit corporation organized under state law.

THE NONPROFIT CORPORATION AND ITS PURPOSE

As its name suggests, a nonprofit corporation is a type of corporation. Like for-profit corporations, they are organized under state law and meet the state's statutory requirements to qualify as a nonprofit. While there are many different types of nonprofit organizations, what they all have in common is they exist to provide some public good that holds a benefit for their community or even globally.

The stated corporate purpose must comport with state nonprofit corporation law. Some states will require nonprofit incorporators to make specific attestations in their *Articles of Incorporation* relating to the organization. These can include provisions affirmatively stating that the corporation is being formed for a charitable purpose; that no individual will personally benefit from corporate profits; that political lobbying, if any is undertaken, will be insubstantial; and that if the corporation dissolves, its assets will be donated to another nonprofit organization within the state or to the state itself.

Before you start drafting your corporate purpose, take a look at the required language in your state and measure that against the charitable purpose language required by the IRS. Charitable purposes under Section 501(c)(3) of the IRC are as follows:

- educational
- religious
- scientific
- literary
- cultural; or
- for the prevention of cruelty to children or animals.[2]

You need to develop language that will comply with both state and federal rules.

Your charitable purpose should be specific and outline how your mission can be achieved.

Here is a sample corporate purpose:

> To advance the rich legacy of traditional Welsh vocal music in the United States through partnerships between American and Welsh universities, arts organizations, and language advancement programs. Specifically, we will advance Welsh traditional vocal music in three strategic ways: (1) we will develop singer-specific Welsh language training materials as part of a free Welsh language training course based on the International Phonetic Alphabet to aid students of singing with Welsh language skills; (2) assemble piano/voice songbooks containing traditional Welsh melodies and poetry in the public domain aligning the song texts with parallel levels from the language coursebook; and (3) partner with Welsh community centers and similar interest groups in the United States to explore community-centered performing opportunities to build audiences for this important, but endangered national music.

You can amend your nonprofit mission later, if necessary, by filing an amendment to your Articles of Incorporation with the state.

OWNERSHIP AND CONTROL

Despite that most nonprofit organizations are corporations, unlike for-profit corporations they are not owned by anyone. So, as the founder, you won't be able to sell your nonprofit business and cash out if you decide to pursue other interests or retire. Nonprofits corporations are generally governed by a board of directors. State law will determine the number and type of directors. For example, in my home state of New York, nonprofit corporations are required to have at least three directors and at least one of those directors must be "disinterested" (not an employee or someone financially benefiting in some other way from their relationship with the entity). For those who like more control, about sixteen states allow for a single-director nonprofit corporation.

PERSONAL LIABILITY

Most nonprofit organizations are formed as C corporations—legal structures that shield owners from personal liability. Therefore, a nonprofit corporation affords the same level of personal liability protection for its employees, officers, and directors in the same manner and to the same degree as a for-profit corporation.

PROFIT AND GROWTH

Many are surprised to learn that nonprofits can (and should) make a profit. The difference between nonprofit and for-profit entities is how profits are utilized. In for-profit businesses, net profits are distributed to the owners/shareholders or reinvested back into the business. In nonprofit organizations, net profits must be retained and reinvested back into the organization in furtherance of its mission. While personal inurement is not allowed, individuals employed by nonprofit organizations are entitled to make a "reasonable" salary. See the Fifth Article from the sample Articles of Incorporation within this chapter.

TAX TREATMENT

Not all nonprofits are tax exempt and federal tax exemption is not automatic. A nonprofit must apply for *charitable organization* recognition by filing an application (IRS Form 1023 or 1023-EZ). The 1023-EZ is a streamlined application, but applicants are required to complete and submit a long worksheet to prove their organization is eligible for the streamlined service. Being exempt from paying taxes allows the charity to reinvest all profits back into the organization in furtherance of its mission. Once officially recognized as a charitable organization through receipt of a *determination letter* from the IRS, the charity is exempt from federal income taxes.

Even if charitable organization status is granted, state tax exemption is not automatic—you'll have to file an application with the state's tax authority to be exempt from paying state corporation income tax as well as an application to be exempt from paying state sales tax on purchases. See New York State CT-247 for an example of an application for exemption from corporate income tax and ST-119 for an example of an application for exemption from paying state sales tax on purchases.

Similarly, charities typically don't pay taxes on property used exclusively for charitable purposes. If your organization purchases real estate, you'll have to apply for exemption from paying real estate taxes if you qualify. If you don't qualify (you are not using the property in furtherance of your charitable purpose), you'll have to pay real estate taxes.

Nonprofit organizations file annual financial reports with the IRS on a Return of Organization Exempt from Income Tax (Form 990). Qualifying smaller-revenue organizations can file a Form 990-EZ or a 990-N (the "e-postcard").

There is no exemption from paying employment tax, and if your nonprofit makes ancillary income that is not directly related to its stated mission, you would have to report that income as Unrelated Business Income and pay income tax on those earnings. For example, income realized from paid advertising in your organization's concert program or from retail rental income received from third parties.

ARTICLES OF INCORPORATION

Individuals undertaking corporate formation are called *incorporators*. The incorporators don't need to be the organization's founders—often the founders will hire a professional to handle the incorporation paperwork. The application is called the *Articles of Incorporation*.

Also referred to as the *Certificate of Incorporation* or the *Corporate Charter*, the contents of the Articles are few and determined by state law. This document is a contract with the state that makes the case for the corporation's legal purpose for being. Most, if not all, states will have an optional online form to complete for submitting the Articles of Incorporation, but you can often draft your own. Realistically, it will likely be a smoother, faster process if you use the state's form because the state employee reviewing your materials will have more experience with their own form than with an unfamiliar form you submit for approval.

Articles of Incorporation Decision Points

- The name of the corporation and any trade name to be used, if any
- The nonprofit corporate purpose
- Whether the corporation is organized on a stock or nonstock basis (where the option is allowed). The majority of states requires nonprofits to be organized on a nonstock basis, which is consistent with the fact that no one "owns" a nonprofit organization. But in the handful of states where stock organization is allowed, it's merely for governance and control in the absence of a Board of Directors.
- How the corporation is expected to be financed

- With respect to governance, whether the corporation is organized on a membership or directorship basis. Membership governance allows members to vote on corporate action; directorship governance means that the organization will elect a Board of Directors to determine corporate action.
- The name and address of the registered agent in the state (may be required to be the Secretary of State)
- Name and addresses of the incorporator(s)
- Other information as required

The incorporators may also be required to make some attestations that affirmatively state nonprofit statutory language. For example, that the corporation will operate for a specific nonprofit purpose; no earnings will inure to the benefit of any person; how corporate assets will be distributed upon dissolution; and anything else required under state nonprofit corporation law.

Sample Articles of Incorporation[3]

Articles of Incorporation of the undersigned, a majority of whom are citizens of the United States, desiring to form a Non-Profit Corporation under the Non-Profit Corporation Law of _____, do hereby certify:

The applicable laws of your state should be inserted above in legal citation format. Usually you'll see something at the beginning of the statute that says "short title," which tells you how you should reference the statute. For example, New York's nonprofit law's short title section says: "This chapter shall be known as the 'Not-for-Profit Corporation Law' and may be cited as 'N-PCL.'"

First: The name of the Corporation shall be _____.

The corporation's name will be the registered, official name that complies with your state's naming rules. For example, requiring the word "Corp." or "Inc." following the corporation's name. You might also be able to show your trade name here, if any, with a "doing business as" indicator as follows: The Buffalo Corporation d/b/a The Blues Shack.

Second: The place in this state where the principal office of the Corporation is to be located is the City of _____,
_____ County.

Third: Said corporation is organized exclusively for charitable, religious, educational, and scientific purposes, including, for such purposes, the making of distributions to organizations that qualify as exempt organizations under Section 501(c)(3) of the Internal Revenue Code, or the corresponding section of any future federal tax code.

This language, relating to the organization's charitable purpose, is required for all nonprofits intending to be recognized as a charitable organization under the Internal Revenue Code—specifically under Section 501(c)(3), the most common recognition under the Code.[4] The language referring to "the making of distributions to organizations that qualify as exempt organizations under Section 501(c)(3)" is added here to include foundations that are themselves tax exempt, but who also make grants to other tax-exempt organizations.

Fourth: The names and addresses of the persons who are the initial trustees of the corporation are as follows:

Name   Address

"Initial trustees" means the incorporators.

Fifth: No part of the net earnings of the corporation shall inure to the benefit of, or be distributable to its members, trustees, officers, or other private persons, except that the corporation shall be authorized and empowered to pay reasonable compensation for services rendered and to make payments and distributions in furtherance of the purposes set forth in Article Third hereof. No substantial part of the activities of the corporation shall be the carrying on of propaganda, or otherwise attempting to influence legislation, and the corporation shall not participate in, or intervene in (including the publishing or distribution of statements) any political campaign on behalf of or in opposition to any candidate for public office. Notwithstanding any other provision of these articles, the corporation shall not carry on any other activities not permitted to be carried on (a) by a corporation exempt from federal income tax under Section 501(c)(3) of the Internal Revenue Code, or the corresponding section of any future federal tax code, or (b) by a corporation, contributions to which are deductible under Section 170(c)(2) of the Internal Revenue Code, or the corresponding section of any future federal tax code.

More required language that parallels federal charitable organization law prohibiting personal financial benefit. Note that persons working in charitable organizations may receive "reasonable compensation" for their services. Political lobbying or political candidate campaign involvement are prohibited.

Section 170(c)(2) of the Code is the part of charitable organization law that authorizes charitable tax deductions by donors.

A note from the IRS regarding language here that might conflict with state law:

If reference to federal law in articles of incorporation imposes a limitation that is invalid in your state, you may wish to substitute the following for the last sentence of the preceding paragraph: "Notwithstanding any other provision of these articles, this corporation shall not, except to an insubstantial degree, engage in any activities or exercise any powers that aren't in furtherance of the purposes of this corporation."

Sixth: Upon the dissolution of the corporation, assets shall be distributed for one or more exempt purposes within the meaning of Section 501(c)(3) of the Internal Revenue Code, or the corresponding section of any future federal tax code, or shall be distributed to the federal government, or to a state or local government, for a public purpose. Any such assets not so disposed of shall be disposed of by a Court of Competent Jurisdiction of the county in which the principal office of the corporation is then located, exclusively for such purposes or to such organization or organizations, as said Court shall determine, which are organized and operated exclusively for such purposes.

Corporate dissolution refers to how the entity officially ceases to be in existence—if you formed a corporation you cannot decide to no longer operate it and simply walk away; statutory formalities must be followed, especially when it comes to legally distributing a tax-exempt organization's assets as part of the dissolution process. This is important—you will need to orderly wind down your business and comply with state laws governing corporate dissolution. Your state will have rules for how the nonprofit corporation's assets should be distributed once the corporation's governing body votes to dissolve. For example, New York nonprofits are required to liquidate corporate assets once all corporate debts have been paid and remit remaining funds to another recognized charitable organization or to the state itself.

In witness whereof, we have hereunto subscribed our names this _____ day of _____, 20__.

Signatures:

Your state might have specific rules regarding the number or manner of signatures including whether the signatures need to be notarized.

CORPORATE BYLAWS

State law will govern the content of corporate bylaws or, at minimum, provide the default rules in instances where the bylaws are silent on a specific topic. Expect to see a lot of redundancies between the content of the Articles of Incorporation, bylaws, and statements required on federal Form 1023 and 1023-EZ.

Bylaw Decision Points

- Nonprofit purpose
- Principal place of business
- Number of board members, their terms, how board vacancies will be filled, compensation, indemnification, insurance, and so on.
- Individual board member titles and responsibilities
- How conflicts of interest will be handled
- Frequency of board meetings, notice of meetings, quorum, voting, and other meeting rules
- Financial details such as the corporation's fiscal year, budget preparation, and budget-related voting
- Other state-required content such as corporate policies relating to whistle-blower protection, sexual harassment, workplace violence, related-party (interested) transactions; the duty to develop and adopt some or all of these policies may be triggered by the size of your organization and/or its budget.

Sample Nonprofit Corporation Bylaws

Bylaws of
<your corporation's registered name>, Inc.
for
<your trade name, if any>
A *<your state>* Nonprofit Corporation

Article 1
Mission Statement/Purpose

1.1 As stated in its Articles of Incorporation, the Corporation's mission and purpose is to *<insert purpose>* and to receive and administer funds for these purposes and reasonably related purposes set forth in Section 501(c)(3) of the Internal Revenue Code (IRC), including making distributions for such purposes to other organizations that qualify as tax-exempt organizations under IRC Section 501(c)(3).

This is where you would insert your nonprofit mission as taken from your Articles of Incorporation. For example:

To realize a global platform for art song that explores the dynamic union of music and text through publication, performance, and commission of new works, enlivening the practice and experience of artful storytelling within its diverse community. We aim to provide and promote education about and appreciation of Art Songs among performers, students, scholars, and fans of this extraordinary art form; to establish and maintain a virtual home, gathering place, and information exchange for the Art Song community.

Article 2
Offices

2.1. The principal and registered offices of the Corporation shall be at such place(s) within the State of *<your state>* as the Board of Directors may designate from time to time.

Article 3
Board of Directors

3.1. Board Membership

The activities of the Corporation shall be governed and managed by a Board of Directors, which shall consist of no less than three (3) persons. The members of the first Board shall be appointed by the incorporators and serve three-year terms. Thereafter, successor directors shall be appointed by the Board of Directors, also for three-year terms. There shall be no limit on the number of three-year terms a Director may serve. A Director may resign at any time by written notice to the Corporation, and any Director may be removed with or without cause at any time by majority vote of the other members of the Board; in either event, the Board shall fill the vacancy created by the resignation or removal by appointing another person for the remainder of the term of the person who has resigned or been removed.

State law will provide for the minimum number and type of directors. For example, many if not all states require a minimum of three directors in nonprofit corporations. Some states may require that at least one of the directors be "disinterested" (for example, not on the corporation's payroll as an officer). Similarly, the actual length of term served by a director is often governed by state default rules but can be changed to provide for an individual entity's needs.

3.2. Meetings

The Board shall meet as frequently as it deems necessary and appropriate, but no less frequently than once every twelve months, and shall hold its annual meeting each year during the month of June. Written notice of all Board meetings shall be given to all Directors at least ten (10) calendar days before the date of the meeting, by postal mail, hand-delivery, or email, but Directors may waive this requirement in writing or by email by so stating during a meeting they attend, provided the oral waiver is recorded in the minutes of that meeting. A Director who is unable to attend any meeting in person may do so by teleconference, and upon consent of all Directors, any meeting of the Board may be held entirely by teleconference, provided such arrangements are recorded in the minutes of the meeting.

It may seem fussy to have specific rules about how and when board meetings will be held, how meeting notices should be made, taking of minutes (meeting notes), and formally waiving certain protocols, but enacting and following these rules is extremely important because it signals to the state that corporate officers and directors are taking their responsibilities seriously. One of the central reasons for forming a corporation is the liability safeguards afforded by the corporate legal structure. For example, if the corporation has outstanding debts it cannot pay, a corporate debtor will attempt to demonstrate to a court that the corporation is a sham and therefore, its directors and officers are not entitled to protect their personal assets from creditors. The first step in making this kind of accusation is attempting to show that corporate formalities like these are not being followed or were never adopted at all.

3.3 Quorum

Three (3) Directors shall constitute a quorum for transaction of any business by the Board. Actions approved by those Directors attending, either physically or by teleconference, shall constitute authorized action by the Board, provided that all remaining Directors have received or waived advance notice of such meeting or action.

A quorum is the minimum number of persons required to be present (including electronically) in order to conduct official corporate business. Establishing quorum rules helps to ensure that the requisite number people affected by the decision being discussed and/or voted on are present and participating in the process that affects them.

3.4 Committees

The Board may appoint such committees as it sees fit from time to time and they may include Board members and other persons, but such committees shall function only in an advisory capacity and have no authority to take official action in the name, or on behalf of, the Corporation.

Some states have rules that restrict the authority a corporate board may delegate to a committee. For an example, see Article 2.9 of the sample New York bylaws provided in Chapter 5.

3.5 Compensation

Board members shall serve without compensation but may be reimbursed for expenses in the performance of their duties as Directors, upon specific Board authorization.

Some states have rules that say it's up to the corporation whether board members are compensated for their time or not. Additionally, it is sometimes the case that only non-compensated board members receive the broadest indemnification pledge from the corporation. See Article 3.7 for an example of an indemnification provision.

3.6 Conflicts of Interest

If a Director has an affiliation with another organization that seeks to provide services or sell products to the Corporation, or has any other duality or conflict of interest, actual or apparent, such affiliation, duality, or conflict shall be disclosed to the Board and made a matter of record. An affiliation with an organization shall be considered to exist if a Director, member of his/her immediate family, or other close relative is an Officer, Director, Trustee, Partner, Employee, or Agent of or has any ownership interest in or other substantial dealings with such organization. A Director with such affiliation or interest should not vote or use his/her influence on any matter related to dealings between the Corporation and the organization in question and should not be counted in determining a quorum for any meeting at which such a matter is voted upon, but he/she may express an opinion on or answer questions from other Directors about the matter under consideration. The minutes of a meeting at which any such matter is discussed or voted on should reflect the Director's disclosure, abstention from voting, and exclusion from quorum count.

Some states require that the bylaws contain a conflict of interest policy that outlines measures to be taken to ensure that all matters voted on by the board are "arm's length" transactions—meaning that no person voting or no person closely related to a voting member will personally benefit from action taken by the board. Similarly, some states also require that the corporation adopt rules for handling related-party transactions, which are transactions in which board members, officers, or key employees (or any family members of any of these) stand to financially benefit from a decision by the corporation.

3.7 Indemnification

All persons serving as members of the Board of Directors shall be protected and indemnified against personal liability for their actions as Directors in the manner and to the extent stated in the Articles of Incorporation, and the Board shall maintain adequate Directors and Officers liability insurance coverage.

Directors and Officers (D&O) liability insurance protects a company's directors and officers from lawsuits alleging that a member of the management team committed a wrongful (negligent) act in service to the corporation.

In this corporation's bylaws, purchasing D&O insurance is an obligation, but it doesn't need to be (changing the word "shall" to "may" would make the purchase of insurance optional). "Adequate" refers both to the limits of insurance purchased (limits of insurance should be high enough in dollar amounts to actually provide protection based on the company's legal exposure), policy language that is broad enough to cover the risks presented, and the quality of the insurance company from which the coverage is purchased. Insurance companies are rated by organizations such as Moody's and Standard and Poor's based on their financial stability/ability to pay claims.

Article 4
Corporate Officers

4.1. The officers of the Corporation shall be a Chairperson, Secretary, and Treasurer. The Board may appoint other officers (such as President, Assistant Chairperson or Vice President, Assistant Secretary or Assistant Treasurer) as it sees fit. The first officers shall be appointed by the Board at its first meeting and hold office until the next annual meeting; thereafter it shall appoint officers to one-year terms at each annual meeting. The same person may hold two (2) offices, but shall not execute, acknowledge, or verify in more than one capacity any instrument that may be required by law to be executed, acknowledged, or verified by two (2) officers.

Not allowing one individual holding two offices simultaneously to do certain important things like sign checks or execute contracts on behalf of the organization is smart. It is generally considered best practice to have dual signature require-ments for check signing over a certain dollar threshold.

4.2 Chairperson

The Chairperson shall preside at all Board meetings and perform such other duties as are typical of the office and assigned to him/her by the Board, in-cluding signing corporate documents; appointing employees, agents, and independent contractors; determining their duties and setting their compen-sation; and having general control over corporate activities in accordance with directives and actions of the Board.

4.3 Secretary

The Corporate Secretary shall keep minutes of Board meetings and actions, provide notices of meetings to Board members if and as required by law, maintain and distribute the Articles and Bylaws, and perform such other du-ties as are usual to such office and assigned by the Chairperson or the Board.

4.4 Treasurer

The Treasurer shall oversee all financial activities of the Corporation and per-form such other duties as are usual to the office and assigned to the Treasurer by the Chairperson or the Board including filing or overseeing the filing of the corporate tax documents as provided in Article 6. All records, papers, funds, and other property of any kind belonging to the Corporation and in the Trea-surer's custody or possession shall be returned to the Corporation upon his/her resignation, removal from office, or death.

Article 5

5.1 Corporate Documents

No Director, officer, agent, employee, or attorney-in-fact shall sign any docu-ment on behalf of the Corporation unless authorized to do so by the Board or these Bylaws.

This clause may seem restrictive, but I like it because it requires regular com-munication between the officers, employees, and the board with respect to the signing of documents, which can include changing bylaws, moving the corporation, or even something as mundane as applying for a letter of credit or signing a venue rental contract.

Article 6
Finances

6.1 Fiscal Year

The fiscal year of the Corporation is *<insert dates>*.

6.2 Budget

The Chairperson and Treasurer shall present a budget for the next fiscal year to the Board at its annual meeting each year, and the Board shall adopt it, with such changes as it considers appropriate.

6.3 Expenditures and Debts

No expenditure shall be made that is not in accordance with the budget, unless approved by the Board. No Director or officer may sign any instrument of indebtedness on the Corporation's behalf without specific authorization from the Board.

6.4 Annual Financial Report

The Treasurer shall present to the Board for its approval within ninety (90) days after the close of each fiscal year an annual report for that fiscal year and shall prepare or cause to be prepared any tax returns legally required to be filed by the Corporation, present such returns to the Board for its review and approval, and after approval shall file them by the applicable due date, original or extended.

Article 7

7.1 Rules of Order

Board meetings shall be governed by and conducted in accordance with Robert's Rules of Order or such other rules as the Board may adopt from time to time.

The Robert's Rules of Order is the operation manual for parliamentary proce-dure commonly used by organizations in the United States. It provides formal rules for running efficient meetings, aims to enable fairness to all participants by providing for a way for all voices to be heard, and ensures any initiatives adopted at a meeting accurately reflect the decisions of those who participated.

Article 8

8.1 Amendments
The Board of Directors may amend or repeal these Bylaws, or adopt new ones, at any Board meeting, but only if notice setting forth the terms of the amend-ment, intent to repeal, or complete contents of the new Bylaws has been given in accordance with Article 3.

It's not uncommon to need to amend your bylaws as the needs and preferences of the corporation change. Providing authority to do this is important and should be captured in the bylaws so all stakeholders are aware that amendments are permissible.

Adopted by the Incorporators this *<insert date>* day of *<insert year>*.

_____   _____

<first incorporator's signature>   *<second incorporator's signature, if any>*

FORMING A NONPROFIT CORPORATION/CHARITABLE ORGANIZATION
The life of a nonprofit corporation begins in the same manner as a for-profit corporation does: by filing Articles of Incorporation with the state, but that's only the beginning.

Formation Steps
1. Incorporate under state law.
   a. Decide on a corporate name (and any trade name, if applicable) and check on availability.
   b. Reserve the corporate names (optional).
   c. Determine your Board of Directors.

d. Pull together the content required for your Articles of Incorporation (also known as the *Certificate of Incorporation* or the *Corporate Charter*) and bylaws.

e. Obtain any state agency consents, if required.

f. Research and obtain any required local permits or licenses.

g. Determine whether you need business insurance (and any insurance required of employers if you plan to have employees).

h. File the Articles of Incorporation with the Secretary of State.

i. Draft corporate bylaws once the content is determined.

j. Hold an organizational meeting with the Board of Directors to vote on bylaws and any outstanding matters.

k. Research and obtain any required local permits or licenses.

2. Apply for federal tax exemption.

a. Apply for a federal employer identification number (EIN).

b. Apply for recognition of tax exemption under IRC (From 1023 or 1023-EZ).

c. Respond to IRS questions, if any.

3. Apply for tax exemption under state and local law.

a. Apply for exemption from state corporate tax.

b. Apply for exemption from state and local sales tax.

c. Register with any required state not-for-profit regulatory bodies.

4. If you plan to solicit funds or apply for government grants, you may need to register in every state (see "Charitable Solicitation Registration").

Appendix A provides a chart that compares nonprofit corporations with federal charitable organization status against other business models.

Tip: For nonprofit formation help, search "nonprofit incorporation guide" plus your state's name and you'll likely find more step-by-step advice for getting started in the state where you're planning to launch your nonprofit enterprise.

CHARITABLE SOLICITATION REGISTRATION

Nonprofit organizations rely on philanthropic giving to obtain the funding needed to carry out their mission of achieving a public benefit. Philanthropy is primarily realized through charitable donations and grants from both public and private sources. Before a nonprofit organization can solicit donations, in many states (and Washington, DC) the nonprofit must first register with the jurisdiction's charities bureau for authority to solicit charitable donations there. Each state has its own rules for what constitutes a charitable "solicitation." Sometimes there are clear instances of traditional solicitation such as when an organization asks for donations through a direct mail program, a phone campaign, or fundraising events in the state, but other forms of soliciting are less obvious. These might include merely having a website that has a Donate Now button.

Some donors and grantors will not or cannot, by charter, donate to nonprofits that are not registered in their state because applying for grants is generally considered "soliciting." Registration often entails filing information about the nonprofit including a copy of the IRS determination letter of tax-exempt status, latest financial information supported by one of the Form 990s, corporate bylaws, the Articles of Incorporation, information about the board, and paying a registration fee. Beyond mere registration, some states take the position that soliciting in the state constitutes "conducting business" and will require nonprofit corporations that solicit charitable donations to apply for authority to operate as a foreign corporation in that state prior to solicitation. The paperwork and fees associated with the applications vary. The registration fee is often fairly low—usually under $100. Registration is usually annual, though a few states allow for two-year registrations. Most states have penalties for registering after you first began soliciting donations there and for late renewal of an existing registration.

Each state will also determine whether any entities might be exempt from registration and under what circumstances (such as number of donors or by revenue size). Even if your nonprofit meets one of the exempting criteria, you likely still need to apply for an exemption—don't assume exemption is automatic based on your analysis.

HELP WITH CHARITABLE SOLICITATION REGISTRATION

Charitable solicitation is a complicated subject, but the National Association of State Charity Officials has an excellent resource on their website containing links to the charities bureaus in each jurisdiction to help you determine what the requirements are in that jurisdiction. Additionally, see "Charitable Solicitation Registration Resources," below, for organizations that specialize in helping charitable organizations with state registration compliance.

THE FISCAL SPONSORSHIP MODEL

While forming a nonprofit corporation under state law is the standard way to launch a nonprofit organization, there is a more conservative, stick-your-toe-in-the-water approach: the fiscal sponsorship model. Fiscal sponsorship, in this context, means that your start-up enterprise holds off on corporate organization and first partners with a more established nonprofit organization with a similar nonprofit mission. Under this model, the sponsoring organization will lend you its charitable organization status pursuant to a fiscal sponsorship agreement and, in exchange, you will share a percentage of your income (often 5–10%) with the sponsoring organization or work out some other compensation model.

There are many different types of fiscal sponsor arrangements, but the two most common are a comprehensive fiscal sponsorship model and a preapproved grant relationship model.[5]

Comprehensive Fiscal Sponsorship Model

Under a comprehensive fiscal sponsorship model, the sponsoring organization typically assumes oversight and control of the sponsored organization's operations including its finances. In exchange for a percentage of its income, the sponsored organization/project can receive access to its sponsor's office and performing space, administrative assistance, advice, training, publicity, and fundraising expertise. More important than any of these benefits, however, is access to the sponsoring organization's charitable organization and solicitation registration status, which allows the sponsored organization to legally conduct its own fundraising even though it has not yet received (or even applied for) charitable organization status with the IRS. A possible downside of this arrangement is that the sponsoring organization commonly owns the assets and intellectual property (IP) of the sponsored organization, but ownership and control of your IP can be addressed in the written Fiscal Sponsorship Agreement that governs the relationship.

Preapproved Grant Relationship Model

In the preapproved grant relationship model, the sponsored organization/ project is a grantee recipient of the sponsoring organization. The sponsor is responsible for seeing that project funds are properly administered. The sponsored organization owns the assets and the intellectual property resulting from its work and is responsible for its own tax and other filings. Because, under this model, the sponsored organization is more independent of the sponsoring organization, it does not get the benefit of the sponsoring organization's charitable organization status, so it cannot independently solicit charitable donations.

MORE INFORMATION ABOUT FISCAL SPONSORSHIP

For more information about these and other fiscal sponsorship models, visit the website for the National Network of Fiscal Sponsors (NNFS) (see "Nonprofit Resources," below). The NNFS site provides excellent information including white papers, tips for choosing the right fiscal sponsor, what your sponsorship agreement should contain, and operational best practices. Note that you can choose a sponsor whose mission closely aligns with that of your organization or project or you can enter into an agreement with an independent, freestanding sponsoring organization.

THE FISCAL SPONSORSHIP AGREEMENT

Regardless of the sponsorship model you choose, you should have a formal, written agreement that lays out the rights and responsibilities of your organization (or project) and those of the sponsoring organization, in the same manner as you would for any other type of contractual relationship. Your agreement should include who owns the assets and IP developed during and after the sponsorship period, a clear path for exiting the arrangement, a transparent fee structure, what happens to interest on funds held on account, and what services are provided to your organization including accounting, compliance reporting, human resources, recruitment and training of volunteers, marketing, fundraising, access to facilities, and office space, among others.

What follows immediately below is a sample comprehensive fiscal sponsorship agreement.

Sample Fiscal Sponsorship Agreement

WHEREAS the non-exempt organization (the "Sponsored Organization"), whose primary business address at _____ wishes to collaborate with the exempt organization ("Fiscal Sponsor" or "Sponsor") whose primary business address is _____ for the purposes of _____ (the "Project").

The project refers to the sponsored organization's mission.

WHEREAS the Fiscal Sponsor has determined that sponsorship of the Project would be consistent with its goals and wishes to make arrangements with the Sponsored Organization for the implementation and operation of the Project;

WHEREAS the Sponsored Organization agrees to be operated in a manner consistent with the Fiscal Sponsor's tax-exempt status and as described in this Agreement;

WHEREAS the Sponsored Organization agrees to not attempt to influence legislation or participate or intervene in any political campaign on behalf of (or in opposition to) any candidate for public office or otherwise engage in the carrying on of propaganda (within the meaning of Section 501(c)(3) of the Internal Revenue Code).

The parties mutually agree as follows:

1. The Fiscal Sponsor agrees to sponsor the Project and
   a. assume administrative, programmatic, financial, and legal responsibility for purposes of the requirements of any funding organizations, if applicable;
   b. receive tax deductible donations for and in furtherance of the Project;
   c. send acknowledgment receipts of Project funds to donors and timely provide copies of such acknowledgments to the Project;
   d. establish and operate one designated interest-bearing account (the "Account") segregated on the Sponsor's books and in the Sponsor's name for Project funds;
   e. prepare all requisite state and federal government reports and returns required in connection to the Project; and

f. cooperate in good faith with auditors selected or engaged by Project donors, if applicable.

2. Subject to 8, below, all amounts deposited into the Account will be used in support of the Project.

Not all sponsorship models look like this one; the services provided by the fiscal sponsor should closely tailor the needs of the sponsored organization. Organizations looking for a sponsor should first make a list of their primary and secondary needs and then shop around to find a fiscal sponsor who can provide those services professionally and expeditiously according to a fee structure that is reasonable.

3. The Sponsored Organization agrees to implement and operate the Project in accordance with the terms of this Agreement and with any requirements imposed by any funding organizations, if applicable.

4. The Sponsor and the Sponsored Organization will maintain all financial records relating to the Project according to generally accepted accounting principles, retain records as long as required by law, and make records available to auditors as required by law.

5. Disbursements will be restricted to the support and implementation of the Project only. The Sponsor will disburse funds from the Account in the following manner:

_____

This is where the fiscal sponsor would commit to when funds will be made available for the project's use (such as "within five (5) business days of receipt").

6. Designated Official
    The Sponsored Organization designates _____ to act as authorizing official. The authorizing official shall act as principal coordinator of the Sponsored Organization's daily business with the Sponsor and shall have authority to sign disbursement requests.

Designating someone with decision-making and financial authority at the sponsored organization will streamline communication and coordination between the two organizations.

7. Ownership of Intellectual Property

   All right, title, and other ownership interests in and to the Project, including tangible and intangible property arising out of the project and all income arising therefrom, shall be for the sole benefit of the Project.

It's important in any collaborative environment that the ownership of assets—tangible or intangible, such as IP—is made clear. For example, in a situation where an organization is sponsoring a project involving commissioned music, the agreement should clearly state which party owns the works commissioned and any future licensing income that flows from those project-funded commissions.

8. Activity Reporting

   a. The Sponsored Organization will provide all information and prepare all reports required by any funding organizations, if applicable, with the Sponsor's assistance and final approval.

   b. The Sponsored Organization will use all funds received from the Sponsor solely for Project expenses and will provide the Sponsor with reports describing programs and services of the Project in accordance with the following schedule:

The reporting schedule should be one that works for both parties. Reporting to the sponsor too frequently may take valuable time away from the project's goals, but the sponsor does have an interest in being sure that the sponsored organization is operating in compliance with the law or risk losing its tax-exempt status. Quarterly reporting may be appropriate if the sponsor will allow it.

   c. The Sponsor and the Sponsored Organization will reflect the activities of the Sponsored Organization, to the extent required, on their state and federal government tax returns and financial reports. All disbursements from the Account shall be treated as payments made to or on behalf of the Sponsored Organization to accomplish the purpose of the Project. The Sponsored Organization will provide the Sponsor with proper documentation to accomplish this, including furnishing the Sponsor with the Sponsored Organization's Federal Employer Identification Number (EIN).

d. Reports reflecting receipts, expenditures, and balances will be delivered by the Sponsor to the Project on a monthly basis within two (2) weeks after the end of each month and, on an annual basis, within three (3) months after the end of the Sponsor's fiscal year.

9. Compensation

In consideration of the Sponsor's agreement hereunder to sponsor the Sponsored Organization and to cover the Sponsor's expenses in connection with the Project as outlined above, the Sponsored Organization will pay the following fees, charges, and expenses:

The financial arrangement between the fiscal sponsor and the sponsored organization can be arranged in any number of ways: by using a flat-fee structure, by using a menu-style of fees for specific services rendered (such as graphic design or human resources-related services), or by percentage of funds received for the project under the fiscal sponsor's tax-exempt status to off-set administrative expenses. You could also include a maximum cap of deductions the sponsor can take from donated funds in a given fiscal year or, for a longer term arrangement, allow for higher caps or larger percentages as the project's funds grow over time.

10. Termination

This Agreement will be subject to review and will terminate if any of the following events occur:

a. The Sponsor requests the Sponsored Organization to cease activities that it deems might jeopardize its tax-exempt status and the Sponsored Organization fails to comply within a period of ten (10) days;

b. The Sponsored Organization fails to perform or observe any other covenant of this Agreement and this failure remains unremedied fourteen (14) days after written notice; or

c. Upon expiration of four (4) weeks after either the Sponsor or the Sponsored Organization has given written notice to the other of its intent to terminate this Agreement.

In the event this Agreement is terminated, funds held for the benefit of the Project shall not be transferred to any individual for any purpose without the prior written consent of the Sponsor. Both the Sponsor and the Sponsored Organization will comply with any termination conditions imposed by funding organizations, if applicable.

The sponsor will always want a way out of the arrangement if the sponsored organization's activities puts the sponsor at risk of losing its tax-exempt status, which is why you see this issue referred to so many times in this sample.

11. Miscellaneous
    No material changes in the purposes or activities of the Project shall be made without prior written permission of the Sponsor and in accordance with any requirements imposed by funding organizations, nor shall the Sponsored Organization carry on activities or use funds in any way that jeopardizes the Sponsor's tax-exempt status.

12. Integration
    This Agreement constitutes the entire agreement between the parties and supersedes all prior agreements, arrangements, negotiations, proposals, and understandings, if any, relating to the obligations and matters set out herein, whether oral or written.

13. Choice of Law
    The laws of the State of _____ shall govern the interpretation of this Agreement.

14. Insurance
    The Sponsor shall maintain a general liability insurance policy that includes the Project and its personnel as an additional insured with limits of insurance, terms, and conditions adequate to cover the Sponsored Organization and the Project.

In witness whereof, the parties hereto have executed this Agreement on the day and year first written above.

Accepted for the Fiscal Sponsor: For the Sponsored Organization:

_____   _____
Printed Name, Title   Printed Name, Title

_____   _____
Signature   Signature

_____   _____
Date   Date

NONPROFIT RESOURCES

The websites, organizations, and readings that follow may be useful for learning more about the nonprofit sector including understanding compliance obligations, grant funding, and obtaining legal assistance. Appendix A provides a comparison chart of legal business structures.

GENERAL INFORMATION

501Commons, www.501commons.org
Americans for the Arts, www.artsusa.org
Candid, www.candid.org
The Chronicle of Philanthropy, www.philanthropy.com
Freelancers Union, www.freelancersunion.org
Grant Space, www.grantspace.org
National Center for Charitable Statistics, nccs.urban.gov
National Council of Nonprofits, www.councilofnonprofits.org
The National Endowment for the Arts, www.nea.gov
The Nonprofit Centers Network, www.nonprofitcenters.org
Nonprofit Legal Center, www.nonprofitlegalcenter.org
The Sparkplug Foundation, awesomefoundation.org
Support Center for Nonprofit Management, www.supportcenteronline.org
Venable, LLP, www.venable.com
Volunteer Lawyers for the Arts, www.vlany.org

CHARITABLE SOLICITATION REGISTRATION RESOURCES

Affinity, www.fundraisingregistration.com
Harbor Compliance, www.harborcompliance.com
National Association of State Charity Officials, www.nasconet.org
Simple Charity Registration, www.simplecharityregistration.com

FISCAL SPONSORSHIP RESOURCES

Fractured Atlas, www.fracturedatlas.org
National Network of Fiscal Sponsors, www.fiscalsponsors.org
Pentacle, www.pentacle.org

BOOKS AND PUBLICATIONS

The Executive Director's Guide to Thriving as a Nonprofit Leader by Mim
    Carlson and Margaret Donohoe
Guide to Proposal Writing from The Foundation Center
IRS Publication 557—Tax-Exempt Status for Your Organization
IRS Publication 598—Tax on Unrelated Business Income of Tax Exempt
    Organizations
IRS Publication 4221-PC—Compliance Guide for 501(c)(3) Public Charities
IRS Publication 4779—Facts about Terminating or Merging Your Tax Exempt
    Organization
IRS Publication 4839—Annual Form 990 Filing Requirements for Tax Exempt
    Organizations
Webster's New World Grant Writing Handbook by Sara Deming Wason

NOTES

1. IRS Statistics of Income, "Charities and Other Tax-Exempt Organizations, Tax Year 2015," www.irs.gov/pub/irs-pdf/p5331.pdf.

2. IRS, "Exempt Purposes - Internal Revenue Code Section 501(c)(3)," www.irs.gov/charities-non-profits/charitable-organizations/exempt-purposes-internal-revenue-code-section-501c3.

3. IRS Publication 557.

4. IRS Statistics of Income, "Charities and Other Tax-Exempt Organizations, Tax Year 2015," www.irs.gov/pub/irs-pdf/p5331.pdf.

5. Gregory L. Colvin, *Fiscal Sponsorship: 6 Ways to Do It Right* (San Francisco: Study Center Press, 1993, 2005).

7

Hybrid Business Models

The terms *social entrepreneurship* and *social enterprise* are buzz words in vogue right now, yet there is no single, commonly accepted definition of either of them. Generally, social enterprises are those that serve purposes intended to better human existence by advancing social, cultural, and/or environmental causes. These can be for-profit or nonprofit organizations, but regardless of that identity, these enterprises tend to measure their impact with metrics typically not used by for-profit enterprises. In the relatively new, hybrid legal structure examples that follow, each is a for-profit enterprise with a social benefit mission, but none of them are tax-exempt organizations.

These business models emerged in the same way that older, more traditional business structures did: they evolved because the existing models weren't adequately responding to what entrepreneurs needed. The now common LLC, for example, is itself a hybrid between a partnership and a corporation because an LLC combines the operational flexibility and tax benefits of a partnership while offering the limited liability long enjoyed by corporate owners.

While the hybrid characterization of the LLC correlates to operational flexibility, tax benefits, and the protections against personal liability, the social enterprise hybrids introduced in this chapter relate to the seemingly polar opposite ideals of being for-profit while pursuing the advancement of a public benefit. These newer statutory entities are notable because, historically, state and federal governments in the United States have treated making profit and advancing a public good as mutually exclusive pursuits.

THREE TYPES OF HYBRID LEGAL STRUCTURES

The hybrid legal structures introduced in this chapter are versions of corporations or LLCs. They are the *benefit corporation*, the *social purpose corporation*, and the *low-profit legal liability company*. For a good place to start your research, check out the Social Enterprise Law Tracker.[1] This tool will show you the states where these business structures are available now, where relevant legislation has been proposed, and the status of that legislation. Also check with the Secretary of State's website for state filing and other ongoing compliance requirements in the state where you're interested in starting your social enterprise.

Benefit Corporations

A benefit corporation is a for-profit business corporation organized under state law in which the corporation self-identifies as a benefit corporation and affirmatively declares its "general public benefit" purpose in its Articles of Incorporation. Benefit corporations are required to consider the environmental and social implications of all corporate decision-making. Identifying as a benefit corporation may not seem particularly important, but doing so is critical for corporate shareholder-investors because in typical C corporations in the United States, the central purpose for organizing as a corporation (aside from the personal liability protections the corporate structure affords) is a profit mandate to increase shareholder value. In other words, the board of directors has a duty to make decisions that are expected to increase profitability for the benefit of its shareholder-owners. So, in a traditional corporation every governance decision undertaken by its board and executed by its officers is ultimately expected to result in profit. Investors in any kind of business need to understand corporate priorities including the considerations reviewed and factors weighed in corporate decision-making in order to determine where to invest.

Identifying as a benefit corporation, however, authorizes—actually mandates—that the board take a broader view of its governance and consider the effects of its decision-making measured in nonfinancial metrics. In other words, *how could today's strategic decisions impact our employees, neighbors, vendors, members of the community, other stakeholders, and the environment?* Thus, identifying as a benefit corporation and maintaining compliance with state requirements afford legal protection for directors and officers who put mission before profits.

In addition to declaring a general public benefit, benefit corporations also have the option of declaring a "specific public benefit," which may include one or more of the following as taken from benefit corporation model legislation[2]:

1. Providing low-income or underserved individuals or communities with beneficial products or services;
2. Promoting economic opportunity for individuals or communities beyond the creation of jobs in the normal course of business;
3. Protecting or restoring the environment;
4. Improving human health;
5. Promoting the arts, sciences, or advancement of knowledge;
6. Increasing the flow of capital to entities with a purpose to benefit society or the environment; and
7. Conferring any other particular benefit on society or the environment.[3]

There are approximately 4,000 legally constituted benefit corporations to-day[4] including famous brands like Warby Parker, Patagonia, Kickstarter, and King Arthur Flour. About thirty-six states have statutes authorizing benefit corporations in some form,[5] but of course statutes are not uniform even though they were all born from model legislation advanced by the same entity, B Lab.

Other Benefit Corporation Characteristics
Another important distinction between benefit corporations and non-benefit corporations relates to transparency. In most states that recognize the model, benefit corporations are required to disclose the degree to which they are meeting their stated public benefit goals measured against third-party standards, although some states allow for an exception in smaller corporations (gauged by number of shareholders). The disclosure requirement includes making the benefit corporation's annual report available to the public via its website. The requirement of a third party standard is about accountability. It is intended to bring conflict-free assessment to the annual report. Requiring an assessment by independent third parties adds expense and effort for these entities but, for investors, the publicly available report engenders confidence in the corporation and its governance.

Regarding ownership and control, growth, exposure to personal liability, and tax treatment, benefit corporation characteristics mirror those of other for-profit corporations. Existing entities (corporations or other legal structures) can become "certified B" by undergoing a B impact assessment in which they are evaluated in a multistep verification process. The impact assessment is done by B Labs, the certifying body behind the model legislation and B advocacy, generally.

Newer businesses, however, must wait until they have a year of financials, which are required as part of the assessment process.[6] So, if you know you want to form a benefit corporation, first organize your business as a corporation in a state that recognizes the model, and after a year, undergo the impact assessment and amend your corporate documents to the requirements of the benefit corporation law in your state of incorporation. The process and filing costs for starting a benefit corporation will be the same as for any other corporation. See Chapter 5 for more information about corporate formation, generally.

Social Purpose Corporations

Another type of hybrid, for-profit statutory entity is the social purpose corporation (SPC).[7] SPCs can have more than one social purpose to advance. They are similar to benefit corporations in that they follow the organizational structure of a corporation, but differ from benefit corporations in two key ways. First, though SPCs are required as part of their stated corporate purpose to have a social mission, they are not required to consider the environmental impact of corporate strategy as benefit corporations are. Second, while SPCs have a mandatory public reporting requirement via their annual report in which they state their financials, objectives, and provide an analysis of their objectives, they are not required to measure their results against a third-party standard as benefit corporations must.

The process and filing costs for starting a social purpose corporation will be the same as for any other corporation. See Chapter 5, "Corporations," for more information about corporate formation, generally.

Low-Profit Limited Liability Companies

Like benefit corporations and social purpose corporations, low-profit limited liability companies (L3Cs) are for-profit organizations with public benefit missions. As the name suggests, L3Cs are a type of LLC. They provide the ownership flexibility (no board of directors) and tax benefits (pass-through taxation) typical of a standard LLC. They are driven to make a positive social impact (like a nonprofit organization) but without the tax exemptions and restrictions on ownership and profit common to nonprofits recognized as charitable organizations by the IRS.

L3Cs are unique in that their capital structure is often designed in a tiered manner to allow for different types of investors including equity investments by private foundations. Private foundations are charitable organizations recognized under the Internal Revenue Code (IRC). They must comply with strict rules to maintain their tax-exempt status. One such rule is that these foundations must make minimum qualifying distributions of at least 5% of their total assets annually.[8] Usually these foundations meet that requirement through grant-making to other charitable organizations such as nonprofit corporations with 501(c)(3) charitable organization status. Another permissible use of foundation funds that qualifies under the "5% rule" is program-related investing (PRI). PRI is the practice where a foundation is allowed to invest funds that further some charitable purpose, but which could yield a return for the foundation as long as the investment meets tax-exempt rules, including furthering its tax-exempt purpose(s) and not being significantly motivated by profit. PRI is an exception[9] to the general rule[10] under the IRC that disallows any investing that could jeopardize the foundation's tax-exempt status (leading to an imposition of an excise tax equal to 10% of the amount improperly invested).

So, L3Cs can attract a diverse group of investors including those interested in mission-centered investing or private foundations with whom the L3C has a parallel mission. In either case, the investor, even a private foundation, is allowed to make a return on its investment in the L3C.

Like standard LLCs, they are governed by state law (where the model is recognized) and founding owners are required to file Articles of Organization and create an Operating Agreement. L3C owners interested in attracting funds from private foundations would be wise to draft their governance documents to comply with the federal requirements that allow for program-related investing.

The process and filing costs for starting an L3C will be the same as for any other LLC. See Chapter 4 for information about LLC formation, generally.

CONCLUSION

Whether one of these models is right for you and your enterprise can only be determined by you. A criticism leveled against these newer business forms is that these structures are merely state-sponsored marketing gimmicks[11] because traditional for-profit entities can (and regularly do) engage in mission-centered activities. Further, one legal scholar expresses concern that an unintended consequence of creating specialized hybrid legal structures like these will be that traditional entities like C corporations will adopt a position that corporate giving should be left to the hybrid entities and abandon their philanthropic practice entirely.[12]

In the end, the decision to form a for-profit entity that incorporates a public benefit mission will depend on several things in addition to the considerations laid out in Chapter 1. These include whether the state in which you want to launch your enterprise enacted statutory authority for the hybrid model, the type of investor you want to attract, the level of transparency and accountability you are comfortable with, the extent to which your mission aligns with what is permissible in the relevant state's authorizing statute, and the types of activities your business will engage in. Appendix A provides a chart that compares these newer hybrid entities against other business models.

HYBRID ORGANIZATION RESOURCES

Americans for Community Development, americansforcommunitydevelopment.org

B Lab, www.bcorporation.net

Benefit Corporation, www.benefitcorp.net

Digital Media Law Project, www.dmlp.org

InterSector Partners, L3C, www.intersectorl3c.com

Small Business Development Center at SUNY Buffalo State, "Benefit Corporation Guide," sbdc.buffalostate.edu/sites/sbdc.buffalostate.edu/files/uploads/Documents/2%20Benefit%20Corporation%20Guide.pdf

"Social Enterprise Law Tracker," socentlawtracker.org/#/map

Yale Center for Business and the Environment, *An Entrepreneur's Guide to Going "B,"* cbey.yale.edu/programs-research/an-entrepreneur's-guide-to-going-b

NOTES

1. Social Enterprise Law Tracker, socentlawtracker.org/#/map. This handy tool is maintained by the Grunin Center for Law and Social Entrepreneurship at NYU School of Law.

2. Model Benefit Corporation Legislation, www.benefitcorp.net.

3. Ibid.

4. Ben Schiller, "Should Your Corporation Be a Benefit Corporation, a B Corp, or What?" *Fast Company*, www.fastcompany.com/3069192/should-my-company-be-a -benefit-corporation-a-b-corp-or-what.

5. Benefit Corporation, "State by State Status of Legislation," benefitcorp.net/ policymakers/state-by-state-status.

6. B Corporation, "Certification," bcorporation.net/certification.

7. Note that in some states SPCs may be referred to as Flexible Purpose Corporations, the name they were originally given in California until the name was later amended.

8. 26 C.F.R. §170(c)(2)(B) and Treasury Regulation §1.501(c)(3).

9. IRC §53.4944(c).

10. §53.4944(a).

11. Mohsen Manesh, "Introducing the Totally Unnecessary Benefit LLC," 97 N.C. L. Rev. 603 (2019).

12. Ibid.

PART IV

COMPLIANCE TOPICS

8

Start-up Compliance

Now that you've decided which legal structure is best for you, you'll need to decide where your business should be domiciled. You are not limited to choosing the state where you live. If you decide that a sole proprietorship or a general partnership structure is best for your plans, then choosing a state is not a critical issue for you—it will likely be where you live. However, if the legal structure of your business requires a state filing, know that you have options: you don't need to file in the state where you live or in which the business's principal office will be located. For example, you can live and work in North Carolina and incorporate your business in Delaware or elsewhere.

There are several reasons entrepreneurs choose to domicile their business out of state:

1. State statutory law—If you want to be the sole owner of a limited liability company or corporation, the state you live in may not allow a single owner, so you could file your paperwork in a state that allows single-owner members, then file paperwork in your home state to operate your business as a "foreign" company authorized to conduct business in your home state.
2. State common law—Whereas statutory law refers to laws enacted by lawmakers such as state legislatures, common law refers to the body of case law that developed in a particular jurisdiction as the result of past legal disputes there. Some states, like Delaware, promote themselves as corporation-friendly jurisdictions with well-developed case law on their books that tend to favor corporate interests.

3. State taxes—States have differing tax schemes. Some states have a corporate franchise tax in which corporations pay for the privilege of doing business in the state. Some states don't tax income, but they will tax businesses in other ways. Similarly, if you launch a subchapter S corporation, some states don't recognize the federal election to pass profits through the entity to its shareholders, so in those jurisdictions, the entity would have to pay the state a corporate income tax despite not having to pay federal tax.

4. State culture—Some states are just heavier with regulations and oversight than others, so in those states you'll be spending more of your time keeping track of deadlines, completing paperwork, and submitting reports to the state with filing fees (you're basically paying a state employee to check in on you periodically to be sure that you are operating your business in compliance with state law). New York State is widely considered to be a regulation-heavy state with many regulations across industries. Where there are rules, there is paperwork and where there is paperwork, there are filing fees, late fees, and penalties for noncompliance.

Before doing any filings to launch your business, first you need to decide on the name (or names) for your business.

NAMING YOUR BUSINESS

Businesses often have two names: (1) a legal, registered name; and (2) the trade name. Your business's legal name is dependent on the type of business structure you choose. For example, if you are a sole proprietor, the legal name of your business will be your full name. If you decide to form a general partnership, your business's legal name will consist of whatever the partners decided upon and stated in the partnership agreement, otherwise it will be the last names of all of the partners. If your business is an LLC or corporation, the business's legal name will be the name you used on your paperwork when you registered your enterprise.

Despite having a legal name, businesses often use other names for marketing and branding purposes without regard to the business's legal structure. These are known as trade names—also known as DBAs ("doing business as") or "fictitious" or "assumed" names. For example, if your name is John Smith, you might be able to use Smith Recording Studios as a business name without obtaining state approval for it. However, if you want your business name to be Dynamo Studios, you'll need to let your local or state authorities know that you plan to conduct business under an assumed (trade) name and obtain approval for it or risk having to change the name later after a costly lawsuit.

For legal structures requiring state approvals like LLCs and corporations, you'll have to follow the state business naming rules and complete a *Certificate of Assumed Name* and pay a nominal fee. Contact your state's Secretary of State office for the requirements. However, if your business structure is a sole proprietorship or general partnership—which are not governed by state law—the process usually involves completing a local or county form.

When choosing a trade name for your business, consider the following:

- Is the name available or is it already in use?
- Is the name unique or could it be confusingly similar to another trade name?
- Is the website domain name available?
- Is the name easy to spell/pronounce?
- Does the name accurately reflect your products or services?

> While driving recently, I was behind a truck that was apparently carrying a brand of bread. The logo was cool: a caricature of a muscled guy playing an electric guitar. While I obviously remembered the logo, I don't remember the trade name of the bread maker because the connection between the name and logo were not clear to me. It definitely wasn't "Rock 'n Roll Rye"!

CLEARING YOUR TRADE NAME

Choosing a good name can be tricky because it needs to be one that accurately reflects your brand, is memorable, and is one people can spell and find in order to pay for your products and services. More importantly though, the trade name must be available for your use. If you plan to launch an LLC or corporation, the state in which you file your paperwork will not allow you to choose a name that is already in use there. Even if the name is available there, it could be in use elsewhere, and this can be problematic if you plan to do business outside of your home state (as most do).

Choosing an available trade name can be challenging. The difficulty arises out of how trademark rights accrue. A trademark is any word, phrase, symbol, and/or design that identifies and distinguishes the source of the goods.[1] When choosing a name for your business, consider whether you plan to trademark the name. The central purpose for trademarking a name is to reduce or eliminate confusion in the eyes of consumers so that when they see your mark, they know who made the goods and have a pretty good idea of the quality they can expect. For this reason, trademarks are an indicator of goodwill once your goods have brand recognition. Similar to trademarks are service marks. Service marks are used for indicating the source of *services* (not goods), though the term *trademark* tends to be used interchangeably for both. For example, if you formed a band, your band's name is a service mark (for musical services), but if you sell merchandise, your band's name and logo, together, constitute your trademark.

In the United States, trademark/service mark rights accrue as soon as the mark is used commercially (used "in commerce"). This right exists even if the mark's owner has never filed it on a state or the federal registry. For this reason, there are both registered and unregistered trademarks. Whether you decide to file your mark or not, the minimum due diligence you should do is to take as comprehensive a search as you can to check on the availability of your chosen trade name.

In addition to doing a basic Internet search, search to see if your proposed trade name is already in use on social media sites (Facebook, YouTube, Twitter, and Instagram). Check online music retailers like Amazon, iTunes, CDBaby, and AllMusic as well as domain registration service providers (Go-Daddy, Whois, etc.).

Contact your County Clerk's office and ask whether that office (or the state) maintains an assumed name database. For registered marks, go to the Secretary of State's website in your state as well as the federal government's Trademark Electronic Search System (TESS) site (USPTO.gov). Finally, you might also search the Copyright Office's database.[2]

Using your preferred Internet search engine, type in "business entity search" followed by your state's two-letter abbreviation to guide you toward your state's database for fictitious/assumed names.

Even if you decide to hire a trademark search firm to conduct the research and register your trademark or service mark for you, doing your own research first may make the process go faster and ultimately save you some money because you will have bypassed many of the name hurdles before you've engaged the professionals for help. Once you've landed on a trade name, if you are starting an LLC or Corporation, check your state's Secretary of State's website for an *Application for Reserved Name*. By paying a nominal fee, you can reserve your proposed name until you're ready to complete the paperwork for your filing. Because trademark law in the United States is based on priority of use, registering your name only puts others on notice that the name is in use. The best way to protect the mark is to use it "in commerce"—using the mark across state lines will provide evidence that your mark is active in the geographic area(s) of use.

Protecting Your Trade Name

It's a good idea to register your trade name as a trademark/service mark. Registering the mark in the business's legal name will make the enterprise the owner of the trade name and guard against an individual business owner using the mark without authority. For example, you and three friends form a band whose legal structure is an LLC registered in your state as Four Guys, LLC. You perform under the trade name Swiftwater, which is registered as a service mark on the federal registry. If two LLC members quit to start another band, they can't operate under the Swiftwater trade name because the name is protected as a service mark owned by Four Guys, LLC. In this example, no one band member/LLC member owns that trade name. Contrast this approach with the one taken by the partnership in Chapter 3.

You can register your mark nationally, via the federal registry, or only in a specific state where you operate. The upside of registering your trade name as a trademark/service mark is that once listed on the federal registry, you have national protection against other businesses using your name/mark in a similar business. This is particularly important once your business grows and develops a loyal following regardless of whether you produce goods, provide professional services, or both. The downside of registering is the upfront cost. Best practices involve hiring a search firm to conduct comprehensive international research on the availability of the name you want to use for your business. The costs can reach $1,000. The University of Central Florida has an excellent guide consisting of six steps for conducting a trademark search.[3] The United States Patent and Trademark Office (USPTO) provides search capability via its Trademark Information Network.[4]

If you decide to register your name on the federal registry, the cost is about $375. That application fee is for a federal employee at the USPTO to check on the availability of the name for registration purposes. If the name or something confusingly similar is already in use, you may have just wasted $375 because your application will be denied and your fee could be lost. You'll have to apply again and likely have to pay the fee again as well. So, to the greatest extent possible, you want to be confident no other business is using the name you want to register.

If you decide to take a chance and forgo trademark registration, you certainly can do that, but you should be aware of the risks you're taking, which include investing money in your business under a name that you may ultimately be legally required to relinquish to someone who started using it before you and/or registered it before you. That challenge could come in the form of an expensive lawsuit as well as lost goodwill (if you have to rename your business) and loss of marketing collateral on any materials printed with the original trade name on it because those can no longer be used.

Protecting Your Trade Name Overseas

It's possible to obtain a Community Trademark (CTM) to protect your mark in certain areas of Europe. A single registration covers only European Union members. At the moment, there are twenty-seven member countries where the CTM applies. The program is administered by the European Union Intellectual Property Office.[5] The registration fee varies depending on what you're seeking protection for and how you file your application.

STATE AND LOCAL COMPLIANCE

If you plan to start an LLC or corporation, you'll need to register your business with the state, file the required paperwork, pay a filing fee, and follow the state's statutory rules for the duration of your business's lifetime. Filing fees vary from state to state. In some states, it's a flat fee, but in others the fee is a percentage of some indicator such as the number of shares authorized to issue (for a stock-based corporation) or the number of members (for an LLC). Some states also allow for expedited filing if you're in a hurry, but this often involves an additional fee.

In most states, you would contact the Secretary of State to determine what the start-up requirements are for registering a new business in that state. The

Secretary of State is the chief clerk of the state and the keeper of important records. Some states don't have a person titled "Secretary of State." Instead, they have the functional equivalent in a Lieutenant Governor or other high-level state employee or employees who have shared responsibility for the varied regulatory oversight commonly assigned to a Secretary of State. I recommend beginning with an Internet search using "Secretary of State" and the name of your state, for example, *Secretary of State Massachusetts*. Despite that Massachusetts is, technically, a commonwealth and not a state, that search query will get you to the general area in state government responsible for business formation. For further searching, try *business licensing, starting a business, business and corporation forms*, or something similar. In this example, the proper division of Massachusetts state government with oversight authority for business formation is the office of the Secretary of the Commonwealth.

The Wikipedia page for "Secretary of state (U.S. state government)" is an excellent starting point for getting to the correct website in your state and ultimately determining what the specific requirements are for starting your business.

> With any kind of research, you will save a lot of time if you can determine who the authority is on a given subject as early in your research as possible. When doing research, don't turn your nose up at Wikipedia as an excellent place to get started. Starting at Wikipedia will point you in the right direction—particularly when you scan the "See also," "References," "Further reading," "External links," and the date the page was last edited at the bottom of each entry to lead you to the authority on a given topic. Generally, any regulating or licensing body will be considered the authority.

Local Compliance/Approvals

Similar to obtaining permission to use a trade name, you'll need to check on the local laws for operating a business in your town—this is especially true if you expect foot traffic or car parking near your business. Some areas of your town are only zoned for residential uses, and you should check to see how that is specifically defined and the extent to which your municipality allows home businesses. Contact your local municipal offices for guidance, likely your Town Clerk.

Check out Fundera's website, www.fundera.com/blog/business -license, for a very handy state-by-state chart for determining what is required in your locality regarding business permits for proprietorships and general partnerships. You can also do an Internet search to help find a Small Business Administration office near you: www.sba.gov/content/find-local-sba-office.

Additionally, some Homeowner Associations' bylaws have restrictions against home businesses. If you are buying a home that is part of a planned community (like a condo association), make sure that you get a current copy of the bylaws so you understand all of the rules—particularly those referred to as *restrictive covenants*. In this context, restrictive covenants are contractual promises you make to other members of the association not to do something that you would otherwise be legally entitled to do (like operating a business out of your home).

If you've decided on a legal structure, chosen a business name (or names), and handled any required regulatory filings for state and local approvals, you're now ready to go to the next step: preparing to make money and report income.

BUSINESS TAXES: GETTING STARTED

There are two instances when the federal government will necessarily play a role in start-up formation: (1) when you apply for an employer identification number (EIN); and (2) if you form a nonprofit organization and want to obtain charitable organization recognition from the IRS. See Chapter 6 for a discussion of charitable organizations.

Tax Identification Numbers

An EIN is a form of Taxpayer Identification Number (TIN); another is a Social Security Number (SSN). Like SSNs, EINs are nine-digit numbers that identify a business entity for federal tax purposes. EINs are assigned only to entities, not individuals. Despite the name, you don't need to have or even contemplate employees to get an EIN. While single-owner businesses don't need an EIN because those owners can use their SSN, musicians and other freelancers should consider getting one because of the nature of their work as independent contractors who regularly complete W-9 forms in order to get paid. Using an EIN will help to keep your SSN private. And you will need an EIN, even as a sole proprietor, if you expand your business and hire employees, start a retirement plan, or change the legal structure of your business to one of the other models. To obtain an EIN (for free), complete the Application for Employer Identification Number (Form SS-4) and submit it by mail or contact the IRS at 800-829-4933.

If you plan to sell branded merchandise, you'll need to be sure you understand your obligations for collecting and remitting taxes to the authorities for whom you are collecting them.

Sales Tax

Before selling merchandise, contact your state's tax authority to see whether you need a *Certificate of Authority* (also known as a state tax ID number). Sales tax is paid by the "end user" of goods and services at the point of sale and collected by the retailer to later remit to the government entity requiring the tax. These certificates are often required before you can legally collect sales tax in the state. If your business model is one that involves selling merchandise on a retail basis, you will need to collect and remit sales tax to the authorities where you operate your business. This is referred to as having a *nexus*[6] with the state or municipality. If you sell merchandise online, you'll collect and remit *use tax* in certain instances as well.

If you plan to buy products (and in some states, services) to incorporate into your products or services, you should look into getting a *resale certificate*. A resale certificate is a document that exempts you from paying sales tax on your purchases because you are not the end user—you are including that product or service in something you will be selling to another person or organization. Some states require that you use their certificate while others will allow you to use a multistate form. Resale certificates can only be used for purchases a business makes as an intermediary. For example, if your business is teaching music to children and you purchase big note music books to sell, you wouldn't be the end user, so you wouldn't be required to pay sales tax on the books; the purchasers would pay the sales tax. Similarly, if your business was making guitars, your purchase of strings would not be subject to sales tax because the strings will be used as a component of the guitars. However, if you purchase office furniture, that would be subject to sales tax because the furniture will be "consumed" by your business.

Note that some resale certificates expire, so you'll want to be mindful of any expiration dates and retain expired certificates until the period of time they cover has been closed for tax audit purposes. A good starting point is to do an Internet search for "resale certificate" with your state's name and "department of revenue."

Use Tax

As noted above, use tax is a form of sales tax. Both types of taxes are applied at the point of sale. What distinguishes the two types of taxes is sales tax is applied in the geographic location where the sale took place; use tax is applied based on where the product or service is intended to be converted to its intended use. For example, if you bought a sound board in a store in Syracuse, New York, you'd pay sales tax in Syracuse and some percentage of that tax might be remitted to the City of Syracuse, some to Onondaga County, and some to New York State. However, if you bought the same sound board online from the same retailer and had it shipped to you in Virginia, you'd pay the Syracuse retailer Virginia's use tax and the retailer would have to remit the tax amount collected from you to Virginia tax authorities as though you had purchased the board there.

New York State famously passed its "Amazon Laws," which require Internet retailers outside the state (with no nexus/offices in the state) to pay sales taxes on sales made to citizens in the state. Contact your state's Department of Tax and ask for a packet of tax-related information for small businesses and reference numbers of available publications to help you comply with your state's tax laws. For example, New York has several publications to help business owners. See Publication 20, *New York State Tax Guide for New Businesses* and Publication 750, *A Guide to Sales Tax in New York State*.

CONCLUSION

While the title of this chapter is "Start-up Compliance," think of these topics as setting yourself up to facilitate the smooth operation of your business while protecting yourself and your investment. First up: you have options for where to locate your business. Choosing a state of domicile is highly individual; take the time to investigate how welcoming the jurisdiction is to business (regulations, zoning, compliance reporting, tax liability, etc.). Second, your business name (or names) is important because it identifies your brand as a trademark. The goodwill associated with your business will have independent value that will grow as your business and reputation grows, so you'll need to be diligent in both choosing and protecting them. Finally, if you elect a legal structure that requires a state filing, the date you file is the date your business is born. Do it right the first time and obtain all the identifying tax identification numbers and approvals to demonstrate the legitimacy of your business.

FEDERAL COMPLIANCE RESOURCES

IRS Publication 15—Employer's Tax Guide

IRS Publication 334—Tax Guide for Small Business

IRS Publication 535—Business Expenses

IRS Publication 560—Retirement Plans for Your Small Business

IRS Publication 583—Starting a Business and Keeping Records

IRS Publication 1635—Understanding Your EIN

IRS Publication 1779—Independent Contractor or Employee Brochure

IRS Publication 4591—Small Business Federal Tax Responsibilities

IRS Publication 4806—Profit-Sharing Plans for Small Businesses

IRS Publication 5170—Taxpayer Bill of Rights Brochure

NOTES

1. United States Patent and Trademark Office, "Trademark, Patent, or Copyright?" www.uspto.gov/trademarks-getting-started/trademark-basics/trademark-patent-or -copyright.

2. United States Copyright Office, "Copyright Catalog," cocatalog.loc.gov.

3. University of Central Florida Libraries, "Trademarks," guides.ucf.edu/trademarks /start.

4. United States Patent and Trademark Office, "Trademark Information Network," www.uspto.gov/trademarks-getting-started/process-overview/trademark -information-network.

5. European Union Intellectual Property Office, "eSearch Plus," euipo.europa.eu /eSearch/.

6. The term *nexus* is most commonly used in a tax context. It means a connection for the purposes of establishing tax liability. Depending on the jurisdiction, a tax nexus can be based on merely having a presence in a state, or it can be established based on reaching a sales threshold there.

9

Employees, Independent Contractors, and Insurance

Employees can have a positive impact on productivity, but they come with significant responsibilities including those associated with complying with state and federal laws enacted to protect workers. Compliance comes in the form of regular reporting to state and federal agencies. For businesses, this translates to increased costs. Additionally, employers are vicariously liable for the actions of their employees during the normal course of their work (see Chapter 1 for a discussion of vicarious liability).

Because of the burden and cost of complying with labor and employment laws, some business owners choose to limit the number of employees they hire and engage independent contractors (ICs) instead. Usually, ICs are short-term talent hired for a specialized skill not held by a business's employees. ICs usually, but not always, work pursuant to a written contract that outlines the scope and terms of their employment. Because ICs are not employees, they are not protected by labor and employment laws, so engaging them does not require the same level of compliance and reporting as is required for employees.

At this point, you may be wondering why a business wouldn't just hire ICs exclusively. The issue is one of control—the amount of control the hiring entity wields over the worker regardless of whether a contract is involved or how the entity classifies the worker. Employers like to set the time, place, and manner of employment for their workers. Sometimes, employers also provide training to their staff. None of these is consistent with how ICs work, and that's the key to understanding the difference between these two types of workers.

EMPLOYEE OR INDEPENDENT CONTRACTOR?

There is no single legal test for determining whether a worker is an employee or an IC. Historically, the common law test to determine whether someone is an IC or an employee is the degree of control the business retains over them and their work.

Ask yourself the following questions:

- How much control do I have over how, when, and where the person works? The more control the business exerts over the worker, the stronger the case is that the worker is an employee. ICs work on their own time, at their own pace, and deliver their services to the hiring entity pursuant to terms agreed to by contract.
- Is there a written contract between you and the worker?
  Most states are *employment-at-will* jurisdictions, which means that employees can be fired for any reason or for no reason at all. While this may appear to disadvantage employees, it allows them the freedom to change jobs as they wish without having contractual liability to their employers. Using well-written IC contracts and requiring them to submit payment invoices will help underscore the distinction between your use of employees and independent contractors.
- How is the worker paid?
  Receiving a regular paycheck suggests that the worker is an employee. ICs usually submit an invoice to the company for payment of services rendered at the end of the job or, if a longer-term project, upon reaching specific milestones spelled out in the contract. Business owners who use ICs should require each IC to complete a Request for Taxpayer Identification Number and Certification (Form W-9) as part of the engagement paperwork. Each year the business owner should send the IC a Miscellaneous Income Form (Form 1099), which outlines the payments made to the IC during the preceding calendar year.
- Are expenses reimbursed?
  Reimbursement of expenses suggests that the worker is an employee. IC contracts usually contain language stating that any costs incurred in the provision of services are to be accounted for in the fee for those services, not paid separately by reimbursement.

- How central to the business are the services being provided by the worker? Employees generally provide the central functions of maintaining a business; ICs are typically engaged periodically for special projects requiring a particular skill set for which the company doesn't have an ongoing need.
- Does your company provide benefits to its workers such as health insurance, vacation pay, or a retirement plan?
  Benefits like these are offered to employees, not ICs.

For help understanding the differences between employees and ICs, the IRS has resources to help,[1] a form you can submit for their review to help with the determination,[2] and another form and process for self-reporting misclassified workers in which you may be granted financial relief if you've improperly classified employees as ICs.[3]

EMPLOYEES

Employers must comply with labor laws including maintaining unemployment and workers' compensation insurance, withholding taxes from employee wages, and making contributions to Social Security and Medicare on behalf of their employees. Employees are required to provide information and documentation to facilitate their hiring. This includes their name, address, and Social Security number via state-approved documentation. The onboarding process includes having employees complete an Employee's Withholding Allowance Certificate (Form W-4) and an Employment Eligibility Verification (Form I-9). Annually, employers are required to provide employees with a Wage and Tax Statement (Form W-2) that shows deductions made from employees' paychecks throughout the year regardless of whether the employee was salaried or paid hourly.

Tip: Outsource your payroll function to a firm specializing in workplace compliance. In addition to payroll, they handle all recordkeeping and reporting and will be responsible for keeping you current with changing employment and labor laws.

Quarterly, businesses with employees (1) file federal Employer's Quarterly Tax Return (Form 941), which describes the amounts withheld from employee paychecks; and (2) deposit withheld funds from employees' paychecks electronically using the Electronic Federal Tax Payment System.[4]

Even after an employee leaves your organization, you will likely continue to receive requests for employment verification from their prospective employers and from financial institutions if the former employee is seeking a car loan or mortgage. Periodically, you will have an employee whose wages you are required to garnish (remit a portion of their pay to the state) to satisfy a legal order to pay child support or for some other form of financial responsibility. As the employer, you will be required to complete paperwork to prove your compliance with the law. Anytime a former employee files an unemployment claim, you may be contacted by a state entity inquiring about the former employee's dates of employment, wages, and other information.

A great place to get started for determining what your responsibilities are as an employer is your state's Department of Labor. Other resources are the federal government's employment law compliance site[5] and its general information site,[6] where you can click on the Small Business tab for an overview of relevant topics.

Tip: Employers are vicariously liable for the actions of their employees, so it's important to have an employee handbook that serves as a manual for employee conduct, operational protocols, and safety. Update your Employee Manual regularly. Require all employees to sign and date an annual statement that each has received a copy and that each has read and understands what is expected of them, and that they will comply with your company's policies and procedures as a condition of continued employment with you.

Because employers are legally liable for their employees, you should perform background checks on prospective employees. Be sure you understand and comply with the Fair Credit Reporting Act and other consumer protection laws. This is an area where you may prefer to hire a professional to do this work for you because they will be sure to stay within the confines of the law and can assist you in interpreting the screening results. Chapter 13 contains a sample release form for conducting a background check on prospective employees.

INSURANCE

Having the right kind of insurance and the appropriate amount of it can help you sleep better at night. And if you rent commercial workspace or a performance venue, you will likely be required to purchase a liability insurance policy with limits high enough to protect the lessor against lawsuits in which both you and they are named.

Business Insurance

There are countless types of insurance products developed to serve the needs of businesses under the category of Property and Casualty Insurance. Property insurance is referred to as *first party insurance* because it reimburses the insured party for covered losses sustained, such as those from a fire or theft. If you own a car, the portion of your auto policy called comprehensive coverage is an example of first party insurance. Casualty insurance is referred to as *third party insurance* because it protects the insured party against lawsuits brought by other people or entities arising out of the insured's negligence. Continuing with the auto insurance example, the state-mandated liability section of your auto policy is an example of third party insurance. Auto liability is designed to protect you financially from lawsuits brought by others alleging you negligently operated your vehicle and caused someone else a physical injury and/or damaged their property.

The most common business insurance purchased is called Commercial General Liability (CGL) Insurance. It is usually contractually required by commercial landlords as a condition of signing a lease. CGL policies are often required of performers or producers by venues rented for performances. This type of insurance provides premises coverage for injuries sustained by your business visitors as well as products and completed operations coverage that is intended to protect your business from allegations that you didn't do something properly. See Chapter 13 for a discussion of the insurance requirements commonly found in a venue rental agreement.

Less common, outside licensed professionals like lawyers, architects, physicians, and real estate agents, is Errors and Omissions Insurance (E&O), also known as malpractice insurance, which protects business owners from lawsuits brought by their customers alleging that the insured business negligently provided a professional service resulting in a financial loss to the customer.

To determine what your insurance needs are (and not be over-sold on insurance products), draw up a list of services and/or products you provide/create for others, the types of clients you serve, and how you expect them to use those services/products. You may find that, based on the nature of your business, a Miscellaneous Professional Liability (MPL) policy would be available for your business. MPL policies are a type of E&O policy—they protect you and your business against lawsuits alleging that you were negligent in providing professional services to a client when that negligence caused the client a financial loss. MPL policies are endorsable to the specific risks presented. In other words, they are tailored to your needs provided the insurance company has a risk appetite for those hazards. Being well-prepared for a conversation with an insurance professional will better help them determine what you need and at what limits of insurance and deductible amounts.

For more information on property/casualty insurance, check out www.irmi.com.

Unemployment Insurance

Though its name can be misleading, unemployment insurance is not purchased via an insurance agent or through an insurance company. It is a federally mandated program that is administered by individual states. The concept of what we know now as unemployment insurance originates from the Social Security Act of 1935. Unemployment insurance is intended to provide temporary income for eligible workers who lose their job through no fault of their own. Each state has its own unemployment laws and legal tests to determine a worker's employment status for the purposes of unemployment compensation eligibility. Most employers are required to pay taxes that flow into a state-controlled reserve fund from which payments are made to those who qualify for them. In a minority of states, employees themselves pay directly into pooled funds reserved for this purpose. For more about unemployment insurance in your state and what your legal responsibilities are as an employer, contact your state's Department of Labor.

Workers' Compensation Insurance

Workers' comp, as it's known, is insurance intended to help employees who are injured in the course of their workday (or injured at some point in their career in the case of employment-related diseases like mesothelioma). This insurance, mandatory in almost every state, covers injured employees' medical expenses and lost wages. Each state has its own set of laws and legal tests to determine a worker's employment status for the purpose of workers' compensation eligibility. These regulations help employees injured at work by requiring that insurance be available and, no less important, does not require the injured employee to prove that the employer was culpable for that injury.

Workers' comp regulations benefit employers by eliminating the need to defend themselves against lawsuits brought by employees injured on the job. However, employers who have not procured workers' comp coverage can be sued directly by injured employees and will likely face state fines and penalties for failure to comply with the law. In some states, employers can purchase workers' comp in the private insurance market, but in others, the only option is to purchase it through a state-fund insurance pool. For more on workers' compensation insurance, contact your state's Department of Labor.

Equipment Insurance

If your business will have expensive equipment, you might want to purchase insurance to protect it from theft or damage. Contact your local insurance agent and ask whether they offer an "All-Risk" insurance policy. These policies protect your equipment against unintentional damage caused by theft, accidental breakage, vandalism, flood, fire, lightning, and anything else that isn't specifically excluded. The important thing to do before buying a policy is to consider what you want insurance protection from and, with an "All-Risk" policy, review the Exclusions section of the policy to be sure that what you're concerned about is not carved out of what the policy actually covers. Things like normal wear and tear and losses resulting from you renting or loaning out your equipment are not usually covered.

Personal Insurance

I'm sure I don't need to convince you that you should have health, dental, and disability insurance, but the costs of these benefits can preclude many of us from purchasing the coverage. If this is your situation, consider joining the national nonprofit Freelancers Union.[7] The organization represents over 56 million independent workers from across the United States encompassing multiple disciplines of people who work for themselves.[8] Membership is free. Its website, which also houses a blog, is rich with useful content including member discounts, tax guides, financial tools, networking tips, and a template for creating certain types of contracts.

INDEPENDENT CONTRACTORS

In contrast to employees, independent contractors (ICs) are often hired to take on special projects for which there is no in-house expertise. Sometimes ICs are hired after submitting a proposal containing a Scope of Work that includes pricing and milestone completion dates for individual elements of the contracted work plan. Once the work is complete and approved by the hiring department, ICs will submit an invoice for payment. Federal and state employment and labor laws don't apply to independent contractors and no taxes are withheld from payments made to them for their services. Some businesses choose to engage independent contractors instead of hiring employees because they don't want all the paperwork, reporting requirements, and insurance costs that come with having employees. Be warned, however, that just because you call someone an independent contractor and have a signed IC Agreement doesn't mean that your state Department of Labor will agree with you.

Independent Contractor Agreements

The terms *independent contractor agreement* and *professional services contract* are often used interchangeably, but an IC agreement is more specific because the title itself identifies the nature of the employment relationship. Professional services can be provided in an IC scenario or in a typical employer-employee relationship.

IC agreements are contracts and because they are general enough to address all manner of professional services, they are all crafted to apply to a specific hiring situation. But, you will see that a basic template exists with the following standard clauses:

- An identification/definition of the parties
- An outline of the services to be rendered
- Duration of the agreement
- Compensation information
- Language that incorporates IC law
- IP ownership clause
- Representations and Warranty clause
- Indemnification clause
- Remedies clause
- Miscellaneous "housekeeping" clauses

Other possible clauses could be a publicity release, confidentiality, conflicts of interest, noncompete, or anything else the drafting party requires. Many of these clauses are provided in the annotated IC sample, below.

CONCLUSION

The moral of this story is to maintain distance between yourself as the business owner and your independent contractors. You don't want to find yourself in violation of employment and labor laws following an audit by the Department of Labor. One serious repercussion of this is that the individual responsible for payroll can be held personally (financially) liable to the government for the amount of taxes that should have been withheld from employee paychecks but was not because the business had inappropriately characterized those workers as independent contractors instead of employees.

For more information relating to employees and independent contractors, check out 501Commons, www.501commons.org.[9]

What follows below is an annotated sample IC agreement for professional services (a term usually defined in the contract). This sample is not industry-specific.

Sample Independent Contractor Agreement
(Agreement for Professional Services)

This Agreement entered into _____, 20___, between _____ ("Company") and _____ ("Contractor").

WHEREAS the Company is in the business of:
<insert nature of company's business, for example: live theatrical production>

WHEREAS the contractor specializes in <insert specialty, for example: lighting design and projection services> and desires to be engaged to perform such services for the Company on an independent contractor basis.

> *These "whereas" clauses are called recitals. Now considered old fashioned, they are not required to be in a contract, but I like them because they provide background context for third party readers regarding who the contracting parties are and why they are entering into a contractual arrangement.*

Subject to the terms and conditions set forth in this Agreement, the parties mutually agree as follows:

> *This is the mutuality provision. While not required, it signals to third party readers that both signatories to the contract are in full agreement of the promises they've made to each other.*

1. This Agreement shall commence on _____, 20___ and shall continue until the satisfactory completion of the professional services (the "Services") performed hereunder as determined by the Company.
2. The Contractor shall perform the following Services:

> *A description of the services to be rendered goes here. An example taken from an artist's contract might read: "Artist will perform Professional Services for the Organization as Rehearsal Pianist, Staff Coach, Assistant Conductor, and Orchestra Librarian the duties of which are provided in Exhibit A, attached."*

> *Using exhibit pages allows for a cleaner contract that companies can use as their baseline IC agreement requiring few amendments. All the details can then be provided in the exhibits.*

3. The Contractor expressly acknowledges and agrees that the Contractor is not an employee of the Company. Contractor will execute the Services in a

good and workmanlike manner in accordance with his or her independent and professional judgment and generally accepted industry practices. The Contractor shall have control and discretion over the means and manner of performance of the Services and shall supply all necessary equipment, materials, and supplies to fulfill Contractor's duties hereunder.

Some of the language contained in this clause is drawn from case law, which provides the legal test for determining whether a worker is an employee or an independent contractor. The test includes the extent of control exercised by the hiring party over the worker, including setting work hours and providing training, equipment, and materials.

As a standard to measure the adequacy of the services contracted for, this contract references "generally accepted industry standards." If a more specific standard exists, that standard should be included. For example, in the accounting world, the standard is "generally accepted accounting principles," but in other industries a specific quality standard may exist.

4. The Company agrees to pay the Contractor a flat fee of $_____, to be paid half upon execution of this Agreement and half upon satisfactory completion of the Services as determined solely by the Company. No federal, state, or local income tax or payroll tax of any kind will be withheld from or paid by the Company on behalf of the Contractor. The Contractor expressly waives any and all claims for unemployment benefits and/or workers' compensation benefits hereunder. Further, any expenses relating to the provision of services hereunder shall be borne solely by the Contractor and not reimbursed by the Company.

Because independent contractors are not employees of the company, no taxes are withheld from their pay. Also, independent contractors are not entitled to unemployment or workers' compensation benefits, or for reimbursement of business-related expenses. This contract provides that the IC receives half their fee upon signing the contract and the balance upon completion of the work. While this payment schedule is not standard across industries, it makes most sense in a scenario where the IC may incur up-front costs at the start of the project.

5. The Company retains the right to inspect, stop, or alter the work of the Contractor to assure its conformity with this Agreement. The Contractor shall, upon the request of the Company, submit information as to the amount and scope of work performed including periodic invoicing as requested.

6. This Agreement shall not be construed to form a partnership or joint venture between the parties. The Company shall not be liable for any obligations incurred by the Contractor unless specifically authorized in writing. Further, the Contractor shall not hold him or herself out as an agent of the Company.

This clause makes clear that the nature of the contractual relationship is not partnership-related (a joint venture is a limited term/purpose partnership between two entities). This clarification is intended to restrict the authority of the contractor because, in partnerships, each partner is considered to be an agent of the partnership and, as such, can bind the partnership contractually.

7. The Contractor agrees that the Services to be performed pursuant to this Agreement, including all tasks, duties, results, inventions, and intellectual property developed or performed pursuant to this Agreement, are considered "work-made-for-hire" as defined under U.S. copyright law. Any such work is by virtue of this Agreement assigned to the Company and shall be the sole property of Company for all purposes, including, but not limited to, copyright, trademark, service mark, patent, and trade secret laws.

This work-for-hire clause makes clear that the nature of this arrangement is work-for-hire, which means that any IP developed by the contractor pursuant to this agreement will be owned by the company and the IC has no rights to it. See Chapter 11 for a discussion of the work-for-hire doctrine.

8. In the event that any work created by the Contractor does not qualify as a work-made-for-hire, the Contractor agrees to assign his or her rights in the work to the Company. The Contractor agrees to execute any and all documents prepared by the Company and to do all other lawful acts as may be required by the Company to establish, document, and protect such rights.

This clause recognizes the murky nature of the work-for-hire doctrine. It backs up the work-for-hire clause by saying that in the event the independent contractor's status is determined to not be work-for-hire for some reason, the contractor will nonetheless assign their rights in the IP developed under this agreement to the company.

9. The Contractor hereby represents and warrants that there is no conflict of interest between the Contractor's other employment, if any, or other contracts, if any, and the Services to be performed hereunder.

This is a representations and warranty clause in which the contractor is required to attest that no conflicts exist to inhibit their work for the company or otherwise subject the company to liability for engaging their services.

10. The Contractor agrees to indemnify and hold the Company harmless from and against any and all claims which may arise out of and in the course of the Contractor's Services hereunder.

This is an indemnification clause. These generally accompany representations and warranty clauses, but they are often broader in scope than merely backing up those clauses. This version is unilateral, which means that only one of the parties is making promises to the other. In this example, the IC is promising to hire an attorney to provide a legal defense and pay any legal judgment awarded to a claimant who might sue the company relating to the services provided by the IC. One example of this could be that the IC provided copyrighted lighting projections without first obtaining rights to them and both the IC and Company were sued for infringement by the copyright owner.

11. The Contractor agrees not to disclose or communicate, in any manner, either during or after the term of this Agreement, any proprietary information about the Company, including but not limited to, the names of its customers, marketing strategies, operations, or any other information marked confidential or proprietary. The Contractor understands that a breach of this provision is material. Upon termination or expiration of this Agreement, the Contractor shall deliver all records, data, information, and other documents produced or acquired during the performance of this Agreement and all copies thereof to the Company. Such material shall remain the property of the Company.

This is a confidentiality clause. It focuses on customer lists, marketing, and operations, but what should be kept confidential is ultimately determined by contracting parties. You should draft yours to include what, specifically, should remain confidential as well as what is not subject to the confidentiality promise. This one is not especially well drafted because it's unclear what constitutes "proprietary information," and this could lead to problems later. The reference to "material breach" is a signal to a court that unauthorized disclosure is not insignificant and, in fact, is so important that it would qualify as an actionable breach of the contract. See Chapter 13 for sample language from a nondisclosure agreement with a confidentiality provision.

12. The Contractor shall not act as an agent for, as a consultant to, or as an officer, employee, or other representative of any subcontractor or supplier to the Company. The Contractor shall not serve in any of the foregoing capacities for any of the Company's competitors or prospective competitors, without giving prior written notification to the Company.

This clause aims to restrict the contractor's professional activities that could potentially give rise to a conflict of interest relating to the contractor's work with the company. If I were the IC, I would find this language too broad because complying with it could unduly restrict my ability to make a living doing similar work for companies like this one. I would ask for a list of their top competitors to review and possibly ask the company to approve future assignments with other companies on a case-by-case basis.

13. Further, the Contractor shall not, during the term of this Agreement and for a period of one year immediately following termination of this Agreement, either directly or indirectly, call on, solicit, or take away, or attempt to call on, solicit, or take away, any of the Company's customers or clients on whom Contractor called or became acquainted with during the term of this Agreement. This restriction applies either for the Contractor's own benefit or for the benefit of any other person, firm, corporation, or organization.

This is a version of a noncompete clause. It restricts the IC from soliciting the company's customers and clients for a year from the date the professional services contract ends. More typical versions of this clause are directed at persons who are in a position to directly compete with a company, not those who are in a position to recommend a customer or client to one of the company's competitors. Regardless, the company intends to protect its client base from being pilfered by the IC.

NOTES

1. IRS, "Independent Contractor (Self-Employed) or Employee?" www.irs.gov/ businesses/small-business-self-employed/independent-contractor-self-employed-or -employee.

2. Form SS-8, Determination of Worker Status for Purposes of Federal Employment Taxes and Income Tax Withholding.

3. Form 8952, Application for Voluntary Classification Settlement.

4. Electronic Federal Tax Payment System, www.eftps.gov.

5. United States Department of Labor, "Elaws," webapps.dol.gov/elaws/.

6. "Resources for Job Creators," www.employer.gov.

7. Freelancers Union, www.freelancersunion.org.

8. Freelancers Union, "About Freelancers Union," www.freelancersunion.org/about/.

9. Though 501Commons is a nonprofit organization whose mission is to assist other nonprofits, its website has a host of helpful information relevant to any type of business including legal resources, human resources, tech, and strategic planning.

PART V

PROTECTING YOUR BUSINESS & PROTECTING YOURSELF

10

Collaborating with Others

One of the grading criteria in my elementary school was "ability to get along with others." The cultural imperatives of sharing and compromise have been drilled into us since childhood. Unlike so many examples in the animal kingdom, we humans still find it challenging to work together (ask any college or graduate student about the dynamics of working on group projects). If collaboration were effortless, there wouldn't be a need for facilitators or dispute mediators (like me).

Collaborating with others can be difficult regardless of the personalities involved or the nature of the project because we all have our own opinions, ideas, impulses, and agendas. But those with experience in creative collaboration will tell you that, without fail, working together will always result in two things: (1) a richer outcome; and (2) invaluable buy-in from those participating in the collaborative process merely because their voices were heard.

Musicians collaborate regularly in all kinds of ways—in rehearsal, in performance, and in creating original content. This chapter is about the latter: the collaborative negotiating that takes place when musicians co-author, co-produce, or join together to form a new enterprise.

With all of the creative decisions that need to be made in these examples, the baseline decisions of how the actual collaborative relationship should work are rarely considered until it's too late. Once a dispute arises, the collaborative process halts, emotions rise, and good sense falls away because people adopt hard-line positions that limit their ability to be reasonable. When we adopt an unreasonable posture, we rule out the possibility for compromise—the cornerstone of effective collaboration. The time to hammer out the details of a collaborative arrangement are up front, before disagreements overtake reason.

The typical organizational structure that emerges from collaborative arrangements is a general partnership even if the terms of the arrangement are never committed to a formal signed writing. In the absence of this formality, the law fills in the gaps, so if a dispute arises among the members, a legal framework is provided to resolve the issues according to a predetermined set of default rules. These default rules are found in state partnership law. The problem is that partnership default rules governing collaborative arrangements may be far from what the member-collaborators ever contemplated. See Chapter 3 for a discussion of partnerships and the application of state default rules.

Enter the collaboration agreement—a contract. Contracts are powerful because they can change what the law provides. While it's unrealistic to suggest that all conflict can be avoided, with a bit of planning much of the negativity resulting from conflicts can be. If we anticipate that conflicts will arise whenever humans work closely together, we can decide how we will address those conflicts before good sense is overtaken by emotion. In other words, deciding in advance of a conflict how your collaborative process should work can greatly minimize stress, provide a solution that you and your co-collaborators had a hand in designing, keep projects on track, and help retain the relationship for future collaborations.

Finally, you don't need to hire a lawyer to draft a collaboration agreement; you can do it yourself. If you do decide you need legal help, preparing a good first draft yourself will save you money in legal fees.

COLLABORATION DECISIONS

It is impossible to lay out all the decisions collaborators need to make without knowing their specific situation, but what follows is a start that will provide you with the basic things you need to think about, discuss, decide upon, and commit to a formal written collaboration agreement.

Contractual Rights and Duties

All contracts must outline the rights and duties of each party to the contract because these will form the basis for the binding promises you make to one another. My first book goes into detail about the four required elements all contracts need to have to be valid: an offer, acceptance of that offer, terms that are definite, and consideration (which is defined as a bargained-for exchange of values). If you are concerned whether a contract provides terms that are definite enough, look for details about what you have promised to do (your duties) and what the contract says that the other party (or parties) promised to do (their duties). For a musician working with others pursuant to a collaboration agreement, their duty may be to collaborate in songwriting sessions, play guitar, transcribe the resulting sessions into a music software program, edit arrangements, participate in booking gigs, attend rehearsals, and perform as scheduled. Their rights under that same agreement likely involve receiving a pre-negotiated ownership interest in the material created and an income percentage generated from it.

Credits and Billing

Your agreement should address how each collaborator's contribution is credited in every instance where credits are given and how such credits should appear in size, style, and font.

Income

Some of the most important decisions you'll need to make relate to the split and distribution of income. Income is often split equally, as would be the case where no written agreement exists, but it's also possible for unequal percentage splits where that makes sense. For example, sometimes one member has contributed more time, money, equipment, or other resources to the extent that income generated from the collaboration would naturally be split unequally and proportionally favor that contributor. Similarly, if one person made a loan to the collaboration and an agreement was reached to fully (or partially) repay that debt prior to a general distribution of income, those details should be spelled out in the written agreement as well.

The sample collaboration agreement provided at the end of this chapter involves three people co-writing a musical: a book writer, a composer, and a lyricist. Those collaborators don't merely want equal sharing of income. In addition to income from the exploitation of the musical through licensing, they also intend that each contributor be able to draw independent income from their own contributed element. In other words, they intend for each of them to be able to exploit their contribution independent of the musical being licensed.

Expenses

You'll need to decide how expenses will be handled. It's not necessary to have a one-size-fits-all approach—you can set rules based on the type and amount of the expense. Like income, expenses that benefit all contributors are likely to be prorated equally among the contributors (such as hiring an agent to market a project), but expenses connected to the development of an individual element may not be shared. You'll need to hash those details out early in your collaboration. If a songwriter needs to update their music-writing software program, should that be considered a personal expense or an expense to be shared among all contributors? What if a band member wants to buy an expensive piece of equipment? Should expenses be allowed to accrue or should they be submitted on some agreed-upon timeframe for reimbursement? As a condition of reimbursement, should there be some cap on larger expenses that can be incurred without approval of all collaborators? For example, each collaborator is authorized to incur up to $500 of reimbursable expenses to be shared among the collaborators, within a calendar year quarter, but expenses that exceed that threshold must be submitted for approval by vote.

Intellectual Property Ownership

If you are working on a project with other collaborators, such as writing a musical, you'll need to decide who owns what. In the annotated collaboration agreement provided below, the composer, book writer, and lyricist each decided that they want to retain copyright ownership in the individual elements that they contributed to the musical so they could each exploit their element independently of the musical as a whole. For example, if the book writer chose to lead an actors' workshop using dialogue from the musical for technical work with acting students, presumably the writer could do that without compensating the composer and lyricist or having to ask their permission to do so because Clause 8.b. grants that right to the composer and lyricist. In lawyer speak, this agreement *is silent* on the specific issue of whether the book writer has that same right, but it can be inferred.

If you want this type of flexibility in your collaborations, you'll need a formal, written agreement that spells this out because, in the absence of a writing, federal copyright law will assume that the works resulting from your collaborative efforts are "joint works." This means that all collaborators own an undivided interest in the whole. For joint works, independent revenue streams like the one provided in the example above are not possible; all income, regardless of source, would need to be split equally among the collaborators.

Finally, while it's always important for creative people to know the basics of copyright law, it is especially important to understand how copyright law works when contributing creative content as part of a collaboration. All collaborators owe it to the others that the content each is contributing is their own original work because if contributed work contains any content from other sources without the content owner's permission, all contributors may need to defend themselves in a legal claim alleging copyright infringement. Contributors of musical content need to understand that music sampling can easily constitute copyright infringement if the contributor didn't first obtain permission from the rightsholder. See Chapter 12 for a discussion of sampling and master use licenses.

One way collaborators may protect themselves is to promise one another, via a *Representations and Warranties Clause*, that the content each is contributing to the collaboration is indeed their own original work or that proper permissions have been secured for its use. (See Clause 5. in the example below.) But that won't go very far should a claim of infringement be brought against a collaborator. In reality, all collaborators would likely be named in an infringement lawsuit. Some collaboration agreements might go beyond the warranty clause to state, via an *Indemnification Clause* (also known as a *Hold Harmless Clause*), that if an infringement claim is made against the collaborators, the contributor who provided the allegedly infringing content promises to defend and indemnify the others against such claims (see Clause 6., on p. 158). Indemnification Clauses say that in the event that we are sued because of something a collaborator is alleged to have done improperly (such as used sampled music without first obtaining and paying for a license to do so), that collaborator will (1) engage a lawyer to provide a legal defense for all of us; and (2) pay any resulting monetary judgment on behalf of all. See Chapter 11 for a discussion of copyright and infringement.

Voting

The voting issues relevant to collaborators are very similar to those in partnership agreements. See Chapter 3 for a discussion of the decisions collaborators need to consider regarding the issues subject to vote and the different types of votes that can be put in place depending on your needs.

Merger Date

The merger date is the date that project collaborators choose for when their individual contributions to the whole become inextricable from it. Once this date arrives, and assuming that the collaborators agree that the date is still relevant for merger, the contributed elements are now merged together for the benefit of the project. Merger does not change the fact that, in the sample collaboration agreement that follows, the contributors retain ownership of their contributed intellectual property for the purposes of exploiting their contributions independently (as indicated in Clauses 7. and 8.).

Pre- and Post-Merger Contingencies

For collaborative projects like co-authoring a musical, the merger date provides a demarcation line for when some rights accrue and when actions concerning those rights can be taken. An obvious example of this idea is where, after the merger date, collaborators can no longer extract their contributions to the project. Another example is that, post-merger, the rules can be different for removing a collaborator after their death, disability, or other reasons (such as being voted off the project). The rules can also differ on replacing the collaborator and how the new collaborator can vote and be compensated. Essentially, anything that can be put up for vote can be made a contingency for differing treatment pre- and post-merger.

Miscellaneous Items

The final section of most contracts is where the miscellaneous ("housekeeping") clauses are found. "Housekeeping Clauses" is the nickname lawyers use to refer to these general provisions. Not all of these clauses are essential, but they are nonetheless included in contracts to remind the parties of what the law already provides. For example, an Amendment Clause says that no party is allowed to make unilateral changes to the contract; a Choice of Law Clause provides for which state law will apply if a dispute arises. Despite their seemingly innocuous nature, never pass over these clauses without a careful reading because this section is a notoriously good place to hide items the drafter doesn't want to draw readers' attention to. See Clauses 19–26 of the sample collaboration agreement below for annotated examples of miscellaneous "housekeeping clauses."

CONCLUSION

Like prenuptial agreements, it can seem antithetical—even distasteful—to spend time talking and thinking about the potential for future conflicts when you are about to embark on an exciting collaboration project with others whose creativity inspires you. But in the context of a business arrangement, it's common practice: this is why the use of contracts has persisted for so long—having a written memorandum of what was agreed to puts all parties on the same page. Well-drafted contracts can remove some of what is unknown or unexpected by providing answers to questions like *what will happen if I break my promise?* Businesses have relied on contracts for hundreds of years. If you feel uncomfortable using contracts, don't be concerned—it's only because you are building new skills.

The sample collaboration agreement annotated below is based on an excellent sample written by attorney, producer, and playwright Charles Grippo.[1]

Sample Collaboration Agreement

This Agreement is made this _____ day of _____, 20___ by and between _____ (BOOK WRITER), _____ (COMPOSER), and _____ (LYRICIST) (collectively hereinafter referred to as COLLABORATORS); all of whom desire to collaborate with each other to create a musical play presently entitled _____ (the WORK).

This lead-in language lays out the date of the agreement, who is entering into this contractual relationship, and the reason for it. In this instance, three people are agreeing to collaborate in the creation of a musical in which each is contributing one element of three: the book, the music, and the lyrics.

You'll notice that some words are typed in all caps. This is one way of indicating to readers that those words have special meaning in the contract. This contract doesn't have a section of defined terms, but it could. Another method of bringing attention to special terms in a contract is providing them within quotation marks. The method chosen is largely based on the drafter's personal preference or custom in the industry, but whatever method is used, the most important thing is to be consistent throughout the contract to avoid ambiguity, which can be fatal to contract interpretation and, under standard contract interpretation rules, will always work against the party who drafted the contract.

Now therefore, in consideration of the promises contained herein, the parties mutually agree as follows:

This is the mutuality provision. Its purpose is to demonstrate to third party interpreters of this contract that those who signed it have a common understanding of its terms and are in full agreement of the binding promises each collaborator made to the others.

1. Each party shall write and create his respective element of the WORK and join with the others to complete it.

This clause lays out each party's contractual duties to the others: to create their individual element of the musical and to collaborate with the other two to complete the work.

2.a. Copyright registration in the respective elements of the WORK shall be the responsibility of its individual creator with ownership interests as follows:
Book: _____ %
Music: _____ %
Lyrics: _____ %

This clause does two things. First, it says that each collaborator is responsible for protecting the element they created by filing an application of copyright (a "claim") for that element with the Library of Congress's Copyright Office. Second, it states that each collaborator shall own their own contribution to the musical and therefore may control how their individual contribution is exploited in the future.

b. Nothing contained herein, including the provisions relating to merger below, shall be construed or intended as creating a joint work, as that term is used under United States Copyright Law, and any amendments thereof. The parties expressly agree that the book, music, and lyrics of the WORK shall each be deemed a separate work for copyright and other purposes. The copyright to each such element shall belong solely to its respective creator as set forth in Clause 2.a., above.

Clause 2.b. further underscores 2.a. The reference to a "joint work" under the Copyright Act is important because, without this clarification, the default rule is that once the three individual elements are merged into the whole, each would lose its individual status and become a "joint work" in which each collaborator's ownership interest would be an undivided interest shared among three people rather than their actual intent (for each to retain full, undivided ownership of their respective elements).

3. All contracts dealing with the WORK, or any of the elements contained therein, shall require that whenever authorship credit is given to one author, all of the COLLABORATORS must also be duly credited and provided for in the same size and style of type as the others. Authorship credit shall appear in the following manner:

    Book by: _____
    Music by: _____
    Lyrics by: _____

    Clause 3. speaks to the manner of credits including order of names/contributions, size and style of fonts.

4. If, pursuant to any of the provisions of Clause 14. (removal of a COLLABORATOR) or 17. (death or disability of a COLLABORATOR) below, the parties agree to add or replace a COLLABORATOR, the new or additional COLLABORATOR shall be required to sign this Agreement and to be bound by it. However, such new, additional, or replacement COLLABORATOR shall not be entitled to any revenues or other receipts earned from the WORK, including advances for uncompleted work, prior to the date of his signing of this Agreement.

    If any collaborator is added or replaced, the new person is not entitled to any revenues/income for work completed prior to the date such person signed onto the project. This clause speaks to death or disability of a collaborator but doesn't address when a collaborator decides to exit a project voluntarily or is voted out for some reason. I think those additional contingencies should be included here.

5. The parties hereby represent and warrant that all material each has or will contribute to the WORK is and will be original to each party (except for public domain sources) and has not been adapted or derived from any other copyrighted and/or trademarked material owned by a third person or entity not a party to this Agreement. Furthermore, to the best of the contributing party's knowledge, his material does not infringe upon or violate the rights of others, including any rights of publicity or privacy belonging to any third persons or entities.

    This is a Representations and Warranties Clause. It is an express statement of promise made by each of the collaborators to the others that the content each is contributing to the project is their own original work and that no person has any reason to believe that a third party can legitimately make a legal claim against any one of them based on the content each is contributing to the project. This is an important clause because while any lawsuit could completely derail this project, allegations of copyright infringement or violations of privacy are particularly expensive and difficult to defend. These issues aside, the mere allegation of contributing non-original material can be damaging to a contributor's reputational capital/personal brand.

6. Each COLLABORATOR shall defend, indemnify, and hold harmless the other COLLABORATORS from and against any and all liability, loss, expense including reasonable attorneys' fees, or claims for injury or damages arising out of the performance of this Agreement, but only to the extent such liability, loss, expense, attorneys' fees, or claims for injury or damages are caused by or result from the negligent acts or omissions of each COLLBORATOR and relates to the content contributed to the WORK.

    This is an Indemnification Clause (aka a "Hold Harmless Clause"). It gives the Representations and Warranties Clause that immediately precedes it in Clause 5. some punch. It says that if the collaborators are sued for copyright infringement or violating a person's right of privacy, for example, the collaborator who provided the offending content will do two things: (1) hire an attorney to provide a legal defense against those allegations; and (2) if that lawsuit is ultimately lost, pay the monetary judgment awarded to the plaintiff on behalf of all persons against whom the judgment is rendered. In essence, each collaborator is promising to back up the creative content they are bringing to the work by saying "I stand by my contribution; it's my work and no one can make a legitimate claim against me or us based on my contribution, but if they do, I'll defend and protect all of us."

7. The parties expressly deny any intention or agreement to form a partnership or joint venture between them, and this agreement shall not be construed as creating either.

    No partnership or joint venture is intended to be formed by this agreement. Even though the individual terms of this agreement deviate from the common default rules that would otherwise apply under state partnership law, it's still a good idea to actually spell this out as a safeguard because the parties to this contract specifically want an arrangement other than what state partnership rules would provide by default.

    In the absence of a formal agreement, would this arrangement more resemble a joint venture or a general partnership?

    When analyzing this contractual arrangement to write a musical together, it would be easy to conclude that these collaborators are forming a joint venture that needs only to exist until the writing of the musical is completed, but that would be a mistake. This scenario is actually closer to a general partnership because while the initial phase of the arrangement is to create the musical and financially exploit it, the "ongoing business" requirement under general partnership rules can be found in these individuals' intent to make money from their work into the future as long as someone is interested in licensing the work or its individual elements.

8.a. After deductions for agent's commissions (as defined below), producer's share of subsidiary rights, and any other percentages of the gross revenues which the parties must share with others, except as provided in Clause 8.b., below, all of the net revenues, monies, and income from the commercial exploitation of the WORK, its adaptations, derivations, translations, and use in any media or format, whether now in existence, or hereinafter developed, shall be divided among the parties as follows:

Book Writer: _____%
Composer: _____%
Lyricist: _____%

Agent's commissions refers to the agent for the WORK, as a whole, and not to the respective agents for the individual BOOK WRITER, COMPOSER, or LYRICIST, each of whom shall be responsible for his own agent's commissions, as applicable.

Clause 8.a. spells out the split of net profits between the collaborators. "Subsidiary rights" refers to rights to future income, usually provided as a percentage, sometimes given to early producers and investors of new theatrical works as a matter of custom. These rights are ancillary to the initial deal to mount the work. Instead, they apply to income generated from later productions and other income that flows from the work such as from licensing. Income from subsidiary rights rewards initial investors who take the risk of mounting new works and building a first audience for them.

b. The parties understand and agree that the music and lyrics may be used separate and apart from the play and said separate uses will earn revenues. Such uses may include, but not be limited to, the separate publication, mechanical reproduction, synchronization, small performing rights, motion picture, television, radio, video, cast albums, recordings of any kind, all of which may occur and be presented in any format of sound reproduction and/or publication, whether now known or hereinafter developed.

Clause 8.b. says that the music and lyrics may be used apart from their use within the musical and, as such, are expected to produce independent revenue for their respective owners, but not for the book owner. Further, subsections i, ii, and iii, below, clarify how different uses will result in different splits of profits.

Synchronization rights are rights to income pursuant to a license when music is synchronized with visual content such as in films, videos, television shows, commercials, and on the Internet.

Small performing rights is a broad category of specific rights that are granted through licensing. See Chapter 12 for a discussion of small rights.

Except as provided in Clause 8.c., below, the COMPOSER and/or LYRICIST, as the case may be (or an entity owned or licensed by each of them respectively), shall have sole control, authority, and direction over such uses, and the BOOK WRITER shall have no control, authority, or direction thereon. All revenues earned from such uses shall (except as provided in 8.c. below) inure to and belong to the COMPOSER and LYRICIST respectively and the BOOK WRITER shall not be entitled to any of said revenues (except as provided in 8.c., below).

All such revenues shall be divided according to the following formula:

(i)   If both music and lyrics are used, then _____% to the COMPOSER and ____% to the LYRICIST;

(ii) If only the lyrics are used, then ____% to the LYRICIST and _____% to the COMPOSER;

(iii) If only the music is used, then ____% to the COMPOSER and ___% to the LYRICIST.

c. In the event _____% of the book is used in any presentation of the separate music and/or lyrics, as stated above in Section 8.b., then the BOOK WRITER shall be entitled to ____% of the net receipts. The BOOK WRITER shall further be entitled to ____% of the direction and authority over the use of the book, in connection therein.

Clause 8.c. lays out profit percentages owed to the book writer in certain situations in which the music and lyrics are presented. It also provides for some authority by the book owner over how the book can be used in those settings.

d. In any publication of the book, net receipts therefrom shall be divided as follows:

   (i)   If only the book is used, then 100% of the net receipts shall inure to the BOOK WRITER. Only the BOOK WRITER shall have direction and authority over the use of the book in such publication.

   (ii) If only lyrics are included in the publication of the book, then net receipts shall be divided as follows: _____% to the BOOK WRITER and _____% to the LYRICIST and _____% to the COMPOSER. The BOOK WRITER shall have _____%, the LYRICIST shall have ____%, and the COMPOSER shall have ____% of the direction and authority over such use of the book and lyrics respectively.

   (iii) If the music and lyrics are included in the publication of the book, then net receipts shall be divided according to the formula, as stated in Section 8.a., above. The BOOK WRITER shall have ____%, the LYRICIST shall have ____%, and the COMPOSER shall have _____% of the direction and authority over such use of the book, lyrics, and music respectively.

Clause 8.d. lays out profit splits if the book is published in various forms.

9. The parties hereby appoint _____ as exclusive agent for the Work. The parties hereby appoint _____ as attorney for the Work.

Hiring an agent to market the work to producers is one expense that is generally shared equally (pro rata) between the collaborators. (See related Clauses 8.a., above, and 10., below.)

"Exclusive agent" means that these collaborators have decided to only work with this one named agent. Such arrangements should be in a separate writing and signed by all parties. The most prudent approach to working with anyone on an exclusive basis is to try to limit the time period of exclusivity so that if that person isn't delivering on the promises made to you or can't get the deal you want, you're not tied up contractually for a long period of time.

This clause can be removed if you prefer to not use anyone on an exclusive basis or if you prefer to make these decisions later. You can write "to be negotiated" on that line or you can replace it with something conditional such as:

"COLLABORATORS agree that in the event COLLABORATORS decide to engage a professional to assist in the exploitation of the WORK, expenses for such exploitation shall be borne by the parties on a pro rata basis."

10. The parties agree and understand that the creation and/or marketing of the WORK may entail expenses. The COLLABORATORS must agree in advance upon any expenses incurred and they agree to share such expenses, pro rata. In the event any party advances expenses, to which all of the parties have mutually agreed, he shall be entitled to reimbursement from any monies earned by the WORK before such revenues are divided up among the parties. In the event it becomes apparent, within a reasonable time, that the WORK may not earn revenues sufficient to repay him, the other parties agree to reimburse the advancing party, in full, pro rata according to their shares in the WORK.

This clause speaks to the equal division of financial responsibility for expenses associated with the project in which the collaborators agree that if the project generates income, the person who advanced expenses will be reimbursed before any income is declared and distributed among the three. There are several ways to handle this based on what the parties to the contract want. One way is to allow each collaborator to incur up to $X of expenses per any time period, such as six months, without having to get permission from the other collaborators up front. In any case, I would build a clause into this contract that requires that any expenses over $X be presented to the others within X days of incurring them to reduce the potential for ugly surprises (such as a large expenditure by one person expecting reimbursement from the others).

11. The BOOK WRITER shall have sole rights of approval to the book element, including any additions and/or deletions thereto. The COMPOSER shall have sole rights of approval to the musical elements, including any

additions and/or deletions therefrom, as well as to the choices of orchestra members, rehearsal pianist, musical orchestrations, and arrangements. The LYRICIST shall have sole rights of approval to the lyric elements, including any additions and/or deletions thereto.

Each collaborator retains final say over their contribution. Composers often get additional say in choosing musicians, orchestrations, and musical arrangements.

12. All of the parties must agree upon and execute any contracts for all productions, presentations, publications of the WORK, and for the sale or license or any rights therein (except as otherwise provided in Clause 8.b.). Except with the consent of the other parties (and as otherwise provided in Clause 8.b.), no party may sell, license, or otherwise dispose of any of the rights to the WORK or authorize or grant the rights to produce or present the WORK in any manner whatsoever.

Here, a unanimous vote is required for exploitation (sale or license) of the work. Note that in the absence of this written agreement, partnership default rules would allow any collaborator to independently dispose of the work without the others' permission (though the partner would need to compensate the others). In a general partnership, each partner is both principal and agent of the partnership, therefore, any partner could bind the partnership to an arrangement that this clause specifically prohibits.

13. Whenever the consent of any COLLABORATOR is required, the parties agree that voting rights shall be apportioned as follows:
    a. Each COLLABORATOR shall have one vote. There shall be as many votes as there are COLLABORATORS.
    b. Except as otherwise provided in Clause 12., all decisions shall be by majority vote.
    c. In the event the parties cannot agree upon a decision, the COLLABORATORS hereby appoint the following persons to break deadlocks:

    Artistic Decisions: _____

    Business Decisions: _____

This clause spells out voting rights. It provides for majority voting, but re-quiring a unanimous vote is another option. Unit voting is also an option in collaborations where there may be more than one person contributing to a single element (such as two lyricists). The clause provides for tiebreaker contingencies relating to voting issues where the collaborators cannot agree. It splits artistic versus business decision-making and allows for different people with differing expertise to break any ties.

14. At any time prior to merger, any of the parties may be removed by major-ity vote of the other parties. The removed party shall be entitled to due written notice. All rights to any of the material created or contributed by the removed party shall revert immediately to him, to use and exploit as he shall see fit, and the remaining parties shall have no claim, interest, or entitlement to the use of same, whether in this WORK or in any other. The removed party shall have no claim, interest, or entitlement to the WORK, or any revenues earned by it.

Pre-merger of content, a majority voting rule applies for the purposes of removing a collaborator from the project (aka "disassociation"). That per-son will retain ownership of the content contributed (because merger has not yet taken place). There should also be a statement here about someone quitting the project such as, pre-merger, if you leave the project, you keep your contribution and are not entitled to any revenue generated from the collaboration. (See the comments under Clause 4.)

15. Any COLLABORATOR hereunder may sell, pledge, lease, assign, en-cumber, or otherwise dispose of his interest of net receipts to a third party, provided, however, he first gives written notice of his intention, including the terms and conditions of said sale or encumbrance, to the other COLLABORATORS. Said notice must be by certified mail, return receipt requested, and shall be effective only upon receipt by the other COLLABORATORS.

The other COLLABORATORS shall have _____ days after re-ceipt, as a first option, to purchase the selling COLLABORATOR's inter-est, on either an individual or joint basis, upon the terms and conditions so stated in the notice. If, during the said time period, the Purchasing COLLABORATORS either fail to exercise said option, or complete the purchase, the Selling COLLABORATOR may offer and transfer his rights to a third party upon the same terms and conditions as contained in the notice to the other COLLABORATORS, provided, however, he transfers only his right to receive the net revenues.

Upon receipt of a copy of the sales contract to such third party, the remaining COLLABORATORS must honor the Third-Party Purchaser's interest in the net receipts. The Selling COLLABORATOR may not transfer voting or other rights to the Third Party. Upon transfer of his interest in the net receipts, the Selling COLLABORATOR's voting rights, in all matters, business and artistic, shall cease. Rights to billing credit shall remain unchanged.

Any collaborator can sell or otherwise dispose of their rights (e.g., the right to receive revenues), but only if the selling collaborator first provides notice to the others with details of the sale offer because the non-selling collaborators are entitled to right of first refusal to purchase those rights at the price preliminarily accepted by a third party buyer. Voting rights do not transfer to the buyer regardless of who that is. Billing credits are unaffected by a sale of rights. Contrast this provision regarding the transferability of rights to future income from the restriction on transferring contractual duties as outlined in Clause 19.

16. Merger of the respective elements of book, music, and lyrics shall, for all purposes, occur on _____, the MERGER DATE. Upon the MERGER DATE, all material—whether elements of the book, music, or lyrics—that the parties have agreed will constitute the WORK, will thereupon be incorporated into and become an essential part of the WORK. Said merged material may not be removed, or otherwise used in any manner outside of the WORK (except as noted in Clause 8.b., above).

Any material created for or considered for the WORK, but not actually a part of the WORK on the MERGER DATE, shall not be merged into the WORK and shall remain the individual property of its creator/

COLLABORATOR, whose control over it shall be absolute. All rights to same are reserved by its creator/COLLABORATOR. None of the other COLLABORATORS shall have any rights, claims, entitlement, or interest thereon.

The merger date is the date the collaborators have set for when all three elements merge into one cohesive work that, post-merger, can never be divided. Once merger has occurred, any unused content remains the sole property of that collaborator who contributed it.

17. In the event that merger has not occurred, and one party dies or becomes disabled such that he cannot effectively collaborate, the remaining parties may continue the WORK. They shall have unbridled discretion to modify or change any or all parts of the WORK, including any material contributed by the deceased or disabled party. If the remaining parties determine that additional material or contributions are needed for the element which the deceased or disabled party had heretofore been creating, they may bring in another person to finish the element, including changing or deleting any material heretofore created by the deceased or disabled party, or otherwise to contribute to the WORK.

In the event the surviving parties bring in a replacement COLLABORATOR, they may compensate that COLLABORATOR by changing the deceased or disabled party's compensation according to the following formula:

<insert formula>

The original collaborators are not required to obtain the consent of the disabled party or his representative or the representative of a deceased party. However, they may not change or reduce any billing credits for the deceased or disabled party. Otherwise, all other compensation due to the deceased or disabled party shall be duly paid as agreed. In addition, copies of all contracts or other agreements affecting the WORK shall be furnished promptly to the disabled party or his representative, or to the legal representative of the deceased.

This clause is for pre-merger contingencies relating to the death or disability of a collaborator. Disabled, in this context, also means mental incompetence. These collaborators have retained a lot of authority over that person's contribution, such that they can make changes to it, hire someone to finish the project (with a predetermined formula for reducing the deceased or disabled collaborator's compensation, and for compensating the new collaborator), and are not responsible for obtaining anyone's consent in order to do so. All payments due to the deceased or disabled person or estate will be made according to the contract's terms. They agree to not change billing credits for the replaced collaborator.

18. In the event of the death or disability of a COLLABORATOR, after merger has occurred, the following provisions apply:
    a. All artistic decisions for which a COLLABORATOR'S decision may be required, requested, or permitted shall be made by the surviving COLLABORATORS, according to the voting formula herein described in Clause 13., above. If a COLLABORATOR is disabled but still competent to make artistic decisions, his voting rights shall not change, and he shall be entitled to vote as if disability had not occurred.
    b. The legal representative of a deceased or a disabled COLLABORATOR shall not be permitted to vote on artistic matters.
    c. All business decisions, which a COLLABORATOR may be required, requested, or permitted to make, shall be made by the surviving COLLABORATORS and the legal representative of a disabled COLLABORATOR who is not competent to make such decisions and the legal representative of a deceased COLLABORATOR.

This clause spells out contingencies, post-merger, for the death or disability of a collaborator when decisions need to be made.

If a collaborator dies, the remaining collaborators make all decisions according to the same voting splits. If a collaborator becomes disabled, but remains mentally competent, they can still vote.

But who decides competency? It may be a good idea to allow for a decision-maker here too, even if it's merely by title if not someone's actual name, such as "a psychiatrist currently holding a medical license in good standing by the State of New York." If you want a specific person, by name, you could include "Dr. Michael Smith residing at XYZ, or his duly licensed designee."

No person's legal representative may participate in artistic decisions.

Legal representatives are allowed to participate in business decisions.

19. This Agreement may not be assigned or transferred (except an interest in the net receipts as provided in Clause 15., above), without the express written consent of the other parties. Nothing contained herein, however, shall prevent a party from transferring or assigning his rights by will, trust, or other testamentary instrument to any person(s) and/or entities, for estate planning purposes.

This is a version of an Assignment clause. Recall that all parties to a contract have both contractual rights and contractual duties that serve as binding promises made between them. These promises are critically important because one promise is said to induce a reciprocal promise from the other party (or parties) and, considered together, provide for consideration (a required element for contract validity).

Assignment Clauses are connected to one's contractual duties. These clauses typically restrict one or more parties to a contract from subcontracting out their contractual duties to another person or entity. The underlying policy for this rule is that each party to a contract like this one is providing personal services of a highly creative nature that are unique to them such that subcontracting those services to another person would defeat the purpose of the contract.

This Assignment Clause says that no collaborator may assign their duties to another (e.g., the duty to create song lyrics), but any collaborator may sign some or all of their rights away (i.e., rights to future income from the project). Clause 15. provides the rules for selling one's financial interest in the project.

20. This Agreement shall bind the parties hereto, their executors, administrators, personal representatives, successors, and assigns.

    This clause aims to bind persons who gain a future interest in the subject matter of this contract to these terms as though they, themselves, signed it.

21. This Agreement constitutes the entire agreement between the parties and shall supersede all prior agreements, arrangements, negotiations, proposals, and understandings, if any, relating to the obligations and matters set out herein, whether oral or written.

    This is a Merger Clause (sometimes also referred to as an Integration Clause). These common contract clauses are important in that they trigger a rule of evidence in a legal proceeding that precludes the introduction of any kind of evidence that contradicts the language in the contract itself. Even if you have evidence that demonstrates that you were promised, for example, more money for additional responsibilities, this clause would prevent that evidence from being introduced in support of that assertion. So, if a side deal is offered to you, be sure that those promises are protected under a completely separate contract that meets the validity requirements as its own standalone contract or ask that the original contract be revised to include the newly negotiated content and that the new contract is signed by all parties to it, per Clause 22.

22. This Agreement shall not be changed, amended, altered, or modified. Similarly, no additions, deletions, or substitutions will be valid unless such additions, deletions, or substitutions are made in writing and duly signed by all parties.

    This is an Amendment Clause. This common contract clause restricts the parties from making unilateral changes to the contract without the others' written consent.

23. The laws of the State of _____ shall govern this agreement.

    This is the Choice of Law Clause. This clause isn't usually required, but it's a good idea to state up front which state's laws will apply to the contract and any future disagreements that might arise. Further, you may want your state's statute of limitations (SOL) for bringing a breach of contract action to apply if your state's statute is more generous than the state in which one of the other collaborators lives. If no Choice of Law Clause is provided, a legal test would be employed to resolve that issue.

For example, if two of the three collaborators live in New York State and the third lives in Pennsylvania, and the post-merger work would be performed in New York City, then the court determining the applicable law(s) for a dispute might determine that the nexus of the contract falls within New York State's authority, so New York's six-year SOL for a breach of contract action would apply instead of Pennsylvania's shorter four-year SOL. Longer SOLs generally benefit aggrieved parties in disputes because it allows them more time to file their lawsuit.

24. Any dispute arising out of this Agreement will be resolved by an arbitrator or panel of arbitrators with recognized expertise in the subject matter of this Agreement. The Commercial Arbitration Rules of the American Arbitration Association will apply unless otherwise agreed upon by the parties. The resolution will be binding upon the parties, and any court of competent jurisdiction may enter judgment upon the award rendered. The losing party agrees to pay the costs of arbitration as well as the prevailing party's (or parties') reasonable costs and attorney fees.

This is an Arbitration Clause. It provides for an alternative to litigation if a dispute arises between the collaborators relating to this contract. Arbitration is one form of alternative dispute resolution (ADR); another is mediation. Both arbitration and mediation are designed to be faster, cheaper, and more flexible than litigation. The nonprofit organization Volunteer Lawyers for the Arts (VLA), with offices nationwide, offers mediation services to both members and non-members for a modest fee. Another benefit of ADR is that, unlike litigation, the proceedings are private and remain confidential.

These clauses can be drafted in any number of ways, but this one provides that once the dispute has been resolved through arbitration, whomever has "lost" the dispute has to pay for the arbitration and all fees incurred in it.

But, it's not always easy to determine who "lost" and casting the proceedings as win/lose doesn't promote compromise.

A preferred option for ADR might be mediation because that process is one that necessarily involves compromise provided the parties mediating are willing to be reasonable and give something up in exchange for receiving something in return. Renegotiating contract terms through compromise will also go a long way toward retaining the professional relationship, which is always a good outcome. Winner/loser resolutions rarely result in a relationship that remains intact for future collaborating.

25. In the event of any default hereunder, the aggrieved party will send written notice to the other party outlining the nature of the alleged default and provide two (2) calendar weeks for the other party to cure the alleged default before taking steps to declare a material breach of this Agreement.

This is a Default Clause with a Notice of Cure provision. It doesn't state what, specifically, would constitute default under the contract, so there is some subjectivity here.

This version of the clause spells out the procedure for taking issue with how one or more collaborators is underperforming or otherwise breaking their promises (contractual duties) to the other collaborators. Default Clauses attempt to keep the parties in conversation to work out any issues that arise rather than jumping to the conclusion that a person is in breach of the agreement. This clause allows two weeks to fix whatever is giving rise to the frustration (for example, one collaborator is not meeting agreed-upon deadlines for completing their element). Clause 26. provides for how such notice is properly delivered.

A "material" breach is one that is serious. It means that a party to a contract has not fulfilled a critically important duty and that failure could give rise to a breach of contract lawsuit.

26. All notices required hereunder shall be in writing and shall be given by personal delivery or certified or registered mail (return receipt requested).

Said notices shall be effective upon the receipt thereof. All notices shall be addressed to the parties at the addresses following their signatures below or to such other addresses as any party may specify in writing.

Clause 26. is a general provision that provides that all notices, including grievances, intentions to sell rights to future income to a third party, or any other official communications, must be made in writing and sent via a service requiring recipient's signature.

IN WITNESS WHEREOF, the parties have affixed their signatures below.

Assume there are three signature blocks here with lines for signatures, addresses, and dates.

The address lines are provided for keeping track of where people live for contacting them with income payments as well as all of the notifications required under this contract when selling an interest, voting on/approving something, or properly notifying a fellow collaborator of a grievance you want addressed.

NOTE

1. Charles Grippo, *Business and Legal Forms for Theater*, 2nd ed. (New York: Allworth Press, 2013).

Understanding Copyright

It seems everyone knows a little bit about copyright, but in my experience, what most people know is inaccurate because copyright myths are so common. In this chapter, I will introduce you to the minimum you need to know about copyright in order to protect yourself and your creative output under existing copyright law.

You'll learn

- what copyright is and its purpose;
- the source of copyright's legal authority;
- the types of things that can be copyrighted;
- how and when your copyright rights accrue;
- the importance of timely federal registration; and
- about preregistration and why that might interest you.

There's a Copyright Quiz at the end of the chapter. Take it to see how well you've grasped this complicated area of the law; an analysis of the quiz questions is provided in Appendix B.

Finally, this chapter has a lot of citations—don't be intimidated. I've included references to the federal copyright statute, so you can find the law if you want to read it for yourself to see where your rights originate or do other research.

TYPES OF PROPERTY

Before we can discuss copyright specifically, you first need to understand that there are different types of property. The two main categories of property are real property (real estate) and personal property (everything else). Personal property can be further broken down into two categories: tangible property like your laptop, goldfish, or guitar; and intangible property such as a melody or a secret formula. Intangible property is known as intellectual property (IP). The four basic types of IP are patents, trademarks (including service marks), trade secrets, and copyrights. Copyright protection is critically important to songwriters, orchestral composers, and other content creators because copyright law provides the springboard mechanism that makes it possible for creative people to make money from their work.

WHAT IS COPYRIGHT?

Copyright is a bundle of rights given to creators of original content. The law provides the copyright owners with a temporary monopoly of those rights. This means, as the owner of the copyright, you can control who uses your content and how. These rights are yours whether you've published[1] your content (released it to the public) or not and whether you've registered your copyright on the federal registry or not. However, if you have not registered your work, your rights are limited; see "Why You Should Register," below.

Contrast this temporary monopoly over content with works that are in the public domain. Public domain works are those owned by the public and freely available to all of us. See Chapter 12 for a discussion of public domain, how works fall into the public domain, and how to search for works with public domain status.

AUTHORITY FOR COPYRIGHT

Copyright law is derived from the United States Constitution, which gives Congress the right to create laws "promoting the progress of . . . the useful arts, by securing for limited times to authors . . . the exclusive right to their respective writings."[2] The federal Constitution authorizes Congress to enact enabling legislation to make this limited duration monopoly possible. America's first copyright laws were promulgated by Congress in 1790 when Mozart still walked the earth. Congress created the Copyright Office, a division of the Library of Congress, and the position of Copyright Registrar to oversee the office and execute Congress's directives. The Registrar issues regulations and opinions pertaining to copyright, oversees the processing of copyright applications and, ultimately, grants or denies registered copyright protection status. The Copyright Act is found in Title 17 of the United States Code (17 USC). Copyright law has been amended multiple times over the years in response to anything from interest group lobbying to fixing problematic loopholes resulting from technological advances.

The Copyright Office's website, www.copyright.gov, has excellent materials to help you understand this complicated area of law; see "Copyright Resources," below.

Applicability

Ideas, in and of themselves, don't qualify for copyright protection. In order to meet the requirements for copyright status, your work must fall within one of eight categories and meet three critical criteria.

Copyright protection applies to the following categories of works:[3]

Literary
Musical
Dramatic
Choreographic
Graphic
Motion picture
Sound recording
Architectural

Criteria for protection is addressed below.

As a musician, the content you create is subject to copyright protection, though what constitutes a "musical" work is not defined in the statute. It's important to keep in mind that there are two completely and unequal levels of copyright protection. In order to benefit from full statutory protection of your compositions, you need to timely register your work with the copyright office by completing the online (or paper) application, paying the fee, and providing sample copies (referred to as a deposit) in support of your application; see "Why You Should Register," below.

COPYRIGHT OWNERSHIP

The owner of a copyright is generally the creator of the content—the *author*[4] (or *authors*). In the context of music, a copyright author is the composer/songwriter. There is no limit under copyright law regarding a maximum number of authors, but there is an important concept those who collaborate with others need to understand: *joint works*. A joint work is a single work created by more than one person in which all contributors intend that their contributions be merged together. For example, a two-person songwriting team whose members share equally in the development of melody, harmony, rhythm, and lyrics. It often makes sense for songwriters who work best in collaborative settings to avoid drawing lines between who does what and who owns what.

Authors of joint works own the work equally and each has an indivisible ownership interest in the whole. Joint owners can always transfer their financial interests in the work to others by contract or will. Each owner can also grant permissions to third parties for *nonexclusive* uses of the work without a joint owner's consent, but the granting party has a duty to compensate other owners in accordance with their ownership interests in it. For example, if two people intending to be joint owners co-write a song, either one of them could license the use of the song to someone else without the other's permission, but the income from the license would need to be shared. A nonexclusive use is one in which the grantor reserves the right to make the same grant to another person or entity simultaneously, so the grantee would not be the only one being given permission to use the same content.

In order to grant *exclusive rights* in a joint work, each owner has to consent to the grant of rights (a license) in writing; see Chapter 12 for a discussion of exclusive and nonexclusive licensing rights. Also, see Chapter 10 for an explanation of why some collaborators will not want their collaborative efforts considered a joint work under copyright law and how contract language can be used to protect against that interpretation.

Ownership rights under copyright law accrue once the statutory requirements for protection are met (see "Criteria for Protection," below). However, there are two instances where the individual(s) who created the content is not considered the copyright owner. These are (1) works made for hire; and (2) when the content creator assigned their rights to a third party such as a publisher.

Works Made for Hire

The work-for-hire doctrine is tricky and works like this: works made for hire generally arise in two circumstances: (1) when an employee creates something in the normal course of employment; and (2) when an independent contractor (IC) creates something pursuant to a commission with the intent that the work created will be completely owned by the person or entity commissioning it.[5] The statute provides for some other very specific instances of work-made-for-hire situations, but those aren't relevant to musicians.

When an employee is paid to create something for their employer, the employer is considered the copyright owner. Think of a scientist who spends years working on a formula. The parallel for musicians is if you are a salaried employee whose job is to score incidental music for a film production company. In this hypothetical, you, as employee, have no legitimate claim to copyright ownership in the music you were paid to score.

It gets a little more complicated in the context of an IC's work. Stick with the same film company hypothetical, except now you are a contract worker paid to score a film. In this amended example, your contract should make clear the nature of your employment as to whether, as an IC, you have ownership rights in your work or not. If you compose music on a commission basis, you should have a written contract that specifically states that you are an IC and whether the work you are creating pursuant to that contract is work made for hire or whether you will retain ownership of it. See Chapter 9 for a discussion of employees and ICs (and a sample IC agreement) and Chapter 13 for a sample commission agreement relevant to this discussion.

Copyright Assignments

A copyright assignment occurs when a copyright owner sells 100% of their bundle of rights. As the author of this book, I assigned my rights to my publisher in exchange for a percentage of net profits from sales (royalty). Similarly, songwriters frequently assign their rights to a publisher who manages the administration of the musician's music catalog and retains a percentage of the money received from the exploitation of the songs. Exploitation usually is comprised of licensing songs to others to record (compulsory mechanical licenses); to underscore television shows, commercials, or films (synchronization licenses); for live performances (public performance licenses); for printed music scores (print licenses); or for some other money-making use.

See Chapter 12 for a discussion of the various types of licenses musicians use to make money from their work.

To recap, a copyright owner can be (1) the person who created the content and retained their rights; or (2) a rightsholder to whom a 100% ownership interest was given by the content creator (such as the publisher of this book). Alternately, a hiring person (or entity) can acquire ownership rights from the content creator (1) expressly by contract (via a commission agreement); or (2) by operation of law (in the context of an employer/employee relationship).

Copyright Reversion

Authors who assign their copyright to a rightsholder (like a music publisher) are given the opportunity to have the grant of assigned rights terminate and have the copyright revert back to them. This right arises thirty-five years after the assignment and ends forty years after the assignment, so there is a narrow window of time to exercise this right. This is an important right to keep in mind for the benefit of your heirs. For example, upon exercising the termination/reversion right, you could create your own publishing company to keep 100% of the proceeds of your licenses provided you're confident that potential licensees can find you to obtain your permission. However, the more likely scenario would be that you would use the reversion of rights to negotiate a better deal with your existing publisher being that now you have more bargaining power than you did thirty-five years ago when you were just starting to make a name for yourself. Copyright reversion does not apply to works made for hire; those works eventually fall into the public domain.

Duration of Copyright

Copyrights last a long time, but the length of time differs depending on whether the work is made for hire or not. Today, the copyright for a work made for hire lasts until the earlier of ninety-five years from the date it was published or 120 years from the date it was created. The copyright term for a work not made for hire is the lifetime of the author plus seventy years. If there are two or more authors, the copyright will last for seventy years after the death of the last surviving authors. So, if you wrote a piece of music in 2020, your copyright would last until seventy years after your death, then would pass into the public domain.

PURPOSE OF COPYRIGHT PROTECTION

The underlying purpose of copyright law is to recognize the competing interests of protecting the commercial interests of creative people, like musicians, and the broader interests of allowing the public access to that creative output to advance creative culture, generally. The statute says *"to promote the progress of the useful arts by giving creators exclusive rights to their works for a while."*[6] This *for a while* language is what people point to when they say that copyright is a "limited duration monopoly" on content.

Criteria for Protection

In order to be eligible for copyright protection, the work must fit the following criteria: a work of originality, showing some degree of creativity, reduced to tangible form. The originality requirement is the crux of copyright protection. The music for which you are seeking copyright protection must be original to you as its owner. Only content owners (including those given ownership rights contractually) can enjoy the bundle of rights that are granted through copyright protection. As an owner, you receive a limited monopoly in determining who can use your creative content and how it can be used. Think of your music in the same way as your car: you can decide to never let anyone else drive your car, or you can set restrictions on who you'll let drive it and under what circumstances.

Further, though it's not explicitly stated in the statute, the expectation is that the content you seek to protect is creative enough to merit protection. The creativity element of copyright protection may seem redundant, but it's actually important because copyright protection can be extended to people who put a new spin on content that is already protected by copyright. For example, a "best of" compilation of love songs or short stories can be copyrighted and sold as a collection because the compilation itself requires some subjective analysis and decision-making. The underlying love songs or short stories themselves are still protected by their creators, and permission to publish them in a collection is still required, but the assembly of the songs or stories into a collection can be copyrighted because choosing and compiling them into a collection demonstrates creativity.

Ideas not reduced to tangible form are not capable of copyright protection, but once the idea has been expressed in a format that can be touched or held, then the content can be protected as an expression of the idea. If you have an idea you want to safeguard, copyright is not the right avenue to pursue; instead, your best option will likely be a confidentiality agreement, also known as a nondisclosure agreement (NDA) that might contain a noncompete clause; see Chapter 13 for a discussion of NDAs and other useful contracts for musicians.

THE RIGHTS GRANTED

There are six basic rights embodied in Section 106 of the Copyright Act. But, like so many rights, they are not absolute; Sections 107–122 of the statute provide limitations on the "limited duration monopoly."

Subject to those limitations, copyright owners have the exclusive right to

1. reproduce the copyrighted work;
2. prepare derivative works based upon the copyrighted work;
3. distribute copies of the copyrighted work to the public;
4. perform the copyrighted work publicly;
5. display the copyrighted work publicly; and
6. perform the copyrighted work publicly by means of a digital audio transmission.

Each is discussed below.

The Reproduction Right

The reproduction right refers to your right to control who can make copies of your work. Under Section 106(1), copyright owners have the sole right to make copies of their work subject to the statutory limitations. If someone makes a copy of a piece of music written by you and reduced to tangible form without your permission, that would constitute copyright infringement because the right to reproduce it is yours alone. For musicians, this right applies to musical compositions in notation and in records—referred to as *sound recordings* in the statute. Sound recordings is defined as follows:

> works that result from fixation of a series of musical, spoken, or other sounds . . . regardless of the nature of the material objects, such as disks, tapes, or other phonorecords, in which they are embodied.[7]

One of the most important limitations on the rights afforded under Section 106(1) is the *compulsory mechanical license* right provided in Section 115. The term *mechanical license* refers to the way wax records used to be made by a mechanical pressing. A compulsory license is a type that cannot be denied by the copyright owner. So, a compulsory mechanical license is the right to make your own recording of a pre-recorded piece of music. In other words, a cover version; see Chapter 12 for a discussion of music licensing and the compulsory mechanical licensing exception under the Copyright Act.

The Right to Creative Derivative Works

Often referred to as an *adaptation right*, Section 106(2) refers to new works created (derived) from one that already exists. The right to create a new work from an existing work is reserved for the copyright owner. Examples of a derivative work include reworking an existing piece of classical music and making a jazz version of it. This is where it gets tricky: while the copyright owner has the exclusive right to make a derivative work based on their own original, musicians who obtain a mechanical license to make a cover recording of it are allowed to make minor changes to your original provided they don't substantially change it to the extent that they are improperly creating a derivative work. Section 115(2) of the statute addresses this specifically as follows:

> A compulsory license includes the privilege of making a musical arrangement of the work to the extent necessary to conform it to the style or manner of interpretation of the performance involved, but the arrangement shall not change the basic melody or fundamental character of the work, and shall not be subject to protection as a derivative work under this title, except with the express consent of the copyright owner.

In other words, if you grant another musician a license to make a cover of one of your songs, that license allows them to make a recording with insubstantial changes to the basic structure of the song and release it to the public. If they wanted to rework the song by changing its fundamental character, they would have to first obtain your permission because substantial changes would constitute making a derivative work.

The Right to Distribute

The right to distribute, provided in Section 106(3), refers to your exclusive right to sell, license, or even give away your copyrighted material to others. However, Section 109(a) of the statute places a limitation on your right as the copyright owner to control all downstream distribution of your work. Specifically, it allows people who have lawfully purchased a copy of your material to sell or otherwise transfer their copy to a third party. Section 109(a) provides the following:

> Notwithstanding the provisions of section 106(3), the owner of a particular copy or phonorecord lawfully made under this title, or any person authorized by such owner, is entitled, without the authority of the copyright owner, to sell or otherwise dispose of the possession of that copy or phonorecord.

So, as the copyright owner, you only get to control the first sale of your material. Purchasers can resell copies of your CD, sheet music, or other copyrighted material provided they obtained those copies lawfully.

The Right to Perform

The right to perform refers to the public performance right, but public performance isn't restricted to live shows—it also refers to transmission of performances through television, radio, and other media. Under Section 106(4), copyright owners have the exclusive right to perform their copyrighted musical compositions in public and to authorize others to perform their material in public. This right includes live and recorded/transmitted material such as playing a recording of your music in a restaurant, bar, or even a supermarket over the sound system.

These public performance rights are often referred to as "small rights" to distinguish them from "grand rights." Small rights are the performance rights for non-dramatic works; grand rights are the rights to perform dramatic works such as Broadway musicals. See Chapter 12 for a discussion of performance rights and the organizations that serve as administrative intermediaries between artists/rightsholders and those seeking to license copyrighted content.

The Right to Display

The 106(5) right to display is a bit odd in the music context, but makes perfect sense for visual artists. Think of it as an exclusive right for musicians to control how their music or lyrics are displayed on merchandise. For example, Billy Idol as the writer of the famous song "White Wedding" has the exclusive right to control the use of the lyrics *Nice day for a white wedding*," so if a bridal shop wanted to use the lyrics on its shop awning, the owners should get permission or risk the chance of being sued for copyright infringement.

The Right to Control Public Performance by Digital Audio Transmission

The newest exclusive right, under Section 106(6), is specific to sound recordings. It was added to the Copyright Act to address a loophole in previous versions of the law relating to digital audio transmission of sound recordings. Technology has evolved quickly in the last two decades, and copyright law has been slow to keep pace. Section 106(6) refers to the exclusive right to public performance by digital audio transmission.

HOW YOUR RIGHTS ACCRUE

The moment your original content is reduced to tangible format, you have limited copyright protection even if you haven't released your content to the public or ever used it. *Limited protection*, in this instance, means you don't have the full power of the copyright statute available to you. Specifically, since you haven't registered your copyright, you'll have to do that before you can initiate an infringement suit[8] and you'll have to prove with specificity that an infringing use caused you to lose income, which may be difficult to do. See "Why You Should Register," below, for details on the benefits of timely registration of your copyright.

COPYRIGHT INFRINGEMENT

Infringement of copyright is a legal claim made by a copyright owner/rightsholder alleging that another person or entity is violating one or more of the exclusive rights spelled out in Section 106 of the Copyright Act. Parties to a lawsuit can be individuals, groups of people, or entities. The party bringing the lawsuit is the plaintiff and, like in a criminal case, the person or entity defending themselves in the lawsuit is the defendant. In a copyright infringement case, the plaintiff is saying that the defendant used or is using the plaintiff's content unlawfully. In order to file a copyright infringement lawsuit, the copyright must first be registered with the Library of Congress and the legal action must be brought within the statutory period for bringing such claims.

Copyright infringement lawsuits are particularly expensive to bring and to defend because of the specialized expertise required to prove or defend against infringement allegations. In addition to needing an experienced trial attorney, you need an attorney well-versed in copyright law who also has a strong understanding of the industry in which the infringing activity is occurring (music, dance, literature, etc.). Additional expenses include those for expert witnesses to break down complicated concepts for juries to help them determine the relevant facts.

Because these lawsuits are so expensive, the usual order in which these things progress is the person or entity with rights to enforce will send the alleged infringer a *cease and desist letter*[9] that spells out that they have rights to enforce; that their rights are being infringed; and that the alleged infringer should immediately stop the infringing activity or face a copyright infringement lawsuit. See Chapter 13 for sample language for a cease and desist letter.

Damages

If someone is infringing your content, you have three to five years to bring a lawsuit depending on whether criminal activity is alleged. If you have registered your copyright in a timely manner, you can be awarded statutory damages instead of having to prove what your actual losses are and how much the infringer profited from your copyrighted material. Statutory damages include up to $30,000 in damages for each work infringed and up to $150,000 if you can prove that the infringement was willful and for financial gain.[10] As noted above, you have to register your copyright in order to sue an infringer, but most important is the timing of your registration: you can register your copyright after discovering the infringement, but the amount of money you could be awarded as damages will be severely limited; see "Why You Should Register," below.

Defenses to Copyright Infringement

You've certainly heard of self-defense in the context of a murder charge. Legal defenses don't say that the activity never occurred; they argue that the activity was justified or otherwise permitted according to one of the defenses available. In the context of a murder charge, defendants claiming self-defense acknowledge the killing, but say that it was justified in a way the law allows.

Similarly, there are several legal defenses available to people or entities accused of copyright infringement. Some of these defenses are built into the copyright statute while others have been interpreted to exist by a court upon hearing both sides of an argument in a copyright infringement lawsuit. Here are the defenses I think you should know about:

1. The statute of limitations has run
2. Parody
3. Innocence
4. The work at issue was independently created
5. The activity was authorized pursuant to a license
6. A Fair Use exception applies
7. The unauthorized use was transformative in nature

Statute of Limitations

Statutes of limitations are prescribed time periods for bringing a legal action. For a basic copyright infringement claim, the statute of limitations is three years from the date of the last infringing activity.[11] There is a longer statute of limitations for criminal claims; these must be brought within five years.[12] Once that time period has passed, the legal action cannot be sustained. This rule encourages you, as a copyright owner, to be vigilant in protecting your interests by periodically searching for unauthorized uses of your content, generally, and closely monitoring the uses you granted to others by license.

Parody

Using others' protected content in a comedic parody does not generally constitute infringement. Parody is considered critical commentary and is tied to one's First Amendment right of free speech. For example, late night television hosts using politicians' own writings to mock them is protected use because the subject matter is newsworthy and a matter of public record (as opposed to constituting a form of fictional, creative expression) and the use is provided for comedic effect.

Innocence

The innocence defense is more than *"I had no idea I was infringing another's copyright."* Pleading ignorance won't get you very far. The innocence defense is available in a situation when the user, exercising good faith, sought and received a license or assignment of rights from the person or entity who claimed to have the legal rights to grant the license or assignment, but who, in reality, did not. So, in this scenario, where the true owner (or other rightsholder) is suing the content user, that user can raise the innocence defense by demonstrating to the court that they thought their use was lawful. For example, if a musician gave you written permission to make an a cappella arrangement of a piece of music they'd written, and you were later sued by their publisher, you might raise the defense that you thought you were obtaining permission lawfully from the composer you had a good faith belief to be the appropriate rightsholder. The innocence defense is not available to those defending themselves in a copyright infringement suit in which a copyright notice was provided on the content infringed. Further, attaching notice may even lend credence to a plaintiff's claims of willful infringement, making statutory damages available to the rightsholder.[13]

Independently Created

This defense is available in situations where a person being sued for copyright infringement can prove that the content at issue did not belong to the plaintiff, but rather was independently created by the defendant. Essentially, *"we both had the same idea; I did not know they created the same thing around the same time."* Another situation in which this defense could be applicable is where a defendant can prove that their content was first in time—in other words, it actually predates the content the plaintiff is alleging was used improperly. A copyright infringement claim may fail under these circumstances because no infringement can be proven.

Authorized Pursuant to a License

This defense arises most often when content licensors and licensees disagree about the scope of the rights granted. For example, if you grant a synchronization license to a documentary filmmaker to use a sixteen-bar cut of one of your songs in a film, but discovered after the film is released that the entire song was used, you (or, more likely, your publisher) would likely contact the licensee to request an additional fee for the expanded use. If the licensee refuses to pay it and you brought an infringement action against them, they would likely raise this defense saying that they properly licensed the content from you and perhaps the parameters of the licensed use were vague.

Fair Use

Fair use is another limitation of the exclusive rights contained in Section 106 of the Copyright Act.[14] A fair use is an unauthorized use of another's protected content that was nonetheless determined to be fair after the issue is determined through litigation.

The question of what constitutes fair use is often murky because there will rarely be a definitive answer and there are no simple rules to follow in order to protect yourself. When considering whether an unauthorized use is "fair," courts look to answer the following questions:

1. What was the point of the use? Was it for generating profit or for nonprofit purposes?
2. Was the source material factual content or was it a form of fictional, creative expression?
3. How much of the original source material was used and how substantial to the whole piece was the portion used?
4. What effect did this use have on the source material's market? In other words, did the use result in a negative impact on the owner's ability to license or sell the source material?

Let's consider a hypothetical situation in which you, as a songwriter, were looking for lyrics for a song you ultimately planned to release. You used one stanza of a poem comprised of eight stanzas in one of your songs without obtaining permission from the rightsholder, the poet's publisher. If the publisher initiates an infringement suit and you raise a fair use defense alleging that your use was fair and does not constitute infringement, the court should apply the following analysis:

The Purpose of Your Use

You used the stanza from the poem as lyrics for a song, which constitutes a for-profit purpose; this works against your fair use argument.

Source of the Material Used

The source material was from a fictionalized poem—a form of creative expression, not a news report or other form of factual content. Factual content like news reports or historical events are generally considered to be more akin to commentary and matters of public interest, and therefore their use would lean more toward being "fair." In this instance, you used fictionalized, creative content, which would work against you in a fair use analysis.

Amount and Substantiality of Your Use

You only used one stanza of eight, but you used a stanza in its entirety. This could go either way. For example, you only used an eighth of the poem, but each stanza will contain refrain material that is repeated several times throughout the poem. The repeated material in a poem serves as a poetic binding agent and will assume the same level of importance as the chorus in a song. So, this fact would lean away from a fair use defense.

Effect on the Poem's Market

Your song will likely not affect the market for a poem; although, depending on your stature as a songwriter, it could potentially have a positive impact on the poem, its author, and the publisher.

In the end, it's a guessing game as to how a court would decide matters like this one. I've heard the fair use doctrine referred to as "a shield, not a sword." This means that you only get to raise fair use as a defense once you're already being sued for copyright infringement. Relying on fair use as a pass from obtaining prior permission is a risky proposition and one you would be wise to avoid.

COPYRIGHT OFFICE'S FAIR USE INDEX

The Copyright Office has a very cool (and free) tool available on their website—a searchable database called the Fair Use Index. You can search it to see how the fair use factors have been used to determine the outcome of copyright infringement cases across the United States by year, jurisdiction, and topic category. You can choose up to sixteen categories, including music, parody, photography, and news reporting, and the search results clearly tell you whether fair use was found or not found. It's very easy to use and understand. Check it out!

Transformative Use

Probably the least reliable of the copyright defenses is *transformative use*. This defense is relatively new and is based on the idea that some unauthorized uses of another's copyrighted material can constitute fair use if the original is transformed to the extent that the new work isn't even a derivative work—in other words, the original has been completely transformed by new expression or additional value resulting in a new use or a new understanding of it.

Case in point: the hip-hop group 2 Live Crew's use of a portion of Roy Orbison's "Oh, Pretty Woman."[15] The group used a section of the Orbison tune's well-known baseline set to different music and lyrics in their song "Pretty Woman." Orbison's publisher sued for infringement and lost. The court held that because the group's use of the distinctive baseline under their lyrics about "hairy woman" and "big hairy woman," 2 Live Crew's use of the source material was "transformative in nature" and therefore constituted fair use. Essentially, the court concluded that when 2 Live Crew put their comedic lyrics over the well-known baseline, their use transformed Orbison's song by poking fun at the emphasis American culture places on appearance.

WHY YOU SHOULD REGISTER

As noted above, you don't need to have registered your copyright or have released your content to the public to have copyright protection. The moment you put your music into tangible form, you have some protection, but registration is where the real muscle is.

Benefits of Copyright Registration

If you discover that your content is being infringed, you'll have to register it in order to bring a legal action, but more importantly, unless you've registered your copyright within three months of publication, you will have to prove with specificity that you've lost money because of the infringement. If you timely registered your copyright, you don't need to prove that the infringing use caused you to lose income; the statute provides a financial remedy (statutory damages) without having to prove actual lost income.[16] In some circumstances, you may also be entitled to additional damages from willful infringement as well as having the infringer pay your attorney fees. So, registration provides substantial benefits that are especially important for those who may be unable to show they suffered actual lost income as the result of an infringing use of their content.

Preregistration

Preregistration is not the same as registration and it's not merely registering early. Preregistration is a special service permitted by the Copyright Office since 2005. It recognizes that some classes of copyright categories, including musical compositions and recordings, are at heightened risk for infringement during the collaboration and development phase. For $140, content creators can preregister their works by submitting an online application without having to also provide a deposit (samples of the work). The conditions for preregistration require the work must be (1) from one of the categories allowed for preregistration; (2) unpublished (not yet released publicly); and (3) in the process of being prepared for commercial release or the reasonable expectation of commercial release.[17] Preregistration is not registration—it's early protection in anticipation of registration. Preregistered works must be registered within one month of you becoming aware of an infringing use and no later than three months after initial publication of the work.

Renewal No Longer Required

Copyright protection used to exist for twenty-eight years and had to be renewed in the twenty-eighth year for an additional term of protection; not anymore. Copyrights registered after 1978 don't need to be renewed. Additionally, since 1978, the © indicator is no longer required to show that a work is protected under copyright, but it is still a good idea to include it in the footer of your material to put people on notice that you have rights you intend to enforce and to preempt claims of innocent infringement.

REGISTERING YOUR COPYRIGHT ONLINE

The Copyright Office will allow paper registrations by mail, but registering electronically through eCO, the Electronic Copyright Office Registration System, www.copyright.gov/registration, will be both faster and cheaper, and allow you to track your registration status.

There are different application forms depending on what you are registering. Form PA (for Performing Arts) is a commonly used form for musicians registering one piece of music. Review the form to familiarize yourself with its questions and instructions. If you plan to register multiple related works, you may be able to do that in one application, but it's not the Collective Works form—that's reserved for registering multiple works by different authors in one collection. Instead, use the Group of Unpublished Works application form to register up to ten unpublished works simultaneously via one application. There are some restrictions for using this form, so you'll need to review the requirements closely.[18] For example, all the works registered using this application must be unpublished, of the same type (e.g., all songs), and by the same author(s). So, if you wrote a group of songs using different lyricists, you likely would not be able to use the Group of Unpublished Works application because the writers are not exactly the same for each song. See "Copyright Resources," below.

You'll likely notice that these applications use odd language—it's because the terminology is taken directly from the copyright statute. For example, when you register your content with the Copyright Office, you are making a copyright "claim." Don't confuse this language with a copyright infringement claim; just follow the instructions closely.

Regardless of the registration route you decide to take, I recommend taking it slow to make a few important preparations.

Preparing Your Music for Registration

1. Finalize Your Content

   Fix any errors and otherwise make sure that the version you are registering is the best version because you will submit copies of it as part of a "mandatory deposit" with the Copyright Office.

2. Catalog Your Content

   Create some form of a cataloging system for organizing your music. For example, if you are a songwriter, you might create an Excel template or Word table for keeping track of your musical works with titles, co-writers, split sheet information,[19] source of lyrics, dates of creation, dates of publication, copyright registration filing dates, and copyright registration numbers. If you've received any permissions including for lyrics or sampling, include columns for those details as well. You'll need all this information if you plan to license your music anyway, so best to start these good habits now.

3. Gather Application Details

   Review the application form and instructions first.

   a. Title of your work(s) including past titles you've used for each

   b. If from a collection, list the pieces this way: Song Cycle Name, Song Title Name

    c. Nature of authorship (indicate whether you are the author, co-author, etc.)

    d. Year the work was completed

    e. Date content was made publicly available, if applicable

    f. Whether the work being registered is a derivative work or not

4. Check Out Circular 4—Copyright Office Fees

    Understand the office's fee structure; get your credit card out or create a deposit account if you plan to register a lot of content.

5. Get Resources Lined Up

    You may want to pull up the Copyright Office's FAQ/helpdesk materials, www.copyright.gov/eco/help, and have them handy in the event any questions arise (as they surely will).

6. Check Your Technology

    Safari and Chrome are not currently certified for use with eCO, so you'll need to review the information relating to browsers the eCO system supports, disable any pop-up blocker, and temporarily adjust your security and privacy settings.

STEPS TO COPYRIGHT REGISTRATION (AKA *MAKING A COPYRIGHT CLAIM*)

1. Create a User Account; consider saving your information as a template for future registration.

2. Complete the online application.

3. Pay the fee.

4. Make the mandatory deposit of copies.

5. Print, sign, and submit your application.

6. Record your receipt information confirming payment and registration submission.

7. File your registration certificate once it arrives in the mail (these are not emailed, so you'll need to provide a valid postal address).

Questions? Contact the Copyright Office at (877) 476-0778, (202) 707-3000, or visit www.copyright.gov/eco/help/.

THE COPY*LEFT* MOVEMENT

Some believe the copyright regime currently used throughout the world is too restrictive and has a stifling effect on creativity and the creative economy. The Creative Commons, a nonprofit organization founded in 2001, is part of a larger movement (known as *copyleft*) whose mission is to provide an alternative to copyright by building a richer public domain.[20] The founders of Creative Commons developed a novel licensing approach that gives creators the opportunity to control their work by way of six different licensing schemes that provide free, automatic use rights with varying degrees of restrictions. For example, of the six licenses, some allow commercial use, some do not; some allow derivative uses; and some control how the content subject to the license is distributed. All require attribution (credit) to the content owner.

It remains to be seen what impact, if any, the Creative Commons or the *copyleft movement*, generally, might have on the music industry and its entrenched position using music licensing as a means for musicians to exploit and draw income from their creative output. We are at a time in history when some musicians intentionally take a pass on traditional pathways for establishing themselves in the industry. These entrepreneurs self-produce and record their work, release their digital music via the Internet, connect directly with their fans via social media, and create and sell their own branded merchandise. In this newer, more direct model where traditional gatekeepers are being circumvented completely, it's possible to imagine a music industry of the future comprised of fewer intermediaries in which music licensing (and copyright) becomes less important. See Chapter 12 for a discussion of both music licensing and public domain.

CONCLUSION

There's no way around it—copyright law is complicated. While the statute continues to be updated to keep pace with evolving technology and the resulting loopholes these advances create, it remains an imperfect solution. To my thinking, the statute's shortcomings result from the breadth of the categories that fall within its scope and the limitations inherent in finding adequate vocabulary to put safeguarding rules around artistic expression. I think the takeaway for musicians is to understand what copyright can and cannot provide you in terms of protecting your creative output. Make peace with its shortfalls and embrace the benefits it is capable of providing you—specifically those you are entitled to from timely federal registration.

COPYRIGHT RESOURCES

Music Copyright Law by David J. Moser and Cheryl L. Slay (Course Technology, Cengage Learning)

Patent, Copyright & Trademark by Stephen Elias and edited by Lisa Goldoftas (Nolo)

In addition to an excellent FAQ section, the U.S. Copyright Office, www.copyright.gov, provides many useful circulars by topic to help you understand this complicated and often murky area of federal law. These are the circulars I think will be most useful to you:

Circular 1, *Copyright Basics*
Circular 2, *Copyright Registration*
Circular 4, *Copyright Office Fees*
Circular 9, *Works Made for Hire*
Circular 11, *Using the Single Application*
Circular 14, *Copyright in Derivative Works and Compilations*
Circular 15A, *Duration of Copyright*
Circular 16A, *How to Obtain Permission*
Circular 22, *How to Investigate the Copyright Status of a Work*
Circular 23, *Copyright Card Catalog and the Online File*
Circular 30, *Works Made for Hire*
Circular 34, *Multiple Works*
Circular 38A, *International Copyright Relations of the United States*
Circular 50, *Copyright Registrations of Musical Compositions*
Circular 73A, *Compulsory License for Making and Distributing Phonorecords*
Circular 73B, *Compulsory License for Making and Distributing Digital Phonorecords*

COPYRIGHT QUIZ

1. Karl showed his musician buddy, Sal, a backbeat he developed, but hadn't yet used or otherwise shared with anyone else. Several months later, Karl heard Sal play the backbeat at a gig without ever asking Karl for his permission. If Karl brings a copyright infringement case against Sal alleging that Sal stole his backbeat, would Karl likely succeed?

2. Continuing with the same hypothetical, with the facts changed slightly: Karl recorded his backbeat and sent it by phone to Sal as an audio file saying "*check it out*." Several months later, Karl goes to one of Sal's gigs and hears the backbeat played. If Karl brings a copyright infringement case against Sal alleging that Sal stole his backbeat, would Karl likely succeed?

3. Same hypothetical as 1, but this time rather than the entire backbeat, only a portion was used in a piece Sal wrote. If Karl brings a copyright infringement case against Sal alleging that Sal improperly used his backbeat, would Karl likely succeed?

4. Same hypothetical as 3 except, in this version, Sal is a public school music teacher using Karl's backbeat in an original school musical. Do you think Sal can safely rely on the fair use doctrine as a defense to a copyright infringement allegation?

5. Maggie, a member of a community cello ensemble, purchased the sheet music for a song written by Alicia Keys and made an arrangement of it for her cello ensemble. If Keys's publisher learns about this and brings a legal action against Maggie alleging that she is violating the copyright, Maggie is probably on the right side of the law because she purchased the music. True or false?

6. Same hypothetical as immediately above, except in this version, Maggie is a high school friend of Keys and received permission from the artist to make the arrangement. What do you think now?

7. Tony is a self-described Beyoncé super fan. He makes a modest income by making and selling Beyoncé mash-up videos and high-quality ringtones. To protect himself against allegations of copyright infringement, Tony uses the phrase "*Ownership is neither implied nor intended*" in all his video and print collateral to make clear he is not the owner of the videos. What do you think?

8. Same hypothetical as immediately above, except Tony donates the income to one of Beyoncé's favorite charities. What difference, if any, would that make?

9. Would your answer be different if, rather than making any money, Tony was making videos and ringtones as a hobby and sharing them with other Beyoncé fans?

10. What if Tony found the video owners' names and provided their credits; how much protection does that give him if copyright infringement is alleged?

An analysis of these hypothetical situations is provided in Appendix B.

NOTES

1. "Published" refers to the statutory definition of publication. In this case, it means the date you distributed the piece by sale or other form of transfer (or the offer of same) to a third party. See 17 USC §101 for the full definition of publication under the Copyright Act.

2. Article I §8[8].

3. 17 USC §102.

4. Remember, an "author" under the Copyright Act refers to any creator of protected content, not just writers. If you wrote a song, under the Copyright Act, you are an *author*.

5. One of the things that makes this murky is that the U.S. Supreme Court, in the case of *Community for Creative Non-Violence v. Reid*, has interpreted "employee" broadly in this context, so there are circumstances of the work situation that could give rise to an employee-employer relationship. Best to use contracts that spell out the nature of the worker-hirer relationship and the parties' intent with respect to ownership of content resulting from the work arrangement.

6. Article I-§8[8].

7. 17 USC §101.

8. 17 USC §411(a).

9. A cease and desist letter is a demand by someone to immediately stop doing something. In the context of copyright, it's a threat of potential legal action by a rightsholder if the allegedly infringing behavior continues. The rightsholder is hoping the threat will work because the cost of the letter is much less expensive and time-consuming than bringing a lawsuit.

10. 17 USC §504(c)(1) and (2).

11. 17 USC §507(b).

12. 17 USC §507(a).

13. 17 USC §401(d).

14. 17 USC §107.

15. *Campbell v. Acuff-Rose Music*, 510 U.S. 569 (1994).

16. United States Copyright Office, "Copyright Basics," www.copyright.gov/circs/circ01.pdf.

17. 17 USC §408(f).

18. Because the Copyright Office's requirements are periodically clarified or changed, I won't provide them here; rather, I'll direct you to the following resources: Circular 2 (Copyright Registration), Circular 34 (Multiple Works), and *The Compendium of U.S. Copyright Office Practices: Chapter 1100*, www.copyright.gov/comp3/chap1100/ch1100-registration-multiple-works.pdf.

19. A split sheet is a simple memorandum signed by all co-writers that spells out each writer's ownership interest in a song.

20. Wikipedia, "Creative Commons," wikipedia.org/wiki/Creative_Commons.

Music Licensing Basics

This chapter is organized as a tool to help you understand the complicated, overlapping areas of music licensing—especially if you are a songwriter/composer or other type of content creator. Licensing provides an important vehicle for songwriters and other content creators to make money from their creative output. People often complain about the restrictions found in U.S. copyright laws, but without copyright, making income through music licensing wouldn't be possible because there wouldn't be any need to obtain permission and pay a licensing fee. Without music licenses, musicians would lose one of their primary sources of income.

This chapter will benefit musicians who license their content to others—either through intermediaries (such as publishers or agents) or directly by handling their own licensing administration. It will also be useful for those interested in lawfully using others' content by providing a framework for the type of license needed.

Throughout the chapter, you'll see reference to music publishers. Music publishers do much more than print sheet music. Music publishers

discover and promote songwriting talent . . . and provide important business services for their songwriters. These services include pitching their song catalog to music executives, recording artists, producers, managers and others to secure placement for the songs on appropriate commercial recordings. In addition, music publishers finance and produce demo recordings, pitch songs for television shows, movies, and commercials, issue licenses, and collect royalties . . . and register works with the U.S. Copyright Office and enforce copyrights they own or administer.[1]

Much more than this however, publishers are the hub to the music industry's many spokes. As the industry's gatekeepers, publishers take a percentage of all licensing fees that pass through them, acting as intermediaries between the musicians who create the music and anyone interested in licensing the rights to use the music.

Before introducing the types of licenses commonly used in the music industry, you first should understand the difference between licenses and assignments. Assignments and licenses are contracts—usually they are written, but not always. The general rule is that exclusive rights (via assignment or license) must be in writing, but a non-exclusive license doesn't need to be in writing to be valid and enforceable.

ASSIGNMENTS

As the owner of content, you can sell your copyright in exchange for a flat fee or, more commonly, you can sell your content in exchange for a periodic payment of royalties from sales. Under copyright law, selling your rights is called an *assignment*. It means you've transferred 100% of the bundle of rights afforded content creators under Section 106 of the Copyright Act (the Act). For example, when I was offered a contract to write this book, I assigned my rights to the publisher in exchange for a royalty on the net profits from sales. Theoretically, I could have only given away *some* of my rights, although in book sales that's rare, if not impossible.

LICENSES

Transferring only some of your rights to a third party is called a *license*. Under copyright law, when you license your content to another person or entity, you are transferring some of your Section 106 rights away while retaining others, including ownership of the content licensed. The person or entity granting rights via a license is the *licensor*; the person or entity being granted the license is the *licensee*.

A Licensing Primer

A license can be as flexible or restrictive as the licensor wants it to be. Often, the broader the rights granted, the higher the cost of the license; the more restrictive the terms of the license, the lower the cost. Licenses can be restricted in any number of ways including by content, duration, geography, use, transferability, manner, and exclusivity. When I was working on the website for my consulting business, Enterprising Artist Consulting, I came across a dictionary definition of the word *enterprising* from the *Collins English Dictionary*. I especially liked the *Collins* definition because I thought it captured the idea that an enterprising musician is one who shows initiative and embraces the idea that they are the CEO of their own personal brand; they are adventurous, energetic, and forward-thinking.

So, I wrote to HarperCollins Publishing and asked for permission to use their definition and its phonetic rendering on my website and, possibly, in the end papers of my first book. After some time, I received permission outlining the terms of the license (called a "print license") and instructions on paying the fee (about $90).

By way of example, here's how Collins restricted the use of their definition through my license (which was a simple one-page contract):

Content

I was granted permission to use their definition provided I didn't make any changes to it or use it in any negative or derogatory context. The latter part of this restriction is called *moral rights*. Moral rights refers to a content owner's right to not have the licensee use the content in any manner that could be considered disparaging to its owner. Moral rights also includes the right of attribution (credit).

Duration

My use is permitted for the life of the first edition of my first book and any revised editions for a print run of up to 5,000 copies. No permission was given for further reprints or a second edition, although a new license could be negotiated for either in good faith.

Geographic

Permission was granted to me for worldwide use.

Type of Use
My permission is for English language only.

Transferability
Transferability is restricted. This means I cannot transfer the rights granted to me to another person. For example, I can't sublicense my right from Collins to someone else.

Manner
Permission was given for Braille, large type, and sound recordings provided no charge is made to the visually handicapped.

Exclusivity
I was granted a non-exclusive license, which means they reserved the right to also license the definition to anyone else who might be interested in using it.

Other
Finally, my license also restricted my ability to confer any benefit or right on any third party relating to the use of the definition. This means, primarily, that if I never used the license or died before I could exercise the rights it gives me, no one else could use the license or pursue a return of the license fee I paid.

I felt the fee was reasonable, but if I wanted to loosen any of the restrictions Collins put on my license, I likely would have been asked to pay more for the expanded use.

MUSIC LICENSING

The terms *music licensing* and *music clearance* are sometimes used interchangeably, but music licensing has a broader meaning. As noted above, a license is a formal way of giving someone permission to do something in which you, as the licensor, retain some of your rights. Music clearance refers to the process of obtaining permission for licenses—most often by music supervisors looking for synchronization rights to use a piece of music for television or film.

Music licensing can be broken down into two categories: grand performing rights (*grand rights*) and small performing rights (*small rights*). There is no statutory definition of these two categories; their distinction has been largely dependent on industry practice. The difference between the two is whether the performance rights involve a dramatic presentation using some form of storyline supplemented by stage action or not.

Musicals, operas, plays, and ballets are considered dramatic works because they involve some form of connective through-story or plot within a dramatic setting. To obtain permission to license rights to a Broadway musical, play, opera, or ballet, you would be asking for a grand performing rights ("theatrical") license. These licenses are typically issued by the rightsholders directly—usually the publisher, administrator of the composer or playwright's estate, or author's agent.

The rights for all other music licenses fall within the category of small rights. Small rights are more complicated because there are several different types and different entities serving as rightsholder intermediaries (administering licensing rights under a contract with the content creators). The general categories of small performing rights licenses are (1) mechanical licenses; (2) synchronization licenses; (3) public performance licenses; (4) master use licenses; and (5) print licenses.

Mechanical Licenses

If you want to record and publicly distribute music (not written by you) by way of a sound recording (records, CDs, ringtones, audio tapes, permanent digital downloads, or on-demand streaming, etc.), you'll need a mechanical license. Mechanical licenses are specific to sound recordings. Think of a mechanical license as the formal permission to record and publicly release a piece of music written by someone else. The Copyright Act provides a bundle of rights to content creators (like musicians) provided certain criteria are met. Section 106(1) of the Act reserves the right of reproduction of copyrighted content to its author/creator. Section 106(3) provides the exclusive right of distribution of those reproduced copies.

Despite the 106(1) reproduction right, Section 115 of the code provides an important exception: the compulsory mechanical license. A compulsory mechanical license is permission to make a cover recording to release publicly—it's "compulsory" because under the copyright code, the songwriter cannot deny you permission. You don't need a mechanical license to record and release music written only by you. If you co-wrote a song, you would need permission from your co-author, but that wouldn't be a mechanical license. The fees paid for a mechanical license are split between the songwriter(s) and the writer's publisher(s), if any. So, songwriters make income by licensing rights to their compositions to others.

It works like this: If piece of music was recorded and released by the person who wrote it, the writer cannot deny you permission to do the same due to the compulsory mechanical license exception found in Section 115 of the copyright statute. If, however, a piece of written music was never recorded and released to the public (or was recorded, but never released), the writer *can* deny you permission to use it. See Chapter 11 for a discussion of the copyright monopoly and this important exception to it under Section 115 of the copyright statute.

The fees for compulsory mechanical licenses are determined by the Copyright Royalty Board. The fee structure contemplates the length of the song and the number of units sold.[2] The amount of money you would owe the songwriter for the license is referred to as the *statutory rate*. Statutory rates periodically change, but the current rate for a compulsory mechanical license is the greater of 9.1 cents per song, up to five minutes in length, or 1.75 cents per minute if longer than five minutes. So, if an artist recorded one cover song of four minutes in length and made 100,000 copies to release to the public, the cover artist would have to pay the songwriter $9,100.[3] For other licensing rates, see the Harry Fox Agency (HFA) website,[4] www.harryfox.com.

Sound recordings have two copyrights: one in the underlying musical composition and one in the recording of it. In the example provided above, if one musician wrote the piece of music, they would likely have assigned their bundle of rights in the composition to their publisher in exchange for periodic royalty payments. That same musician likely also assigned their rights in the recording to the record label in exchange for funding and marketing the recording. Compulsory mechanical licenses only apply to sound recordings—not printed music or public performance rights. Mechanical licenses allow only minor changes to the composition to suit a musical artist's style. If you wanted to make substantial changes to another writer's composition, a mechanical license would not apply; you would need to go to the rightsholder (likely the writer's publisher) to obtain permission to create a derivative work. See "Print Licenses," below.

- a film;
- a television show;
- a television or Internet commercial;
- a video (including on YouTube); or
- a video game.

Typically, the publisher is the rightsholder to the musical composition and the record label holds the rights to the sound recording. So, if you wrote a piece of music that a filmmaker heard and wants to use in a new film, the filmmaker would be required to obtain a synch license from your publisher, who would negotiate a fee on your behalf. Once the publisher agrees to the license, the record label will often also allow the license provided it is compensated at the same amount. For example, if the publisher agrees to accept $2,500 for use of the composition, the record label will usually also agree to $2,500 for use of the recording.

This contract-related practice of sharing equal payment information—whether oral or written—is nicknamed *Most Favored Nations*. While it's not specific to music licensing, it's common to synch deals in which the publisher will share with the record label the amount they are charging for use of the composition, so the label can charge the exact same amount for use of the recording.

As noted above, your publisher can deny a synch license, but if someone wants to make a cover of your song, a compulsory mechanical license cannot be denied—as long as you recorded the song and released it to the public, another artist can do the same provided they pay you the statutory royalty rate.

Public Performance Licenses

The public performance right is granted exclusively to authors (content creators) under Section 106(4) and (6) of the Copyright Act. The 106(4) right is for public performance, generally, while the newer, 106(6) right is specific to the digital audio transmission of sound recordings. Public performance licenses are granted by one of the PROs with whom a songwriter/composer has an affiliation (a contractual relationship). The purpose of the PRO is to protect the financial interests of the writers (and, by extension, their publishers) whenever their music is *performed in public*. Performed in public is not

If you are looking to make a cover recording, your first stop in obtainin or even investigating a mechanical license is the HFA. HFA is a rights admir istrator and serves as the primary gateway for obtaining mechanical right in the United States. The agency has contractual relationships with musi publishers of all sizes. Typically, HFA administers licenses for rights under it control to record companies and remits royalty payments to rightsholders– usually publishers who then split the royalty with its songwriter-member pursuant to their individual agreements.

The HFA website will help you to determine who the copyright owner rightsholder is—usually it's the songwriter's publisher. The agency set up search portal at www.songfile.com for determining whether they have been authorized to license the rights to a given song. It's important to note that the agency may not have 100% of the rights to a given song. For example, if a song was equally written by two people with different publishers and only one o the publishers has a relationship with HFA, then the agency can only give you licensing rights to 50% of the song; you'll need to figure out who the rights holder is for the other writer. To figure that out, you can do a Copyright Office search and then contact the rightsholder directly or search the Performing Rights Organizations (PRO) sites. In the United States, the three main PRO; are (1) ASCAP; (2) BMI; and (3) SESAC.[5] For digital transmissions, the pri mary intermediary is SoundExchange.[6] The AFM & SAG-AFTRA Intellectua Property Rights Distribution Fund[7] distributes royalties collected from digit; performance in foreign territories and distributes them to affiliated feature and non-featured musicians (session musicians). For more information o PROs, see Public Performance Licenses on p. 208.

Synchronization Licenses

A synchronization ("synch") license is one in which the rightsholder gran permission to a third party to use music synchronized with visual acti((synch rights). A synch deal consists of two sets of rights: one for the use of t musical composition and one for the use of the sound recording of it. The fe for synch licenses are negotiated directly with the rightsholders—there is set statutory rate, and permission to use the music doesn't have to be grant(In other words, synch licenses are not compulsory. Synch fees are usua granted for individual uses instead of on a blanket basis. Synch licenses : required anytime a piece of music is synchronized with visual action in:

limited to live performances; it also includes the playing of recordings in public spaces.

PROs keep track of how frequently and where their members' music is performed publicly. They control access to the compositions and collect and distribute a portion of the licensing fees to the writers and their publishers. A public performance license is required to perform a piece of copyrighted music in the following ways:

- in a live public setting;
- in a recording played at a restaurant, bar, sports area, supermarket, and so on;
- over the radio or on television (live or via recording);
- via streaming;[8] or
- via satellite and cable.

Of the three primary PROs, ASCAP and BMI are easier to join. Generally, once you have a piece of music published (or recorded with the expectation of commercial distribution), you're eligible to join for free. A SESAC affiliation, also free, is by invitation only. Songwriter/composers can only be affiliated with one PRO at a time, while publishers have independent relationships simultaneously with all the PROs.

PROs issue one of two license types to radio stations, television networks, food and drink establishments, universities, and so on—per program or blanket licenses. Per program licenses are those in which a licensee has permission to use something less than the PRO's full music catalog. For example, a per program license would be more appropriate for a talk radio station where music is not the focus. These licensees would purchase access on a menu basis. Larger commercial users like music radio stations purchase blanket licenses for a single license fee, which gives the stations full access to a PRO's entire music catalog.

For venues, PROs determine the cost of the blanket licenses based on factors that can include venue size, types of performances (live or replay), number of patrons, business hours, and whether a cover charge is required. For broadcasters, pricing factors can include the nature of the use (television or film), size of the broadcast market, and time of day among other considerations. Each PRO has a proprietary formula for calculating licensing fees and royalty payments due. Royalties are usually split 50/50 between writers and publishers, minus the PRO's percentage. PROs make payments directly to writers and their publishers pursuant to their contracts with each.

It's impossible to say which PRO is "the best" for writers/composers. You'd have to weigh your interests and ask other musicians about their experiences. For example, choosing a PRO based solely on the percentage of royalty payments quoted would be shortsighted because that amount doesn't take into consideration other factors such as the proprietary formulas and sampling strategies used for determining the number of radio plays a song gets, how it's used, and when it's used (for example, during rush hour periods or on Sunday afternoons). So, sampling formulas directly impact royalty payments.

Recording artists and record labels are not paid public performance royalties except for digital audio transmissions (Spotify, Pandora, etc.). Sound-Exchange collects royalties for digital performances in the United States for music streamed via satellite, cable, webcasts, and other Internet transmissions (non-interactive use of the sound recordings). In other words, if a listener can download music and create playlists, that use is considered interactive (on demand), and while digital, those uses are contemplated under a mechanical licensing scheme.

Master Use Licenses

A master use license (or "master license") is granted for master use rights—in other words, the right to use some or all of a preexisting sound recording (a "master"). Sometimes a master license is as simple as permission to re-release a recording made previously, but the most common purpose for a master license is for sampling. Sampling is the practice of using a section of a preexisting recording, usually via a sampler or another type of digital audio device, and incorporating it into another piece of recorded music. Because sampling necessarily involves using preexisting recorded music, it involves getting two permissions: (1) a mechanical license from the rightsholders of the underlying musical composition (usually from the music publisher via their agent—most often HFA); and (2) a master license from the rightsholder of the sound recording (usually the record label). Two permissions are required because all sound recordings contain two copyrights—one for the composition and one for the recording of it. If you unlawfully sample without permission from the rightsholders, you are violating at least two copyrights.

For example, if you sample from two or more compositions in one song, you'll need mechanical licenses from each of the writers and master licenses from each of the labels.

Master licenses are negotiated based on the stature of the original artist, popularity of the song, the amount of the recording to be used, the purpose of the use, and distribution plans for it, among other considerations. Because master use licenses are not compulsory, your request can be denied. Rights-holders can ask you for a demo copy to see how you will be using their content and to assist them in determining a license fee. Fees for a master license can take the form of a percentage of the mechanical statutory rate, a flat fee, a request for royalties (including an advance against them), an ownership interest in the piece of music and/or the recording, or some combination of these. Typically, you'd go to the publisher first to ask for permission to use the composition. If the publisher provides a quote, the terms will likely include a Most Favored Nations clause, and if the rightsholder to the master agrees to the license, you'll pay the label the same fee you'd pay to the publisher.

As an alternative to sampling, some artists will interpolate instead. An *interpolation* is where a recording artist will obtain a mechanical license to use a portion of the composition they want to sample and then record it to sound like the portion they wanted to sample. As compared with sampling, interpolating is a cheaper approach—no master license is required because none of the preexisting recording is used. An interpolation strategy is useful if an artist can't get permission from the label to sample or can't afford the fees demanded.

Print Licenses

Print licenses are required anytime copyrighted music notation or lyrics appear (e.g., printing a melody on a T-shirt or adding song lyrics in the footer of a music video on YouTube). Typically, print license permissions are given to publishers to publish sheet music and lyrics. Traditionally, you, as the songwriter/composer, have signed with a publisher to serve as the gatekeeper for the world to access your music. Sheet music fees are split between writers and their publishers according to the individual agreements negotiated between them. For writer/composers without publishers, www.taxi.com and www .newmusicshelf.com provide a platform for people to find your music. Print licenses are also required in instances where your music and/or lyrics would appear on a poster, T-shirt, or coffee mug, or in a video or streamed over audio as is sometimes seen on YouTube fan videos.

If you've read Chapter 11 on copyright basics, you know that Section 106(2) of the code reserves the right to make a derivative work to the owner/rightsholder. A derivative work is one that takes an existing piece of work and uses it as the basis for another. For example, taking a pop song and making a choral arrangement of it. The choral arrangement is "derived" from the existing pop tune, so making a derivative work without the rightsholder's permission constitutes infringement. To make the arrangement lawfully, the arranger should first obtain permission for a print license from the rightsholder.

PERMISSIONS

Requesting rights to use others' content can seem daunting, but consider how you might feel if someone asked to use your content in their artistic work: you might feel honored that your work is valued and you would likely appreciate that the person requesting permission extends their respect beyond the work to you.

To request rights to use another's content, you'll need to tell the person/entity

- who you are;
- why you are contacting them;
- what you are asking permission for (be specific);
- how and where you plan to use it; and
- when you plan to use it.

What follows is a simple template for asking for permission. Send your request via registered or certified mail so you can track it. You may need to send it more than once, and you should always have a backup plan in case permission is not granted or the person from whom permission is being requested asks for a fee you can't afford. Include a self-addressed envelope as well as an email address in your request so they can give permission in the manner that is easiest for them.

You don't need to ask permission to use public domain material. See "Music Licensing Resources," below, for information on determining whether something is in the public domain.

Sample Rights Request Letter

September 3, 2018

16 Columbus Avenue
Albany, NY 12207
(212) 555-5555

Rowman & Littlefield Publishing, Inc.
4501 Forbes Blvd, Suite 200
Lanham, MD 20706

Dear Sir/Madam:

I'm writing you to request permission to use an extract from *The Enterprising Musician's Guide to Performer Contracts* by David R. Williams. Specifically, I'd like to use _____ contained on pages XX–XX of ISBN 978-1538106761.

I teach a course called *Entrepreneurial Musicianship* at Big Conservatory in which students are encouraged to embrace the idea that each is the CEO of his own brand and to approach their careers from the vantage point of a small business owner. I'm writing a book for musicians and theater makers to help them plan and pursue entrepreneurship. The target audience is those interested in collaborating on a theater piece, starting a festival, forming a band, or some other arts-related enterprise.

The requested pages would appear with annotations in the following work to be published by Academic Publishers, an academic press based in New York: *<Your Name, Author, The Work's Title>*.

Kindly sign and return this document in the enclosed stamped, self-addressed envelope at your first opportunity.

Thank you.

I/We grant permission for the use requested above.

Person granting permission: _____

Holder of copyright: _____

Date: _____

Thank you,

<Your Name>

<Your email address>

PUBLIC DOMAIN

The term "public domain" refers to the body of creative work that is owned by the public and, as such, freely available for anyone to use without first seeking permission from a rightsholder. For example, if a university is interested in mounting a production of Beethoven's *Fidelio*, no grand rights license is required because Beethoven's works are part of the public domain. Works fall into the public domain once their copyright protection has expired (including because the rightsholder failed to renew copyright protection),[9] or the work was intentionally placed into the public domain—a practice known as a *dedication*. Stanford University provides an excellent resource for information relating to the public domain and for the application of the fair use doctrine. For example, there's a chart for determining public domain status by year of publication.[10] See Chapter 11 for a discussion of the fair use doctrine.

Also, see Copyright Office, Circular 22, *How to Investigate the Copyright Status of a Work*, which provides a wealth of information for conducting searches of copyrighted works. Because copyright law is so old, most of the documents are not online, but they can be searched in person at the Copyright Office or you can pay someone at the Office to do a search for you. The rates are hourly and set by statute. Upon request, the office can provide you with a cost estimate (copysearch@copyright.gov). One important piece of information contained in Circular 22 is a listing of the information required for the Office to conduct a search for you. The more details you can provide, the cheaper the research costs will be.

Here's the minimum of what you'll need to engage the Office for a copyright search:

- title(s) of the work
- author(s) names
- name of probable owner(s) (for a piece of music or literary work, this could be a publisher)
- approximate year of publication or registration with the copyright office
- type of work (musical, literary, recording, motion picture, etc.)
- any copyright data you might have, such as a registration number

Note that the Copyright Office doesn't maintain a list of public domain material or a list of works by subject matter. The office cannot provide you with an opinion of its research findings, nor can it provide legal advice.

LICENSING AGREEMENT DECISION POINTS

Contractually speaking, music licenses are usually not very complicated. Because there are so many different types and they can be drawn so specifically, it's impossible to contemplate every possible scenario. However, in the list below I've included some things you'll need to consider whether you are the one granting a license for use of your content (as licensor) or you are the potential licensee asking for permission to use another's content.

These examples are taken from different types of actual music licenses. They should not be construed as being the best language for your needs, but they will provide you with a starting point.

1. Defined Terms. Are there terms you'd like defined in the agreement? Whenever a term is defined in a contract, its meaning is being narrowed to something more specific than its colloquial or dictionary meaning.

   Example 1: "Musical works," for the purposes of this Agreement, shall mean musical compositions and dramatico-musical-compositions, words and music, arrangements, and selections thereof.

   Example 2: "Net Revenues" means all revenues recognized in accordance with generally accepted accounting principles relating to the distribution or sale of Licensed Products by licensee or any affiliated or subsidiary companies, less any units returned as defective or as the result of errors in billing or shipping.

2. Grant of Rights. What rights are being granted? Are sublicensing rights included? In other words, is the licensor giving the licensee the right to assign these rights to another person or entity or is the license restricted (non-transferable)?

Example 1: Licensor permits the use of the "Musical Composition," in whole or in part, in connection with _____ (the "Sound Recording") by "Artist." Licensor further grants Licensee permission to make a musical arrangement of the "Musical Composition" to the extent necessary to conform it to the style and manner of interpretation necessary for Licensee's purpose hereunder.

Example 2: The Publisher hereby grants to Licensee the nonexclusive limited right to record on film _____ (the "Musical Composition") in synchronization or timed relation with the following film whose working title is _____ .

3. Term. How long will the license be in effect?

Example: The term of this Agreement shall be twenty-four (24) months commencing on the execution of this Agreement by all parties.

4. Early Termination. Under what circumstances, if any, can the parties to this agreement terminate the license earlier than the stated termination date?

Example 1: This Agreement shall end and all rights granted revert back to Licensor:
a. upon thirty (30) days' written notice by either party;
b. if Licensee ceases to manufacture, sell, or distribute Licensed Products in the Licensed Territory during the term of this Agreement; or
c. upon Licensee's bankruptcy or merger with another entity.

Example 2: This Agreement may not be terminated for any reason.

5. Reserved Rights. What rights are being reserved to the licensor? In other words, which of the Section 106 rights (and other rights owned or controlled by the licensor) are not included in this grant of rights?

Example: Licensor does not permit, and Licensee shall not allow or permit, any use of the "Musical Composition" not otherwise expressly granted herein including, but not limited to changes to its fundamental character or lyrics without the express written consent of Licensor.

6. Exclusivity. Is this license exclusive or non-exclusive?

   Example: Licensor hereby grants Licensee nonexclusive authority, license, right, and privilege to use the following copyrighted material: _____ ("the Musical Composition") written by _____ ("the Writer").

7. Royalties and Royalty Statements. What is the royalty amount and payment schedule? Are periodic royalty statements required? If so, how frequent?

   Example 1: Royalties shall be recouped by Licensee from first dollar revenue. No royalties shall be paid to Licensor under this Agreement until such royalties exceed the aggregate amount of the Advances paid to Licensor.

   Example 2: Royalty statements and payments shall be due within thirty (30) days after the end of each calendar quarter. Royalty statements shall contain a detailed accounting of the number of phonorecords made and distributed during said quarter.

8. Advances. Is an advance required? If so, how are future royalties deducted from the advance?

   Example: Licensee agrees to pay Licensor the following nonrefundable Advances in accordance with the following schedule:

9. Approvals. Will licensor require any approval rights of the licensee's use of the licensed content?

   Example: All Promotional and Packaging Material and all Licensed Products on which Licensor's Trademarks are used shall contain the following legal notices:

   _____

   _____.

   Approvals shall only be made, in writing, by Licensor prior to commencing the design of the Licensed Products or Promotion and Packaging Material.

10. Warranties. Will licensor provide any warranties relating to the licensed content? For example, warranting that the licensor has the authority to enter into the licensing agreement free of any legal challenges.

Example: Licensor warrants and represents that it has the full right, power, and authority to enter into this Agreement and that no part of the Musical Composition infringes upon any right held by another whether under common law or statute.

11. Indemnification. What kind of indemnification promises are made between the parties?

Example: Licensee hereby agrees to defend, indemnify, and hold Licensor harmless against any and all claims, demands, causes of action, or judgments arising out of this Agreement.

12. Remedies. What limitation of remedies, if any, for breach of contract are included?

Example: If Licensee receives notice of any claim, demand, or suit, or becomes aware of any facts leading Licensee to reasonably believe Licensor has been in breach of its warranties as set forth herein, Licensee shall have the right to withhold payment due to Licensor under this Agreement and deposit in an interest-bearing escrow account reasonable amounts as security for Licensor's obligations hereunder.

13. Default and Notice. Should notice of default be included? If so, should what constitutes default be defined in the agreement? Should a cure period be included? How shall notices be given?

Example 1: Written notices including statements (other than Royalty Statements), payments or other matters shall be given to Licensor or Licensee only by registered or certified mail. Royalty Statements may be sent by regular mail.

Example 2: Licensee shall not be deemed in breach hereunder unless Licensor shall notify Licensee thereof in the manner prescribed herein. Licensee shall have thirty (30) days after receiving such notice to completely remedy the alleged breach unless the parties otherwise agree.

14. Confidentiality. Confidentiality requirements—if the other party will have access to proprietary information you'd like kept confidential, you should have a broad confidentiality clause followed by a list of situations or classes of information that would not be subject to the confidentiality requirement.

> *Example: Neither party of this Agreement shall disclose any Confidential Information of the other party during or after the term of this Agreement. Information shall not be deemed confidential if it:*
> a. *is now or hereafter becomes generally known or is now or later enters the public domain through no act or omission on the part of the receiving party;*
> b. *was acquired by the receiving party before receiving such information from the disclosing party and without restriction as to use or disclosure;*
> c. *is information which the receiving party can document was independently developed by the receiving party;*
> d. *is required to be disclosed pursuant to law; or*
> e. *is disclosed with the prior written consent of the disclosing party.*

See Chapter 13 for a discussion of confidentiality clauses and nondisclosure agreements (NDAs).

15. Exhibits. Are there any sample documents that should be added to the license as an exhibit or otherwise incorporated by reference[11] in the license?

> *Example: "Licensed Products" means only those products indicated as Interactive Products in Exhibit A as attached hereto.*

CONCLUSION

Licensing represents several ways musicians—especially writer/composers—make money from their music. Writers earn royalties whenever their music is covered or interpolated (mechanical rights), is performed live or via recording in public (public performance rights), appears on television or in film (synchronization rights), is sampled by another artist (master use rights), appears in printed sheet music, appears on merchandise, or is arranged for ensemble (print rights). Recording artists earn royalties when their recordings are digitally transmitted through non-interactive media. Appendix C provides a quick reference music licensing chart.

MUSIC LICENSING RESOURCES

ASCAP, www.ascap.com

BMI, www.bmi.com

The Choral Public Domain Library, www.cpdl.org

Cyber Hymnal, www.hymnary.org

Harry Fox Agency, www.harryfox.com

The Plain & Simple Guide to Music Publishing by Randall D. Wixen
(Hal Leonard Books)

The Public Domain Information Project, www.pdinfo.com

SESAC, www.sesac.com

SoundExchange, www.soundexchange.com

NOTES

1. Harry Fox Agency, "What Is a Music Publisher?" www.harryfox.com/#/faq.

2. See www.crb.gov/rate/ for more information on the Copyright Royalty Board and its rate rulings.

3. 37 CFR 385 §11(a).

4. Harry Fox, "Rate Charts," www.harryfox.com/#/rate-charts.

5. There is a Canadian performance rights organization called SOCAN.

6. SoundExchange is a nonprofit music industry collective authorized by Congress. It administers digital performance rights and collects and distributes digital performance royalties to recording artists and their labels (as opposed to songwriters and publishers).

7. AFM & SAG-AFTRA Intellectual Property Rights Distribution Fund, "Do We Have Royalties for You?" www.afmsagaftrafund.org.

8. Music streaming services pay both public performance rights (in which royalties are paid to writers and publishers through PROs) as well as digital performance rights (in which royalties are paid to record labels and recording artists through SoundExchange).

9. Under older copyright law, the duration of copyright protection was only twenty-eight years, but the copyright could be renewed for a second twenty-eight-

year period. Failure to exercise the renewal right in the initial twenty-eighth year would result in the work falling into the public domain.

10. Stanford University Libraries, "Welcome to the Public Domain," fairuse.stanford .edu/overview/public-domain/welcome/.

11. "Incorporated by reference" is the practice where a completely separate document (or other item such as a website) is referred to in a contract.

Other Contracts Useful for Musicians

In this chapter, you'll find samples of contracts that might be useful to you at different stages in the evolution of your music business. While still planning to launch your business, you should become familiar with basics like nondisclosure agreements, rights requests, and releases and assignments. Depending on the nature of your artistic practice, you may also find commission agreements, venue rental agreements (including the insurance requirements commonly required in these), and a cease and desist letter useful.

The sample contracts provided in this chapter only contain the body of the content to show the basics to make the contractual relationship work. Assume all samples have a preamble at the top of the contract that identifies the contracting parties as well as required signature lines at the end of each contract for signatures, addresses, and dates. Additionally, contract drafters often like to include recitals near the top of the contract to provide some context for why the contracting parties are entering into an agreement. For example, see the two WHEREAS clauses near the top of the Sample Unilateral Nondisclosure Agreement. Some drafters also include clauses lawyers nickname "housekeeping provisions." These are general clauses that appear frequently in any type of contract. Though not required (because they often only restate what the law already provides), they are nonetheless common. These include amendment clauses, merger/integration clauses, choice of law clauses, forum clauses, savings clauses, severability clauses, headings/construction clauses, and others. I have not included these clauses in the samples provided below to save space, but you'll find annotated examples of these in both the sample partnership and collaboration agreements provided in Chapters 3 and 10.

NONDISCLOSURE AGREEMENTS

While most people refer to them as *confidentiality agreements,* lawyers tend to refer to them by their nickname: NDAs (nondisclosure agreements). NDAs are contracts designed to maintain the confidentiality of information that may be disclosed to another party. The information subject to the NDA can be anything, but is usually focused around proprietary information such as customer lists, trade secrets, or the results of a confidential legal settlement.

There are two basic types of NDAs: unilateral and bilateral agreements. In a unilateral NDA, only one side is promising to keep information confidential. In a bilateral (mutual) agreement, both sides are disclosing information they want to remain private, so both parties are making promises of confidentiality to the other.

Some examples of when you might want to use an NDA:

Example 1—Development Deals
You plan to meet with potential funders or other collaborators to discuss a development idea you're working on. A situation like this might warrant a noncompete clause as well. For an example of noncompete clauses, see the Independent Contractor (IC) agreement in Chapter 9.

Example 2—Working with Vendors
You're hiring a vendor, such as a computer expert, to perform professional services in or around your work area.

Example 3—Employees or Independent Contractors
You're hiring people to help during busy periods, and they will necessarily have access to private information your business needs to keep confidential (such as celebrity contact information), and if that information becomes public, it will damage your business's goodwill.

NDA Contents
The contents of an NDA are typically (1) who is subject to confidentiality; (2) what should be kept confidential; (3) what is NOT included in the scope of

confidentiality; (4) the duration of the confidentiality promise; and (5) other clauses specific to the situation.

Covered Parties

The parties to an NDA are the disclosing party (the party sharing proprietary information) and the receiving party (the party who will be given the proprietary information). When you draft an NDA, you'll want to be sure that the entity, itself, not just the specific person(s) you are sharing information with, are subject to the promise of confidentiality. You should also ask the recipient who, within their organization, might come in contact with the information, and whether the receiving party anticipates the need to share the confidential information outside their company (such as with a subsidiary company, affiliate organization, or in anticipation of a documents request associated with a company merger).

Confidential Information

The NDA may define what's confidential by type (work product protected under attorney-client privilege, items actually marked "confidential," trade secret files, customer lists, etc.). For musician businesses, the scope of confidentiality might look like this:

> "Confidential Information" means (a) confidential or trade secret information, without regard to how such information is marked, and owned by Employer or any of its affiliates, or licensed from third parties regarding (b) music, lyrics, songs, music concepts, lyric concepts, and song concepts; (c) lists of artists and other clients including artists' and clients' contact information; (d) research, development, products, services, marketing, selling, business plans, budgets, unpublished financial statements, licenses, prices, costs, fees, contracts and other agreements, suppliers, customers, and customer lists; (e) the identity, skills, and compensation of employees, contractors, artists, writers, and consultants; and (f) any specialized training.

Excluded Information

Typically excluded from the scope of what should remain confidential is information that:

1. is publicly known and generally available in the public domain;
2. becomes part of the public domain after disclosure (except if disclosure is unlawful or by breach of the NDA);
3. is intentionally disclosed without restriction;
4. is independently created and which can be readily proven;
5. is received by the recipient from another source that the recipient didn't know was required to be kept confidential; and
6. the recipient already had knowledge of.

Duration of the Agreement

The term of an NDA is ultimately negotiated by the parties, but it will also be influenced by custom in the industry. Regardless, this is one area in which there is an inherent conflict: the disclosing party will usually want the promise of confidentiality to be as long as possible while the receiving party will want the duration to be as short as possible so it's not under this obligation longer than necessary. When you're considering the length of an NDA, consider whether the need for confidentiality will change over time or whether it will remain as it is now. If you're trying to keep client lists confidential, those might eventually become public anyway, so you may be ok with a two-year duration as opposed to trying to negotiate an NDA that lasts in perpetuity. In the end, be reasonable. Once the NDA term has expired, you might want to include a clause that requires the return or destruction of confidential documents, if relevant.

What follows are two sample NDAs: (1) a unilateral version; and (2) a bilateral version. Both contain explanatory annotations where necessary.

Sample Unilateral Nondisclosure Agreement

The agreement provided in Example 13.1, below, would be used in conjunction with a contract for professional services. The NDA elements could be a standalone contract like this one, or these clauses could be folded into and made part of the contract for professional services; see the IC agreement in Chapter 9.

Example 13.1:

WHEREAS the parties to this Professional Services Contract mutually desire to explore the potential for a transaction in which the Contractor would provide "Professional Services" to the Company and its affiliates.

WHEREAS the Company is the Disclosing Party and the Contractor is the Receiving Party.

In consideration of the relationship with the Company <*name of company*>, I <*contractor's name*> hereby agree and covenant as follows:

1. I, the Receiving Party, acknowledge that during the course of my association with the Company, I will be given access to Confidential Information and that the unauthorized disclosure thereof could significantly harm the Disclosing Party.

2. Confidential Information is defined as <*trade secrets and other proprietary information including market data, training materials, customer lists, etc.*>. Confidential Information does not include and no duty of confidentiality exists for matters of public knowledge resulting from disclosure by the Company or by operation of law; information rightfully received by me from a third party without duty of confidentiality; and information disclosed by me with the Company's prior written consent.

3. I agree not to use, or to permit the use by any person or entity, any Confidential information except (1) as expressly authorized by the Company in support of the Company's interests; or (2) as required by law. I agree to immediately notify the Company if I become aware of any unauthorized use or disclosure of any Confidential Information, and to assist the Company in remedying such unauthorized use or disclosure.

4. I understand that the Company's Confidential Information has been developed or obtained by the Company through investment of money, time, and effort and represents a valuable, special, and unique asset of the Company. These assets provided the Company with a significant competitive advantage and, as such, must be protected from improper disclosure which would result in irreparable harm to the Company. Because damages relating to improper disclosure would be difficult to ascertain, I understand and agree that the Company will not have an adequate remedy at law and shall be entitled to seek injunctive relief without the posting of a bond. Nothing in this Agreement is meant to in any way limit any other legal remedy available to the Company.

An injunction is a form of equitable relief in which a party asks a court to flex its muscle and force someone to do something or restrain someone from doing something. For example, a temporary restraining order is a form of injunction in which the court is telling someone to cease doing something that is infringing the rights of another.

The language in this clause referring to "special and unique" is commonly used in contract clauses where the option of injunctive relief is included. Because injunctions are considered extraordinary forms of legal relief, it can be difficult to make the case for them. Typically, the moving party (the one making the request) must convince a judge that special and unique circumstances exist that call for this kind of remedy and the requesting party would be irreparably harmed unless the injunction is granted.

The reference to posting a bond refers to a surety bond. In this context, the surety bond guarantees that if the requesting party inappropriately obtained the injunction (such as misleading the court), a financial guarantor (the surety company) would step in to make sure the requesting party pays the court fees, costs, and damages sustained by the defendant if the court later determines that the injunction should never have been granted. If the requesting party can't pay those costs, the surety will step in and do so as guarantor. This clause, however, says that if the company resorts to seeking injunctive relief (to enforce confidentiality), the parties agree that no bond is required.

<signature lines>

Example 13.2:

Sample Mutual Confidentiality and Nondisclosure Agreement

This Mutual Confidentiality and Nondisclosure Agreement (the "Agreement") dated _____, is entered into by and between _____ (the "Service Provider") and _____ (the "Company").

In consideration of the promises and covenants contained herein, as well as other good and valuable consideration, the receipt and sufficiency of which are acknowledged, the parties mutually agree as follows:

1. I understand that during the course of my providing professional services for the Company, I may receive confidential and proprietary information relating to the Company and its clients as well as both the Company's and the Company's clients' trade secrets or other proprietary information.

2. Both parties agree that for a period of two (2) years from the date of this Agreement, neither party shall disclose any information contained in any written document that is marked as "Proprietary" or "Confidential" to any person, firm, or company, or use it for its own benefit except as noted herein.

This clause provides the promise not to disclose the confidential information and the duration of the confidentiality promise. The lines about not using confidential content for its own benefit is a promise not to compete or otherwise financially benefit from it. The promise is not very forcefully made in this example.

3. This provision shall also apply to information conveyed by the Company to the Service Provider, including, but not limited to, information in tangible and intangible form relating to and/or including released or unreleased products, the marketing and promotion of any product, the Company's business policies or practices, and information received from others that the Company is obligated to treat as confidential.

This clause outlines the manner of conveyance of the information including oral communications (although it's not specifically spelled out as such).

4. The parties agree that information not deemed proprietary hereunder and which shall not be the subject of this nondisclosure hereunder is information that
   a. is now or hereafter becomes generally known or is now or later enters the public domain through no act or omission on the part of the receiving party;
   b. was acquired by the receiving party before receiving such information from the disclosing party and without restriction as to use or disclosure;
   c. is information which the receiving party can document was independently developed by the receiving party;

d. is required to be disclosed pursuant to law; or

e. is disclosed with the prior written consent of the disclosing party.

This clause spells out what is not subject to a promise of confidentiality.

5. Neither party shall have any liability or responsibility for errors or omissions in, nor any business decisions made by the other party in reliance on, any Proprietary Information disclosed under this Agreement.

This clause suggests that if some information intended to remain confidential is made publicly available in error, the disclosing party will not be held liable to the other.

6. The parties agree that, in the event of breach of this Agreement, either shall be entitled to injunctive relief and any such relief shall be in addition to and not in lieu of, any available remedy at law including monetary damages. The parties acknowledge that Proprietary Information is valuable and unique and that disclosure in breach of this Agreement will result in irreparable harm to the parties.

This is a remedies clause that states that all remedies are available to the Company in the event that the receiving party breaches its duty of confidentiality, including injunctive relief. Injunctive relief is a special remedy in which someone asks a court to compel a person or entity to take some action or refrain from taking some action.

<signature lines>

RELEASES

A release is a grant of permission. There are countless purposes for releases, but the most common for those in creative industries are releases used for publicity and content (namely, artwork and music). Additionally, some employers ask employees to sign releases to facilitate pre-employment background screening that often includes credit checks, criminal background checks, driving records, education credentials, and previous employment. In the employment context, the release might include a liability waiver should a prospective employer rely on incorrect or inadequate information provided to it by a third party and rescind a job offer.

What follows are four sample releases: (1) a publicity release; (2) a content release; (3) a musician's session work release; and (4) a background check release for employment.

Publicity Rights

Arts organizations need to obtain publicity rights from participants in order to market their programs and services. To most effectively do that, they need a broad grant of rights. The release should list all manner of publicity, and the rights should be granted for as long a duration as possible—the longest being "in perpetuity" (forever).

The grant of rights, however, should also balance participants' interest in wanting control over how their image is being used and for how long. Sometimes artists will request approval rights to photographs or videos or have other questions relating to how the images will be used. Don't dismiss these as mere vanity points; artists should have control over their image which, of course, is the brand they are putting out into the world.

In some cases, it may be easier to just not include that individual in photography or videography or allow them to choose the image(s) they are comfortable with, and other photographs or videos of them should be destroyed. It's also possible, as was the case in my work recently, where a participant requested that her name and image not be included in promotional material because she was living under an active domestic abuse restraining order and didn't want her whereabouts made public. When I ask for a publicity release, I give the option of discussing the purpose and use of the publicity materials in private, so they feel comfortable telling me about their concerns without sharing their situation publicly.

Example 13.3:

Sample Release 1: Publicity

1. Welcome to *<program name here>*! To the greatest extent possible, we document our work for educational and promotional purposes in furtherance

of our mission to *<your organization's mission statement here>*. We rely on this documentation for educational purposes and to develop promotional materials for donor development via our website, social media, and print media activities. Please read and sign the following document, which includes information about audio recording, video recording, live streaming, and still photography.

2. When at all possible, we will endeavor to identify individuals. In promotional videos, we will identify individuals who are performing or speaking in the most appropriate place (e.g., supertitle or at the end of the video). We will obtain permissions to use any copyrighted materials.

3. We will audio/video record most events including, but not limited to: *<list events here>*

4. Many of our events will be live streamed. Such events will be available via *<insert URL>* and via Facebook Live.

5. Still photography will be taken daily during *<list events subject to photography>*.

I *<print name>* have read and understand the above information. I grant *<name of your entity>* permission to take photos of me at both formal and informal events; make audio/video recordings of my performances and rehearsals; and live stream events. I agree that the materials may be used for any lawful purpose including, but not limited to educational archival purposes, publicity, donor development, social media marketing, and other web-based marketing in perpetuity.

<signature lines>

Content Releases

Content releases are commonly used by documentarians and others who conduct oral interviews. They are usually fairly simple, as is the one provided in Example 13.14, and contain the project name, purpose, identification of the content for which consent is being given, and the nature and duration of the release.

Example 13.4:

Sample Release 2: Content

I, _____, am a participant in *<insert project name>*. I understand that the purpose of *<the project name>* is *<insert purpose>*.

I hereby grant *<project owner>*:

a. ownership of *<insert name of content>* and the right to use *<content description>* that is the product of my participation;

b. my absolute and irrevocable consent for any photographs provided by me or taken of me in the course of my participation in *<name of project>* to be used, published, and copied by *<project owner>* and its assigns in any medium; and

c. use of my name, video, photographic images, likeness, statements, performance, and voice reproduction, or other sound effects without further approval from me.

I release the *<project owner>* and its assigns and designees, from any and all claims and demands arising out of or in connection with the use of such recordings, photographs, and documents, including, but not limited to, any claims for defamation, invasion of privacy, or right of publicity.

<signature lines>

Musician Session Work

Musicians are often hired for session work where they participate in rehearsals and recording sessions in a studio. The common practice is that the musicians are paid for their time without being given an ownership interest in the composition or in the recording of it. Session work can be handled contractually as a release or via a work-for-hire agreement. The release will look much like the sample releases provided above—the musician grants permission to be recorded (audio and visual) and waives all their rights and claims to the images and music captured in recording sessions. See Example 13.5, below.

A work-for-hire agreement functions the same way as a release, but will follow the format of an independent contractor agreement that has a work-made-for-hire clause. See Chapter 9 for a sample IC agreement with a work-made-for-hire clause.

Example 13.5:

Sample Release 3: Musician Session Work

1. I grant *<insert recording company/studio>* permission to use my Performance, in whole or in part, as part of the Project at its sole and absolute discretion. Such use includes, without limitation, any and all recordings of my Performance and the display, distribution, publication, transmission, or other use of recordings and/or video captured of me during my Performance in connection with the Project.

   Note that video capture of the recording session is also included for possible use on television or film.

2. I hereby waive all rights and claims to my Performance including music, recordings, vocals, reproductions, copies, transmissions, broadcasts, telecasts, or webcasts by any media now known or hereinafter developed of any and all audio, visual, or audio-visual aspects of my Performance in connection with the Project.
3. I further grant *<insert recording company/studio>* permission to use my voice, photograph, image, or likeness in printed materials including, but not limited to record labels, marketing materials, brochures, news releases, newsletters, videos, or digital images as *<insert recording company/studio>* deems necessary in its sole and absolute discretion to promote the Project.
4. I further waive all rights and claims to the use of my voice, photograph, image, or likeness in connection with my Performance as captured in any audio, visual, or audio-visual format in connection with the Project.

<signature lines>

Employment Background Screening

A background screening release form will resemble a sample publicity release form. It will contain some background on the purpose of the request, a grant of rights, and a release.

Example 13.6:

Sample Release 4: Employment Background Screening

1. I, <prospective employee>, in connection with my application for employment with <organization> (the "Employer"), hereby authorize Employer and any agent it authorizes to perform a pre-employment background check. I understand that the Employer may obtain a credit report which consists of information having a bearing on job performance and may include information from public and private sources including court records, driving records, schools, former employers, and other sources.

2. Under the Fair Credit Reporting Act, should an employer rely upon a consumer report from a Consumer Reporting Agency in taking adverse action regarding employment, before taking that action, I will be provided with a copy of the Consumer Report and a summary of my rights. Upon written request to any Consumer Reporting Agency, I may obtain a copy of my report as provided by law.

3. I would (_) would not (_) like a copy of any consumer report prepared on me.

4. I authorize and release any person, company, references, current and former employers, schools, and credit bureaus to provide all information that is released to the Employer or its authorized agents. I further release and hold harmless all of the above, including Employer, to the full extent of the law, from any liability or claims arising from the retrieving and reporting of information concerning me. I further agree that a copy of this document shall be as valid as the original.

5. I certify that the information contained in my application for employment is true and accurate. I further understand that any misrepresentation or omission of fact may be considered as cause for rejection of my application or termination from employment at any time. I understand that nothing

contained herein is intended to create an employment contract between *<organization>* and me.

6. I authorize *<organization>* to verify all information contained in this application for employment and any supplement thereto.

<signature lines>

COMMISSION AGREEMENTS

Commission agreements are contracts used by commissioning bodies in which a musician is hired to create a piece of music—often for the commissioning body to perform. These are fairly simple documents that should always contain or address the following at minimum:

- Information that identifies the parties
- Purpose for the contract (the contractual duties)
- Due date(s) delivering the score
- Number and types of copies
- Manner of delivery
- Payment details (how, when)
- Ownership details
- Performance/premiere date, if applicable
- Any exclusivity issues
- Inscription requirements and credits
- Other clauses (other rights, early termination, remedies, representations and warranties, indemnification, publicity, and force majeure)

The sample commission agreement provided in Example 13.7, below, is for an orchestra commissioning a work for a specific group of players.

Example 13.7:

Sample Commission Agreement

1. The Organization commissions Composer to write an orchestral piece (the "Work") to be titled *<working title>*. The Composer shall have the

right to alter the title prior to delivery provided Organization approves the change in writing.

Clause 1 outlines the composer's duty to write the piece of music.

2. The Work and all published editions shall bear the following inscription on the title page: "Commissioned by <*organization's name*>." Composer will be credited as follows: <*composer's professional name*>.

In some instances, the commission body will ask that a specific donor/funding source be recognized. For example: "Commissioned by The Saint Paul Chamber Orchestra with funding provided by the AT&T Foundation."

3. The length of the Work shall be of a minimum of twelve (12) full minutes in duration up to a total maximum duration of fifteen (15) minutes.
4. The Work shall be composed for Full Symphony Orchestra (3.3.3.2 – 4.3.3.1 – timp – 3 perc. – harp – piano – min. strings 14.12.10.8.6).

Clause 4 provides the scoring requirements.

5. The Organization agrees to pay the Composer the gross fee all-in (score + parts both digitally and hard copy, per classical music library industry standards) $18,000 (eighteen thousand dollars) for the Work. Half of the fee ($9,000) shall be due upon full execution of this Agreement. The remaining half ($9,000) shall be paid within thirty (30) days of delivery.

Payment may also reference PRO licensing fees, for example: "Composer affirms that a performing rights license is not required for the performance of the Work." Alternately, the licensing fees could be referenced as follows: "There shall be no additional performing rights fees, royalty fees, or rental fees payable beyond those covered by <composer's affiliated PRO>." See Chapter 12 for a discussion of PROs and music licensing.

6. Composer shall deliver the Work:
   a. as a computer-engraved full score with a full set of parts (both digitally and in hard copy) as per classical music library industry standards;

b. to the Organization no later than <date> (for the score) and <date> (for the individual parts). Any delays must be mutually agreed upon and contained in a writing signed by both parties; and

c. via email (for digital copies) and courier service (for hard copies).

Clause 6 provides the standards, date, and manner of delivery.

7. The Organization agrees to give one (1) performance of the Work on or about <performance date>.

8. All rights in the Work not granted to Organization herein are reserved to Composer. Organization acknowledges that Composer is not an employee of Organization and agrees that the Work resulting from this Agreement is not a "work-made-for-hire" as defined under U.S. copyright law and any subsequent amendments thereto.

This is the ownership clause. It is critically important to composers/ songwriters that commission agreements clearly spell out ownership of a commissioned work. The clause immediately above makes clear that the organization does not intend that the piece composed for it pursuant to this agreement be owned by the commissioning body; rather, the intention of the parties is that the composer retain a 100% ownership interest in the composition. This clause makes it possible for the composer to earn licensing income from the work; see Chapter 12.

Another option is to share ownership. Contrast the version above with the following example in which the commission body requires co-ownership:

Option 2:
"Composer shall own the copyright to the Work; however, Composer agrees to co-publish the Work on an equal share basis (50/50) with <name> for the lifetime of the copyright."

In this second example, the commissioning body intends to participate in future licensing of the work—likely with the hope of recouping its commission fee. This approach is a compromise to commission agreements that state that the work is a "work-made-for-hire" and that the composer, while entitled to a copyright credit, has nonetheless assigned all their rights to the commissioning organization.

A less artist-friendly clause would state that the commissioning body retains all ownership interest in the commissioned work. That clause might look something like this, but it too will make clear that the commissioned work is a "work-made-for-hire":

Option 3: Composer Gives Ownership to Commission Body
"Both the Organization and Composer agree that the Work shall be a work-made-for-hire. Organization shall be the sole and exclusive owner of the Work and shall also be considered the author of the Work for the purposes of U.S. copyright law and any other applicable state or federal laws. Further, if for any reason the Work shall be deemed not to be a work-made-for-hire, the Composer hereby transfers and assigns all rights and ownership interest in the Work to the Organization, including all interest in the copyright and any other intellectual property rights in the Work."

Works-made-for-hire are not subject to the right of copyright reversion; see Chapter 11.

9. The Organization shall have the exclusive right to perform the Work for a period of eighteen (18) months following delivery of same.

   This is an Exclusivity Clause. Note that this clause doesn't require the organization to perform the work; it merely gives it the limited, exclusive right to do so for 18 months. This means the composer cannot grant another organization the right to perform the piece during that period of time unless the commissioning organization provides a release (which should be in writing).

10. Composer agrees to make herself available, at reasonable times and with advance notice, for interviews and other publicity events at the request of the Organization for the purpose of publicizing the Work and its commission.

11. In the event of "Acts of God" or other unavoidable, extenuating circumstances, Composer must negotiate an extension of any delivery date with the Organization; such extension will be invalid unless contained in a writing signed by both parties.

This is a Force Majeure Clause; see Example 13.8, below, for an explanation of these common clauses.

12. Composer represents and warrants that the Work is original to the Composer; Composer is the owner thereof; and Composer is authorized to enter into this Agreement. Composer further warrants that nothing contained herein contravenes any preexisting agreement with a publisher or any other party.

This is a Representations and Warranties Clause in which the composer is affirmatively stating that the music being written is original, wholly owned by them, and that no third party can make a legitimate legal claim against the organization (such as one for copyright infringement).

13. If for any reason beyond the control of the Composer, including illness or accident, the Composer is unable to fulfill the terms of this Agreement, the Composer's sole liability to the Organization shall be the refund of the fees paid. If for any reasons the terms of this Agreement are not fulfilled by Composer according to the schedule provided in Paragraph X, all monies paid by the Organization shall be returned to the Organization, in which event neither party hereto shall be under any further obligation to the other unless a mutually agreeable date can be arrived at for delivery of the Work on or before the date scheduled herein.

The following remedy is artist-friendly in that in the event a legitimate reason exists that hinders the composer from timely delivering the work, it limits the composer's liability to the commissioning body to a return of the commission fees already received.

14. Organization retains the right to cancel performance of the Work if delivery requirements are not met.

A clause spelling out that the commissioning body doesn't have to mount a performance of a work delivered late will accomplish two things. First, it will preempt a composer alleging that the contract was breached by the organization for not performing the work (after the composer has taken the position that late delivery was immaterial to the contract). Second, it's a form of quality control—if the piece is delivered late, the organization may not have adequate time to prepare a reasonably good performance of it.

15. Organization shall have the right of first refusal of any form of recording of the Work for a period of eighteen (18) months after its first performance. Further, Organization shall have the right to record the Work for possible radio broadcast and archival purposes.

It's common for commissioning bodies to want to get the most out of their commissions—including recordings. But, they may not be in a financial position to commit to making a recording, so the safer position is to wait and see how the piece is received and then possibly look for funding for a recording of it. The right of first refusal should be reasonable, but what is reasonable will be determined by custom. Eighteen months seems more than adequate. In the sample clause above, radio and archival recording is not subject to the right of first refusal because it's not considered a commercial release. In other words, the commissioning body will not make money from those uses, so they don't count as recordings for the purpose of this clause.

<signature lines>

PERFORMANCE VENUE RENTAL AGREEMENTS

Venue rental agreements are used for renting performing or rehearsal space. The content for these is usually fairly uniform, but there are a few clauses to look for and read closely. Some clauses are confusing because they contain unfamiliar, stylized language. What all the clauses provided below have in common is they are intended to limit the venue's financial liability in one way or another. This means if something relating to the rental goes wrong, the financial burden is shifted from the venue to you, the renter/lessee.

At minimum, expect to find clauses addressing the following:

- Event details (name of event, rental dates, load in/out times, contact information)
- Lighting, decor
- Services provided by venue, if any (box office, food & bar staffing, merchandise sales)
- Breakdown of fees (deposit and final payment amounts and due dates)
- Property-specific rules relating to usage and safety
- Fitness of property
- Use of venue's trademarks
- Technical/production-related clauses
- Number of expected guests, guest lists
- Condition of space upon rental termination
- Publicity, programs, photography, and videography
- Cancellation details
- Insurance requirements
- Representations and Warranty clause
- Indemnification clause
- General housekeeping provisions (force majeure, choice of law, forum, merger/integration, waiver, etc.)
- Other clauses

The clauses I'm focusing on below are those relating to force majeure events, insurance requirements, fitness of property, cancellation, and others.

FORCE MAJEURE CLAUSES

Force majeure clauses (also known as *Acts of God* clauses) are commonly found in most any kind of contract. They say that if some event completely outside the control of the contracting parties takes place making performance under the contract impossible, neither party can be held legally liable to the other. For example, if you were hired to play a gig at a venue that was inaccessible due to a landslide, you can't be held liable for not performing and the hiring entity can't be held liable to pay your fee. So, a force majeure clause, when appropriately used, excuses both parties from performing their contractual duties.

Example 13.8:

> *Neither Lessor nor Lessee shall be liable for the failure to appear, present, or perform if such failure is caused by or due to an Act of God.*

The purpose of force majeure clauses is to excuse performance under the contract for unexpected events beyond the parties' control rendering performance impossible. Example 13.8 is standard. There's no reason to enumerate things like landslides, hurricanes, floods, or blizzards because doing so would surely result in an incomplete list.

Today, it's not uncommon to see these clauses expanded to include acts of terrorism, civil unrest, regulation of public authorities including those resulting in delay or interruption of transportation services, epidemic or pandemic and labor strikes. Read these clauses carefully and try to gauge the likelihood that the events listed in the clause could cause your event to be canceled leaving you without any financial recourse (and the likely loss of your deposit). Some venues will include a clause that says that if your event is cancelled due to a force majeure event, the venue may be able to reschedule it though additional fees may apply. For example:

Example 13.9:

> *Should Lessee's event be canceled, postponed, or otherwise adversely impacted as the result of a force majeure event, there shall be no refunds for payments already received by Lessor. Lessor will use all reasonable efforts to work with Lessee to produce the event at a later date if necessary, subject to availability. Additional fees may be incurred as a result of a rescheduled event.*

The issue is that, over time, these clauses have been ripe for abuse by some because the unscrupulous drafter will slip things into these clauses that are not meant to be there. For example, unexpected budget shortfalls or other contingencies that would excuse performance under the contract. In the context of venue rental agreements, it doesn't matter what the contingency is because if the lessee can't put its performance on, it can't make income through ticket sales and could potentially lose its deposit.

In instances in which the loss would be especially high should a force majeure event take place (loss of your deposit, rescheduling costs, reprinting programs, amended promotional materials, and other costs) another possible safeguard may be to purchase event insurance. Insurers use rating actuaries to determine the statistical likelihood of certain events taking place and then try to determine the financial loss that is likely to result from that event. The premium charged for that insurance would be based on the amount of insurance purchased, the likelihood of the event happening, and the resulting costs to you if it did.

Did you know that there is something called "hole-in-one insurance"? Think of games of chance in which large prize money is given to amateurs who get a hole-in-one in golf or score a mid-court basket. Technically, this is called *prize indemnity insurance*. There's also an insurance product called *pluvius cover* (after the Roman god of rain), which will respond if a ticketed outdoor event is negatively affected by rain. Insurance company employees called rating actuaries provide mathematical data comprising just one of the factors used in determining what insurance premium to charge.

INSURANCE CLAUSES

As is usually the case in commercial property rental scenarios, venue rentals also come with requirements that the renter have insurance and name the venue as an additional insured under their policy. Example 13.10, below, provides a sample insurance clause.

Example 13.10:

Lessee warrants that it carries and pays for Workers' Compensation Insurance for company employees; that it carries or shall obtain Fire and Theft

Insurance for full replacement value of all scenery, costumes, electrical and sound equipment, literary and musical material, and all other properties and materials owned, rented, or brought into Lessor's property by Lessee, which Fire and Theft Insurance policy shall include a waiver of subrogation against Lessor and that it carries and pays for Public Liability Insurance with a limit of not less than One Million dollars ($1,000,000) naming Lessor as Additional Insured against all losses and claims for personal injury.

This is a long clause containing a lot of stylized, industry-specific language. In it, the venue requires (1) the purchase of three specific types of insurance (workers' compensation, fire and theft, and public liability insurance); (2) with specific terms (*full replacement value* and *waiver of subrogation*); (3) at specific limits (one million dollars); and (4) to be named as Additional Insured.

Here's a breakdown of each of these:

Workers' Compensation Insurance Requirement

Workers' compensation insurance covers a business's employees who are injured on the job. With this request, the venue wants to make sure of two things: (a) that you are in compliance with the law; and (b) that your insurance is available to your injured employee so that person doesn't turn to the venue with their legal claim.

Fire and Theft Insurance Requirement

Fire and theft insurance provides first party coverage, which means that the insured (the purchaser of the insurance policy) has coverage for loss of or damage to property it owns (or property that it doesn't own, but is on loan or rented and in its care, custody, and control) due to fire, theft, or other enumerated hazards.

Public Liability Insurance Requirement

Public liability insurance is the older name used for commercial general liability (CGL) insurance, which is third party coverage. Third party coverage refers to insurance intended to respond to legal claims made against you by others—including by way of a lawsuit. CGL policies contain a few insuring agreements, but the most important one is intended to respond to claims of bodily injury sustained by a business's visitors (non-employees) due to the insured's negligence. For example, if a customer comes to your place of business and is injured after tripping over electric cables on the floor, your CGL policy would be called upon to pay for the legal claims made against you and, if necessary, provide you with a legal defense against those claims. These claims would typically say that you owed your business invitees a duty to exercise reasonable care in maintaining a safe workspace, but you breached that duty by leaving electric cables on the floor and that breach resulted in bodily injury to your customer.

Full Replacement Value

Full replacement value is a clause commonly found in property insurance policies that says that, in determining the amount of the claimed loss, the insurer will pay the amount it would cost the insured to replace the items lost or damaged, not merely the likely value of those items as reduced by age or use.

Waiver of Subrogation

A waiver of subrogation is a clause lessors often ask lessee to add to their property insurance policies. Property policies often have provisions that say that if an insurer has paid a claim to you and you have the legal right to recover monetary damages from someone else for causing that financial loss, that right is transferred to the insurer. Transferring that right to the insurer allows it to recoup the claim money it paid to you. For example, if you rented a venue and your expensive sound and lighting equipment was destroyed because the venue had a water pipe disaster, your property insurer would, after investigation, pay your claim for the damaged equipment, then sue the venue for reimbursement. This contractual right is called a *right of subrogation*—in your insurance policy, you gave the insurer the right to "stand in your shoes" and exercise certain rights that you, yourself, would be able to exercise. In Example 13.10, above, the venue is requiring that you remove the subrogation right so that if a water pipe break damages your equipment, your insurer cannot "stand in your shoes" and sue the venue to recoup the amount of the claim payment to you.

One Million Dollar Limits

The limits of insurance required by the venue is one million dollars, which, while being a lot of money, is a standard amount for commercial insurance policies.

Additional Insured Requests

Requests to add an entity as an Additional Insured under another's commercial insurance policy are common. Giving an entity additional insured status merely allows them to receive the benefit of your insurance coverage on your dime for a limited period of time. The requesting party benefits in the same way you would benefit under your policy. Usually your insurer will ask for the entity's legal name and the duration of time for the addition. Sometimes venues will ask to be added as a Named Insured, which would give them more status and decision-making authority under your insurance policy, but this is not necessary and your insurer would not likely allow it. Most likely the venue doesn't fully understand what they are requesting.

Some venues might ask to be added as a *loss payee* under your policies. A loss payee refers to the party the proceeds of the insurance policy claim are paid to in the event of a loss under the policy. Speak with your insurer in detail about these requests to be sure you understand the consequences of complying with requests like these. Your insurer will likely ask to see the venue rental agreement to review the request in order to underwrite and price for it.

Requiring that lessees have adequate insurance gives venue lessors some measure of comfort that they are renting their venues to entities that comply with the law and conduct their business in a professional manner with attention paid to managing the risks inherent in their business models. Having a comprehensive insurance program is one indicator of a business's legitimacy.

Chapter 9 provides more information about business insurance.

FITNESS OF PROPERTY CLAUSES

Sometimes there are clauses in venue rental agreements that disclaim the fitness of the property (or elements of it) for any purposes—sometimes these clauses are tucked into a representations and warranties clause. In essence, the fitness clauses require the lessee to take the property at their own risk with no promises that it will serve the purpose for which it is rented. They also disclaim any liability for damage to the renter's property during the term of the rental (for example, a power surge that damages light equipment).

Example 13.11:

> *Lessor makes no representation or warranty as to the fitness of the property for any purpose or the condition or state of repair of the property. Lessee takes the property at its own risk and shall not hold Lessor liable for any defects. Further, Lessor shall bear no responsibility for any damages or loss of any property of the Lessee during the rental.*

Clearly, the venue is trying to limit its liability to its renters in the event that the property doesn't end up being suitable for the purpose rented or for damage or loss of equipment used or stored on the property during the rental term. In reality, these clauses will likely only serve the purpose of mitigating the venue's financial responsibility for renters' losses because if the property is ultimately and objectively not as advertised, the renters can make a case for breach of contract or fraud in advertising. If renters' property is damaged or stolen due to the venue's negligence (such as failure to safeguard the property or a water pipe leak), they may still be held liable despite this clause. But, these clauses should be carefully reviewed and, where possible, negotiated to reflect terms that are better aligned with your interests.

Example 13.12 provides some especially troublesome language.

Example 13.12:

> *Elevator service to the property may be provided and may be interrupted or discontinued at any time before, during, or after the engagement in the sole discretion of the Lessor. Lessor shall not be liable because of Lessor's inability to provide heating or air-conditioning to the facilities.*

Some patrons rely exclusively on elevators to reach their seats; not having access to working elevators is unacceptable except in the most severe circumstances. Depending on the time of year and the geographic location of the rental property, not having adequate heat or air-conditioning could cause serious issues including health concerns for the audience, performers, and back-of-house workers as well as damage to the renter's reputation. Property lessors should be required to provide assurances of baseline, reasonable ranges of expectations of elevator operations and heating and air-conditioning levels.

CANCELLATION

Carefully review the agreement's cancellation language. The cancellation clause will spell out each party's financial liability to the other in the event that the agreement is canceled for a reason other than one of force majeure, for example, poor ticket sales or incapacity of a key performer. Some agreements will provide a payment schedule for cancellation (see Example 13.13) in the form of liquidated damages, which means the parties are agreeing, in advance of a cancellation event, what the financial liability will be.

Example 13.13:

> *If the event is canceled with less than X days' notice, Lessor will retain a cancellation fee equal to Y% of the initial deposit as specified in Section A of this Agreement.*

Other agreements will take a more severe approach and completely disallow cancellation or assignment of the rental rights granted; see Example 13.14, below, which is unilateral in that the lessor reserves the right to cancel the agreement, but the lessee has no cancellation right.

Example 13.14:

> *Lessee shall make no assignment, sublease, or sublicense of this Agreement. This license may not be canceled in whole or in part by the Lessee.*

OTHER CLAUSES

Look for other fine-print type language:

- Look for revocation of the rental agreement if a fully executed copy of it is not returned within a specified period.
- If you plan to sell merchandise, check the agreement for restrictions on sales or for consignment language in which the venue takes a commission on sales of your merchandise.

- Some venues have preferred vendors for things like food, beverage, or party rental equipment, so be sure to know whether you can use your own and what the pricing structures are if required to use a firm from the venue's preferred list.

If you are in the early stages of event planning, you might see whether you can purchase an option from the venue to hold your dates for an extended period of time, allowing you more time before making a commitment.

CEASE AND DESIST LETTERS

A cease and desist letter is a type of demand letter. Demand letters forcefully but professionally request a recipient to do something or refrain from doing something. A cease and desist asks recipients to stop doing something currently underway and refrain from doing that same thing again in the future. These are commonly used in the context of intellectual property rights—especially instances alleging copyright, trademark, or service mark infringement in which an owner informs a recipient that the owner has IP rights to enforce; the recipient is infringing those rights; and the rightsholder intends to protect their rights against such infringement.

Typically, a cease and desist letter will contain the following:

- An identification of the parties
- Details concerning the rights at issue including the nature of the rights and how and when the rights accrued
- The nature of the recipient's unauthorized use
- The demand to cease the infringing activity
- The threat of legal action if the infringing use persists or starts again in the future

For example, if you performed a song you wrote at a coffeehouse and later heard a recording of your song played over another establishment's sound system, you have rights to enforce even if you never filed a copyright claim in the song. Copyright violations are about one person or entity's unauthorized use of content created by someone else. Even if you gave the coffeehouse permission to record your performance, if it or another establishment plays that recording without your permission, it is violating your exclusive right to public performance under Section 106 of the U.S. Copyright Act. In this example, you should first contact the establishment and the coffeehouse and request they discontinue the use. If they persist, you could send them a cease and desist letter. See Chapters 11 and 12 for a discussion of copyright and music licensing. Example 13.15 provides a sample cease and desist letter.

Example 13.15:

Sample Cease and Desist Letter

Dear <name>,

I am the owner and author of <name of piece of music (the "Work")> in which I reserved all rights under Title 17 USC §106 of U.S. Copyright Law (the "Act").

This sentence establishes your ownership of the content and your reservation of rights in it.

I understand that <name and/or organization> is currently using the Work without authorization in contravention of the protection afforded under United States copyright laws. Infringement of copyright is serious. In addition to attorney fees, you can be held liable for statutory damages up to $150,000 as set forth in §504(c)(2) of the Act.

This sentence references damages available for willful infringement of copyright which is the highest dollar amount available and reserved for situations in which the infringer was aware of the infringing use and persisted. If the infringed content carried the © symbol, that is evidence of willful infringement because the symbol, while no longer required, provides evidence of ownership which precludes infringers from raising an innocence defense.

If the infringing use is in the form of an unauthorized derivative use of your content, you should spell out how your content was improperly adapted. With derivative uses, you could state the following:

I understand that <name and/or organization> is currently using the Work without authorization in contravention of the protections afforded me under 17 USC §106(2) of United States copyright laws.

I demand you immediately cease the infringing use and any uses derived from the Work including any electronic copies. I further demand that you immediately deliver to me any and all unused, undistributed copies of same and that you desist from this or any other infringing uses of the Work in the future by affirmatively indicating your intent to comply with the foregoing by <date>.

This is the demand part of the letter where you spell out what, specifically, you want the recipient to do. You could also ask for the destruction of the infringed content. If you suspect there is a lot of content, consider hiring an attorney to subpoena documents and, potentially, a premises search.

If I have not received an affirmative response from you by <same date as above> with indications that you have or will fully comply with these demands to my satisfaction, I will commence legal action against you to remedy the situation.

It's important you provide a specific date for complying with your demand and be prepared to take action if you don't hear back.

Sincerely,
<your name>

CONCLUSION

Having a basic understanding of how contracts and contracting works as well as some facility with contract drafting and interpretation will help your business immeasurably—you'll know how to protect your interests and how to exercise your rights in a business-like manner. If you have invested the time to carefully read the samples included in this book, you'll recognize common themes that can be repeated or amended to suit your needs. The resources provided below will also be helpful regardless of your artistic practice.

I wish you great success in designing, launching, and operating your music business!

GENERAL RESOURCES

Music Industry Law/Contracts

All You Need to Know about the Music Business by Donald S. Passman (Simon & Schuster)

The 11 Contracts That Every Artist, Songwriter, and Producer Should Know by Steve Gordon (Hal Leonard Books)

The Enterprising Musician's Guide to Performer Contracts by David R. Williams (Rowman & Littlefield)

The Musician's Business and Legal Guide edited by Mark Halloran (Pearson Prentice Hall)

This Business of Music: The Definitive Guide to the Music Industry by M. William Krasilovsky and Sydney Shemel (Watson Guptill)

Contract Law, Generally

Contract Law for Dummies by Scott Burnham (John Wiley & Sons)

Contracts: The Essential Business Desk Reference by Richard Stim (Nolo)

Contract Forms

Business and Legal Forms for Theater[1] by Charles Grippo (Allworth Press)

eForms, "Free Electronic Forms," eforms.com

HDTRZ Mastering Studios, "Free Contracts," www.hdqtrz.com/free-contracts/

NOTE

1. Includes a CD-ROM of over thirty contracts.

Appendix A

Business Structures Comparison Chart

	State Filing Required	Formation Paperwork	Formation Costs[1]	Owners	Governance	Ongoing Compliance[2]	Federal Tax Treatment	Personal Liability
Sole Proprietorship	no	none	very low	only one owner	self-governed	very low	pass through taxation	un-limited
General Partnership	no	not required; partnership agreement recommended	low unless attorney is engaged to draft a partnership agreement	consists of only general partners (no investor partners)	governed by the general partners	low	pass through taxation automatic, but corporate treatment option	un-limited
Limited Liability Company (LLC)	yes	articles of organization and operating agreement	moderate	unlimited in number and type	options include member-managed or manager-managed	moderate	pass through taxation options	limited
Low-Profit Limited Liability Company (L3C)	yes	articles of organization and operating agreement	moderate	unlimited in number and type	options include member-managed or manager-managed	moderate	pass through taxation options	limited
C Corporation	yes	articles of incorporation and bylaws	moderate	unlimited in number and type	governed by a board of directors	moderate	taxed at entity and individual levels	very limited
S Corporation	yes	articles of incorporation and bylaws	moderate-high	limited to 100 and limited by type	governed by a board of directors	high due to annual election	pass through taxation common	very limited
Benefit Corporation	yes	articles of incorporation and bylaws	moderate initially	unlimited in number and type	governed by a board of directors	very high	taxed at entity and individual levels	limited

(continued)

255

	State Filing Required	Formation Paperwork	Formation Costs[1]	Owners	Governance	Ongoing Compliance[2]	Federal Tax Treatment	Personal Liability
Social Purpose Corporation	yes	articles of incorporation and bylaws	moderate	unlimited in number and type	governed by a board of directors	moderate	taxed at entity and individual levels	limited
Nonprofit Corporation/ Charitable Organization	yes	articles of incorporation, bylaws, state and federal tax exemption filings, and charitable solicitation registrations	moderate– high depending on breadth of charitable solicitation plans	nonprofit organizations don't have owners	governed by a board of directors	high due to charitable solicitation registrations	charitable organizations don't pay tax, but exemption is not automatic	limited

1. Formation costs don't contemplate the variable of hiring an attorney or other professional to assist with paperwork preparation or filing.
2. For statutory entities, the level of ongoing compliance and reporting is highly dependent on individual state requirements, so this is only a relative overview.

Appendix B
Copyright Quiz Analysis

When lawyers discuss scenarios with clients, they ask a ton of questions to gather the relevant facts, determine which law (or laws) applies, apply the law(s) to those facts, and then make a prediction of how the dispute would likely be resolved in court. It's impossible to guess with certainty how any legal challenge would be resolved—particularly when a jury is involved—but here are my thoughts on these hypotheticals.

1. Karl showed his musician buddy, Sal, a backbeat he developed, but hadn't yet used or otherwise shared with anyone else. Several months later, Karl heard Sal play the backbeat at a gig without ever asking Karl for his permission. If Karl brings a copyright infringement case against Sal alleging that Sal stole his backbeat, would Karl likely succeed?

Analysis:

Karl would likely not succeed because he didn't reduce his backbeat to a tangible format. Copyright protection is only afforded to original works showing some level of creativity that are put into some tangible format. Merely playing it doesn't rise to the level capable of copyright protection.

2. Continuing with the same hypothetical, with the facts changed slightly: Karl recorded his backbeat and sent it by phone to Sal as an audio file saying "*check it out.*" Several months later, Karl goes to one of Sal's gigs and hears the backbeat played. If Karl brings a copyright infringement case against Sal alleging that Sal stole his backbeat, would Karl likely succeed?

Analysis:

In recording his backbeat, Karl put it into tangible format so, as a purely technical matter, he is afforded copyright protection even though he hadn't yet registered it with the Copyright Office; however, the issue is this: what monetary damages can Karl prove that he's entitled to as a result of the infringement? Because Karl hadn't yet registered it, he would first have to register it in order to bring an infringement suit and he'd also have to prove lost income due to Sal's infringement.

3. Same hypothetical as 1, but this time rather than the entire backbeat, only a portion was used in a piece Sal wrote. If Karl brings a copyright infringement case against Sal alleging that Sal improperly used his backbeat, would Karl likely succeed?

Analysis:

Karl could, theoretically, succeed in proving that Sal improperly used his content, although the question of damages looms large. Using only a portion of the backbeat is no less infringing than using the entire backbeat. Recall that copyright infringement hinges on unauthorized use, not the amount of content used. Unless a fair use defense is raised, the amount used without authorization isn't relevant. The argument often goes like this: "the amount I used was only *de minimus,*" meaning insignificant. However, the counter argument is if the unauthorized user now believes that the content used was insignificant, why use it in the first place?

4. Same hypothetical as 3 except, in this version, Sal is a public school music teacher using Karl's backbeat in an original school musical. Do you think Sal can safely rely on the fair use doctrine as a defense to a copyright infringement allegation?

Analysis:

Relying on the fair use doctrine's *teaching purposes* is risky because what constitutes teaching can be subjective. The better course is to ask for written permission to use others' material.

5. Maggie, a member of a community cello ensemble, purchased the sheet music for a song written by Alicia Keys and made an arrangement of it for her cello ensemble. If Keys's publisher learns about this and brings a legal action against Maggie alleging that she is violating the copyright, Maggie is probably on the right side of the law because she purchased the music. True or false?

Analysis:

False. Maggie has violated the copyright owner's rights by making the cello arrangement without permission. An arrangement of an existing piece of music is called a *derivative work*. Section 106(2) of the copyright code reserves that right to the copyright owner; in this example, Keys's publisher.

6. Same hypothetical as immediately above, except in this version, Maggie is a high school friend of Keys and received permission from the artist to make the arrangement. What do you think now?

Analysis:

This is a bit trickier because the hypothetical's facts don't tell us who the rightsholder is. If Alicia Keys self-publishes her songs, the permission may be adequate, but the more likely scenario is that she has assigned her rights to a publisher who now controls the rights to her music in exchange for royalty payments. If a publisher is the rightsholder, Ms. Keys has no authority to give Maggie permission to make the arrangement because she has no right to license her songs—she contractually gave that right to her publisher.

7. Tony is a self-described Beyoncé super fan. He makes a modest income by making and selling Beyoncé mash-up videos and high-quality ringtones. To protect himself against allegations of copyright infringement, Tony uses the phrase "*Ownership is neither implied nor intended*" in all his video and print collateral to make clear he is not the owner of the videos. What do you think?

Analysis:

Tony is violating rightsholders' copyrights. Copyright infringement isn't based on claims of false ownership; it's based on allegations of unauthorized use. Like Maggie, if Tony doesn't have permission to use the content to make compilation videos or ringtones, he is violating the owner's rights and subject to a charge of copyright infringement from each of the rightsholders whose content he used without permission.

8. Same hypothetical as immediately above, except Tony donates the income to one of Beyoncé's favorite charities. What difference, if any, would that make?

Analysis:

Same answer as number 7; it doesn't matter what the money is used for because the use was not authorized.

9. Would your answer be different if, rather than making any money, Tony was making videos and ringtones as a hobby and sharing them with other Beyoncé fans?

Analysis:

Unauthorized use of another's content is not based on commercial or non-commercial use. The issue is whether the content was used without rightsholders' permission.

10. What if Tony found the video owners' names and provided their credits; how much protection does that give him if copyright infringement is alleged?

Analysis:

Same answer as number 7; Tony is violating rightsholders' copyright because he doesn't have permission to use the videos for any purpose.

Appendix C

Quick Reference Music Licensing Chart

	Rights Granted	Examples	Typical Licensor
Mechanical License—compulsory	to make a recording to release to the public of a piece of music already recorded and released to the public by its author	a cover of a Billie Eilish tune; sampling (including ringtones, video games, mobile apps, and novelty items with music: greeting cards, toys, etc.)	Harry Fox Agency
Mechanical License—non-compulsory	to make a recording of a piece of music not written by you and not recorded and released publicly by its author	recording a song written by someone else who never recorded it, or recorded it but never released it publicly	rightsholder—the songwriter or the writer's publisher
Synchronization License	audio-visual projects in which music is synchronized with visuals	video (including YouTube and streaming video), TV shows and commercials, film, websites, video games	rightsholder—publisher
Public Performance License	live performances, playing recorded music publicly, radio (terrestrial/analog, digital, interactive/on-demand services)	TV shows, restaurants, supermarkets, sports areas, radio, Pandora, Spotify	one or more of the PROs (ASCAP, BMI, SESAC) or SoundExchange (for digital performance rights)

(continued)

	Rights Granted	Examples	Typical Licensor
Master Use License	using some or all of a preexisting sound recording in another recording (including interactive audio), reproduce and distribute existing sound recordings	audio-only uses; sampling (including digital sampling and ringtones), Pandora, Spotify	rightsholder—typically record label
Reprint License	using music notation or lyrics in printed format	sheet music, derivative works (music arrangements), using lyrics or music notation on merchandise or synchronized under visuals	rightsholder—typically publisher
Theatrical (Grand Rights) License	story-themed dramatic works on stage	musicals, operas, ballets, plays	rightsholder—typically the collaborators, their estates, or their agents

Disclaimer: The licensing and permissions provided in this chart reflect the traditional pathways for licensees to obtain permissions from rightsholders; however, the music industry is constantly in flux. Some intermediaries, such as the Harry Fox Agency (HFA), look for ways to leverage existing relationships with publishers and record labels by expanding the services they offer. For this reason, potential licensees might not need to always go to different rightsholders for multiple license types. For an example of this, check out HFA Licensing FAQs.[1]

NOTE

1. Harry Fox, "Licensing FAQs," www.harryfox.com/#/faq.

Index

About the Author

David R. Williams, founding principal of Enterprising Artist Consulting, is a former professional musician with a doctorate in music and in law. An active guest lecturer, he has delivered talks on music industry law at Yale University, Tanglewood, Manhattan School of Music, New England Conservatory, and the University of Wisconsin-Madison, among others. His 2017 book, *The Enterprising Musician's Guide to Performer Contracts,* uses plain language to introduce emerging artists to the complexities of music industry contracts and empowers them to embrace their role as CEO of their own brand.

He is a former faculty member of the Crane School of Music, where he continues to serve as Executive Director of the Fall Island Vocal Arts Seminar. David Williams holds a JD from New York Law School, and degrees in vocal performance from the University of Wisconsin-Madison (DMA) and the New England Conservatory of Music (MM), as well as a BM in musical studies from the Crane.

Currently, he is a faculty member at the College of Performing Arts at The New School in New York City, where he teaches a graduate seminar in entrepreneurial musicianship for the Mannes School of Music as well as classes in business modeling, contracts, copyright, and music licensing for The New School's MA program in Arts Management and Entrepreneurship.